EGYPT DIARY 1914–1915

BY THE SAME AUTHOR

Gallipoli Diary 1915
Netley Diary 1915–1916

ALEC RILEY

EGYPT DIARY
1914–1915

Edited by
Michael Crane & Bernard de Broglio

Diary text
© copyright Alec Riley

Annotations, biographies and maps
© copyright Michael Crane, Bernard de Broglio

Images copyright expired or no known copyright restrictions

Cover images: Battalion signallers, 6th Manchesters, August 1914; sunset on the river Nile from Kasr El-Nil Barracks; men of the Manchester Regiment explore a village near Sidi Gaber, Alexandria, 1914

All rights reserved. No part of this book may be reproduced in any form by electronic or mechanical means, including information storage and retrieval systems, without permission in writing from the publisher, except by a reviewer who may quote brief passages in a review

First edition, August 2022

ISBN 978-0-6452359-3-7 (hardback)
ISBN 978-0-6452359-4-4 (paperback)
ISBN 978-0-6452359-5-1 (ebook)

Little Gully Publishing
littlegully.com

CONTENTS

Foreword		vii
Timeline		1
Chapter 1	July 1914	3
Chapter 2	At headquarters	5
Chapter 3	Hollingworth	13
Chapter 4	On the 'Saturnia'	23
Chapter 5	Cairo — Polygon Barracks	39
Chapter 6	Abu Zabal	55
Chapter 7	Polygon Barracks again	71
Chapter 8	Alexandria	95
Chapter 9	Cairo again	105
Appendix I	Biography of Alec Riley	129
Appendix II	Biography of 'M' — Margaret Isherwood (née Riley)	139
Appendix III	Soldiers' biographies	141
Appendix IV	Biography of General Sir Ian Hamilton	187
Appendix V	East Lancashire (42nd) Division, Field State at embarkation, Southampton, 10 September 1914	215
Abbreviations and acronyms		221
Bibliography		225
Acknowledgements		233
Index		235

MAPS

Map 1	Manchester and environs	2
Map 2	Egypt and Sinai	38
Map 3	Cairo and environs	54
Map 4	Alexandria	92

FOREWORD

THIS BOOK IS THE FAITHFUL TRANSCRIPT of a soldier's diary. It is the first of three written by Lance Corporal Alec Riley, a signaller in the British Army's 42nd (East Lancashire) Division.

When war broke out in Europe in August 1914, Riley was 27 years of age and working as a clerk in his merchant father's salt warehouse in Manchester. He was also a part-time soldier with nine years' service under his belt.

Riley had joined the 2nd Volunteer Battalion of the Manchester Regiment as an eighteen-year-old in 1905 when tales of the Boer War were still fresh in popular memory. Writing to Sir Ian Hamilton in 1923, Riley recalled being part of the honour guard when the general unveiled the regiment's South African war memorial in St Ann's Square.

> In those days young volunteers were reared on the romance of the S.A. War, and I remember reading several times some passages in Conan Doyle's book, in which you were very intimately concerned. Now, we don't think very much of the romance of war.

On 1 April 1908, the old Yeomanry and Volunteer units were incorporated into the new Territorial Force. Riley's unit was redesignated the 6th Battalion of the Manchester Regiment and he re-enlisted that same day, being issued the very low service number of 10.

The Territorial Force required its soldiers to attend about 40 drills and range practises each year. These were held on weekday evenings and

Saturday afternoons, earning them the nickname 'Saturday Warriors.' The drills were supplemented by occasional weekends on regimental exercises, and an annual training camp with the division. For many 'Terriers,' this fortnight-long camp under canvas was the highlight of their year.

As a battalion signaller, Alec Riley would have been proficient in telegraphy, Morse Code and telephone communications, as well as visual signalling with flags, lamps, lights and heliograph. Some signallers also acted as despatch riders, using motorcycles and bicycles for transport. (Riley would later sign up his Sunbeam bicycle for service in Egypt.) This mobility gave the signallers, in particular 'old volunteers' like Riley, an autonomy that they regularly exploited. In one of his letters to Hamilton, Riley described the independent attitude that characterised him and his 'old T.F. friends.'

> We belonged to that "free-lance" type of Territorials, and I'm afraid it was a type quite incomprehensible to many. However, we enjoyed it as much as possible.

In contrast to the Territorial Force, Britain's regular army was properly equipped and well trained. However, it was relatively small in size. When Britain declared war on Germany on 4 August 1914, the regular army numbered about 247,500 men, of which a large proportion was based outside the United Kingdom, in India and other outposts of Empire. An additional force of 209,350 regular and special reserves could be mobilised in time of national crisis, giving the British Army a nominal strength of 456,850. The Germans maintained a standing army of 850,000 which expanded to 4,500,000 on mobilisation of its reserves. The 100,000-strong expeditionary force that Britain despatched to France in August 1914 was tiny by comparison and woefully inadequate for the task it faced.

An appeal was made, famously fronted by the Secretary of State for War, Lord Kitchener, for 100,000 volunteers. The figure was quickly surpassed. By 12 September 1914, almost 479,000 men had answered the call. Thus the 'New Army' was born. However, this rapid influx of untrained men presented huge logistical challenges to the military authorities, who struggled to clothe, arm, train and accommodate them. The War Office knew that it would be many months, if not years, before these raw recruits could be trained and organised into effective units. A stop-gap solution was urgently required. Britain turned to the 269,000 men of the Territorial Force who had been mobilised on the day war was declared.

Territorial soldiers were not obliged to serve outside the United Kingdom but when asked to volunteer, many came forward to sign Army Form E.624, the Imperial Service obligation. By war's end, the Territorial Force had fielded 25 divisions on foreign soil. The 42nd (East Lancashire) Division was the first to embark for overseas service, despatched to Egypt to defend the Suez Canal against Turkish troops massing in Palestine. Riley sailed with the division from Southampton on 10 September 1914.

On embarkation, Riley was attached to the 1/1st East Lancs RE Signal Company. At this time, army communications were the responsibility of the Royal Engineers Signal Service. One signal company, comprising a headquarters and four sections, was assigned to each infantry division. No. 1 Section handled communications for divisional HQ and the division as a whole. Sections 2, 3 and 4 were allotted to the infantry brigades. These sections also handled communications between infantry and artillery. Riley served in No. 4 (Manchester Brigade) Section.

During his time in Egypt, and subsequently at Gallipoli and in hospital in England, Riley kept detailed notes, which he later compiled into three diaries. The first, the subject of this book, covers the events around Riley's mobilisation in August 1914 and his time in Egypt from September 1914 until his embarkation for Gallipoli on 3 May 1915. The second diary recaps Riley's last few days in Egypt and details his time at Gallipoli from 6 May until his medical evacuation on 11 September 1915. The final diary describes his evacuation from the peninsula, suffering from diphtheria, jaundice, enteritis, dysentery and nine septic sores. It records his time in hospital on the island of Lemnos, his onward evacuation aboard *Aquitania* in October 1915, and his treatment and 11-month-long convalescence in the Royal Victoria Hospital, Netley. Collectively, the diaries offer a unique window into the experiences of a pre-war territorial soldier, before, during and after Gallipoli.

Riley presented the diaries to the Imperial War Museum in 1957 or 1958 but they lay unregarded in its archives for more than 60 years.

In 2019, the editors identified Alec Riley as the anonymous author of 'The Silent Nullahs of Gallipoli', a soldier's account of his return to the peninsula in 1930. With a name, the editors were able to track down the man. Hiding behind a nondescript catalogue entry at the Imperial War Museum were these three diaries. They proved a revelation, not only for their vivid eyewitness record of the Gallipoli Campaign, but also for Riley's narrative style and perspective. The editors resolved to get all three of his diaries into print, and the central work, *Gallipoli Diary 1915*, was published in November 2021.

Riley had ambitions to write an account of the Gallipoli Campaign in more literary form. He attended Max Pemberton's school of journalism and creative writing. He made at least two trips to the Gallipoli peninsula, travelling independently to gather material. And he opened a decade-long correspondence with Sir Ian Hamilton, the former Commander-in-Chief of the Mediterranean Expeditionary Force. Hamilton treated Riley's work seriously, agreeing to write (and re-write) the introduction for a manuscript titled 'Return to Cape Helles.' But the public's appetite for Great War memoirs had abated by the 1930s and Riley searched in vain for a willing publisher.

Fortunately, Riley did enjoy some success as a writer during his lifetime, most notably the evocative 'Silent Nullahs of Gallipoli' that appeared in the 1930s magazine *Twenty Years After: The Battlefields of 1914–18, Then and Now*. (Readers will find this article reprinted in *Gallipoli Diary 1915*.)

Riley also had a piece published by *The Telegraph and Morning Post* on 23 April 1938 to mark the 23rd anniversary of the Gallipoli landings. It drew attention to a 'new' Gallipoli exhibition at the Imperial War Museum featuring photographs and artefacts donated by Riley. The carefully-labelled battlefield relics collected by Riley in 1930 continue to feature in the museum's Gallipoli displays.

Riley was not only a talented writer. His camera bore witness to both his 1915 service at Helles and his 1930 return to the battlefield. Some of these photographs he sent to Hamilton. At least two were included in the

British official history of the campaign. Twelve accompanied the article 'Silent Nullahs' in *Twenty Years After*, with a further 29 illustrating two other Gallipoli-related articles in that magazine.

Unfortunately, his photographs from Egypt have been lost. Riley purchased a small camera, probably the ubiquitous Vest Pocket Kodak, in anticipation of war being declared. When in Egypt, he twice received film sent from home. But when the division embarked for Helles in May 1915, soldiers were ordered to leave their kit bags behind. These were invariably looted or lost, and a disgruntled Riley tells us, 'I never saw mine again after leaving Abbassia.'

In the absence of a pictorial record made by Riley, the editors have combed other soldiers' photo albums for images to illustrate this account. The soldier-tourist, like the civilian, followed a well-trodden path through the attractions of Egypt, and both found their camera drawn to pharaonic temples and statues, Nile River palms, and contemporary street and village life. The sources for these photographs are listed at the back of the book. The editors hope they provide pathways into new material for fellow researchers.

Egypt, in 1914, was notionally an autonomous province of the Ottoman Empire. However, Britain's military involvement in Egypt stretched back to 1882 when, during a period of political instability, warships and land forces were sent to protect British interests, including the trade route through the Suez Canal, and the lives of European nationals. Britain maintained a strong military presence in Egypt thereafter, imposing what became known as the 'veiled protectorate.' This de facto occupation had no legal basis and consequently many Egyptians resented the British being there. As a result, British and Empire troops in Egypt often faced open hostility and the threat of violence from some elements of the local population.

Local antipathy aside, the culture shock experienced by the Lancashire lads should not be underestimated. Before embarking from Southampton, few had strayed beyond England's borders. Most would have known little of the country, its people or its culture. The sights, sounds and smells of Egypt must have seemed very strange to them indeed.

Imperial Britain promoted a hierarchy of cultural superiority, and its soldiers frequently adopted attitudes that bordered on racial arrogance. Riley was no exception, and on occasion uses racist slang. Today this language stands out as gratingly offensive and profoundly unacceptable. As editors, the principle of 'neither to laugh, nor to cry, but to understand' has determined our approach to his work. Therefore, we have not redacted any words or descriptions in Riley's diary except for one epithet that is clearly marked. We invite you to judge Riley's account by the standards and influences prevailing in the early 20th century.

What follows is Riley's own account in his own words, with only minor corrections to spelling and punctuation. For context, the editors have provided separate footnotes, maps and appendices.

Michael Crane, Bernard de Broglio

TIMELINE

Egypt, 1914–1915

Mobilization of Territorial Force	August 5, 1914
At Headquarters, Manchester	August 5 — August 20
Hollingworth Camp, Rochdale	August 20 — September 7
Chesham Camp, Bury	September 7 — September 10
Embarked Southampton	September 10
Disembarked Alexandria	September 26
Cairo (Abbassia)	September 26 — October 7
Abu Zabal	October 7 — October 9
Cairo	October 9 — November 2
Abu Zabal	November 2 — November 14
Cairo	November 14 — December 5
Abu Zabal	December 5 — December 19
Cairo	December 19 — December 28
Alexandria	December 28 — January 19
Cairo	January 19 — May 2
Left Cairo	Sunday May 2
Embarked Alexandria for Gallipoli	Monday May 3

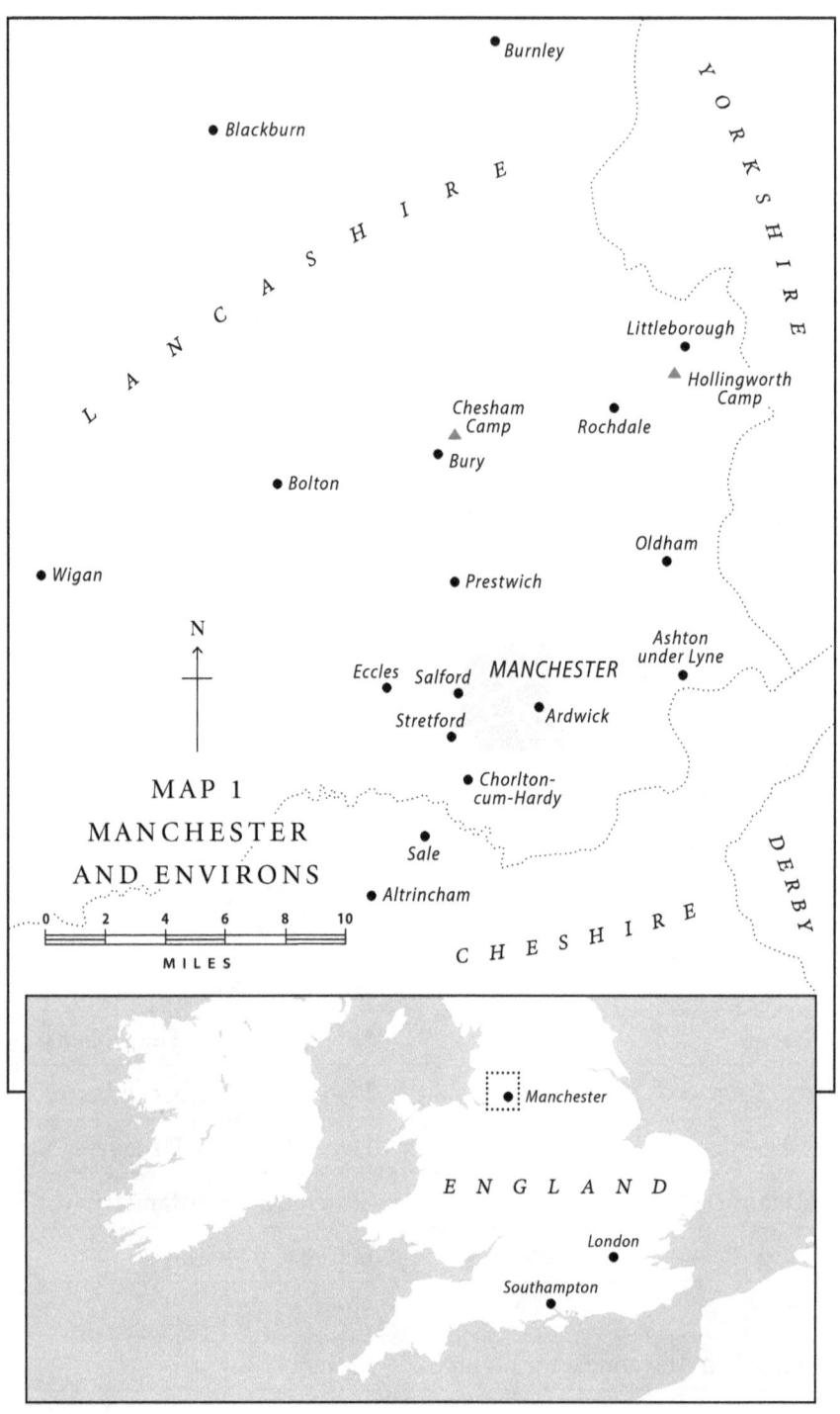

CHAPTER 1

July 1914

BY THE END OF JULY, war was probable.
I called at our headquarters to find out how much the orderly room could tell me. Nothing had happened—but it would, before long. At home, I laid out uniform and kit ready for packing.

My holidays started on July 31st, when I took the train to Bristol, intending to cycle some hundreds of miles in south-west England. I had no holiday feeling.

There were sentries posted at both ends of the Severn Tunnel.

On the morning of Saturday, August 1st, I called at the nearest territorial headquarters, in Bristol, where I was told that the order to mobilize was expected at any time.

My route was through Axbridge, Cheddar and Wells to Bridgewater, but the ride had small interest when one long, glorious camp was in prospect. On Sunday I rode through Taunton to Exeter, where a very obliging officer on duty at the Wessex Command Headquarters gave me what advice he could. The staff was waiting for the word 'go!' In Exeter Cathedral that night, I listened to a red-hot war sermon.

On Monday, August 3rd, I rode over Dartmoor to Plymouth, helping myself to a hold on a motor-lorry, and to a ride on a Dartmoor pony after a meal at a roadside inn.

There was great activity about the forts and barracks near Plymouth. The regulars were getting ready to leave, and many were saying goodbye to wives and children.

At night the Hoe was bright with fairy-lamps. Searchlights beamed upwards, and on two small war-vessels off Drake's Island.

On Tuesday, August 4th, I called at a Plymouth drill hall, but our time had not yet come. I had a steamer-trip up the Hamoaze to Saltash Bridge, passing Devonport Dockyard and the grey warships. After lunch I had a trip to the Eddystone. Returning in the early evening, we passed a long line of warships leaving Devonport, their signal lamps flashing brightly.

We waited impatiently for the hour when war would be declared that night. In my hotel I looked up the trains for Manchester. There was one at 12.10 a.m. I went out into Union Street, a cheerless place that evening, and called at the drill hall. Men, lying about on straw, looked rather fed up. The colonel was far too busy to tell me how to get hold of a free railway ticket to Manchester. In Union Street again, I bought a small camera, some rolls of film, and a body belt, and then returned to the hotel to wait until it was time to leave for the station. Midnight came. The 12.10 a.m. train to Bristol started. After a tiring journey, I had breakfast in Bristol. Many reservists were standing near the booking office just outside the station.

At most of the stations where the train stopped between Bristol and Manchester, the platforms were crowded with men in uniform, and others who would soon be wearing it.

Tired and dirty, I was back in Manchester by 1.30 p.m. on Wednesday, August 5th. The city was grey and depressing as I made my way from London Road Station to the 6th Battalion Manchester Regiment headquarters at 3, Stretford Road, where I found that I had made a mistake in paying my fare back. I could have claimed a free ticket.

CHAPTER 2

At headquarters

The corridors were crowded with men. In the large drill hall, men sat on the floor or on anything they could find. They were making a lot of noise, whistling or singing the popular songs of the day:

'Who'll go to France with me?'
'Who were you with last night?'
'Who's your lady friend?'
'We are the Deep Cut boys'
'The Blue-Ridge Mountains of Virginia'
'Hold me tight, George dear!'

And the shed echoed these songs many times daily for the next week or two.

There was a pleasant buzz of excitement. Officers and NCOs bustled about checking men from lists. Outside the orderly room I met Newton who said that he was after a commission. I found some of my colleagues of the signals. 'Pilk,' the officer in charge of us,[1] handed out a welcome of sorts, but had nothing original to say. We had not much to say to each other, either, except to profess astonishment that it had happened at last. We greeted our acquaintances in the battalion, but our greetings

---

1 Capt. Edward Fielden Pilkington, the battalion's Signals Officer. 'Pilk' did not go with the battalion to Egypt but stayed at home to command a reserve battalion. See Appendix III: Soldiers' biographies. His brother Capt. Hugh Brocklehurst Pilkington, also 6th Manchesters, died on 4 June 1915 at Helles. Both were nephews of Maj. C.R. Pilkington, CO of the 6th Manchesters for most of that battalion's time at Gallipoli.

did not go much further than 'Hullo, so-and-so!' There was not much to be said. We envied Tommy,[2] who had already signed on for imperial service, at 10/- per annum, and wore a breast-plate with 'Imperial Service' on it.

As I had not been home for my uniform I felt improperly dressed. During the afternoon some of us were examined by the MO, who told us to cough twice, and asked if we were 'home' or 'foreign.' We said we were 'home.'

Men who lived within the penny car-stage were allowed to go home, and those with cycles were released after being warned that roll-call would be at 9 a.m., or 10 a.m. if we had cycles, next morning. On my way to Eccles, I called at R.N.'s in Hodge Lane, to see why he had not turned up.[3] Then on to Rosthwaite for khaki and kit,[4] and, as there was nobody at home, to my brother's for the night.[5]

Next day we drew our identity discs, and had our kits inspected by Pilk and Joe (our sergeant) to see if we were entitled to an allowance of 10/- for providing our own kit.[6] We were all for the 10/- but later on we found that we had lost on the transaction.

On Friday we each drew 50 rounds of ammo and our field dressings. With the battalion we marched to the university ground at Fallowfield, where we played about for an hour or two, doing no work that mattered. In the evening we were released again.

The official order for mobilization had not been sent to me. Someone had blundered. There was an alarm at 9 p.m. that night. I heard about it in the morning, when *The Manchester Guardian* reached my brother, and I turned up at headquarters 11½ hours late. There had been a rumour about the German fleet and the east coast. We thought of our 50 rounds and field dressing, and hoped not.

---

2 The identity of 'Tommy' is not known. He may be Pte 2341 (later Pnr 11367 and 400528) Richard Thomas. See Appendix III: Soldiers' biographies.

3 Pnr 1392 George Richard Noble. See Appendix III: Soldiers' biographies.

4 The Riley family home: 'Rosthwaite', Stafford Road, Eccles, Salford, Lancashire.

5 Thomas Alfred Riley, Alec's half-brother.

6 Sgt 262 Graham 'Joe' Royle. See Appendix III: Soldiers' biographies.

CHAPTER 2

Figure 1. Territorial Force Imperial Service Badge. Officers, NCOs and men of the Territorial Force who assented to service outside the United Kingdom were entitled to wear the Imperial Service Badge on their right breast.

Ormesher had been sent to find me and others.[7] He met the postman, who said it was no use calling at Rosthwaite as the house was closed. Those who had stayed at headquarters, or turned up early, had been sent out to find the missing ones. Some of them stayed out for so long that Joe and Pilk had words.

It was late on Saturday night when we were released. Ormy, S. Ridings, Hopkinson and I found ourselves looking for somewhere to sleep.[8] The Clarendon, a pub in Oxford Street, would not have us. Ormy rang up one or two hotels, but they did not want us either. So we went out into the night and Piccadilly where the Albion sheltered us. It was a dingy mid-Victorian hotel. Ormy and I shared a room and bed. We did not sleep much, and were up early for a badly cooked breakfast.

---

7   Sgt 764 Charles 'Ormy' Ormesher. See Appendix III: Soldiers' biographies.
8   Pte 3271 Sidney Ridings and probably Pnr 1883 Harry Hopkinson respectively. See Appendix III: Soldiers' biographies.

Sunday in Manchester, and a dull, wet day. We felt miserable as we stood fast at headquarters. The novelty of mobilization began to wear off. Andrews had not reported, so I called to find out what was wrong. Mrs Andrews, his mother, showed me up to his room where I found him in bed. Later, he told me the cause—half a pint of Hyde's beer. We could not go home, but we were allowed out for an hour or two, and we felt much better when we had had tea at the Cecil Café in Oxford Street.

Monday, August 10th, was brighter. We painted our cycles a dark colour, adding crossed flags and other decorations of our own designs. Our cycles had been before a board. For mine, a Sunbeam, I received £10. It had already done two years hard work. Tommy got £10 for his Raleigh. Ormy got £5 for a very old and tried friend, and Haworth £4 for an antique which cost him one and which was known as Jimmy's camel.[9] He could only ride it when somebody had given him a start, and he had difficulty in getting off.

Our parade ground was lined with crates, boxes, stores, field kitchens, boilers, dixies and all sorts of litter. Vans and carts, commandeered from well-known firms, were being painted grey.

As signallers, we lived on the gallery of the large shed. Here also were our signalling stores and equipment, and quite a lot of our private possessions. Officers passed along our gallery to or from the mess. We spent a few nights in this uncomfortable place. Another night was spent in the small shed, lying on kit bags, but not sleeping. Hard boots and other hard things in the bags were too much for us.

Our red tunics and blue peaked caps were parcelled and handed in. I ripped off my badges and kept them, as well as my old spiked helmet.

We were not allowed out of the headquarters during the day, except on business. We found business in the shape of OHMS envelopes, fictitiously addressed, and these were passed by the sentries who knew nothing about signallers and their ways. Nor did the average officer.

---

9 Probably Pnr 1102 James Haworth. See Appendix III: Soldiers' biographies.

CHAPTER 2

We leaned on the balcony railing, watching the men in the hall below. Through the smoke haze the morning sun shone on them as they sat on their kit-bags, polishing buttons or talking, or singing or whistling.

We had known Manchester all our lives, but there was something different about it now—some strange atmosphere. And the people seemed different, too, though how, exactly, we could not say.

Tram-rides were free to us, and some of the theatres offered free seats to men in uniform. This was such a new experience that we could hardly believe it. Some of us took advantage of the chance to see, for nothing, Bombardier Wells give a show of exhibition boxing at the Palace.[10]

Behind all the activity and excitement was the restful background of Eccles and my home and family.

One morning I was told that I was wanted at the door by a lady. It was M—— who had come to see how I was getting on.[11] I don't know if she understood how glad I was to see her. Most of us had an idea that before long we should not have any more opportunities to see our people.

I had two accidents. Riding to Manchester one morning, I skidded on a tram-line in Regent Road, but managed to reach Stretford Road with a limp that frightened me. The fall had bent a crank, but I knocked it back again that night with my brother's coal hammer. The other misfortune was the breaking of a whisky flask which I carried in a bag on my cycle. Bag and contents were soaked in good liquor.

On August 11th, Pilk asked for names for active service. There were none. He looked disappointed. We made excuses. The need was not urgent enough; we wanted to go as a section, and not individually. Joe suggested marking time for a bit, to see if anything more to our liking turned up. For some, it was a serious decision to make at short notice.

---

10 The Palace Theatre on Oxford Street, Manchester. William Thomas Wells, who fought under the ring name of Bombardier Billy Wells, was the British and British Empire heavyweight champion from 1911 until 1919.

11 Alec Riley's sister, Margaret. See Appendix II: Biography of Margaret Isherwood.

Pilk asked each one of us, privately, about our intentions. He told us he was not going himself. As we knew the reason, we sympathised with him. If we had been given an order to go, we should have gone. We objected to free will for once. We went to the Kardomah in Market Street to talk about it, and talk (with coffee and cakes) was all that resulted.[12]

Next morning we paraded with the battalion in the large shed. We faced the gallery, where Brigadier-General Noel Lee, Colonel Heywood and Captain Holberton, the adjutant, were standing.[13] One by one they addressed us, telling us what we knew—that the need for volunteers was urgent, and that every available man would be wanted. We saw anxiety in their faces, and we knew why they were anxious. What was said to us was understood, perfectly, by all. Few names were given. We wanted more time to think over what must have been already decided. We were obstinate; but we knew we must say something definite sooner or later. I told my brother and family what was going on, and how we were holding out—exactly for what I could not say. They were sympathetic, naturally, but could not help me. It was a matter in which we had to be our own judges.[14]

We were doing elementary signalling jobs; cycling here and there. Most of the work was useless, but it gave us something to do. We drew our small pay, and, on August 15th, our Mobilization Bounty of £5. I spent one night in the band-room, to free C—— for a few hours, and I had an excursion to Ardwick Drill Hall on the carrier of one of our DR's motorcycle.[15] As he took all possible risks in busy streets, it was exciting for me if not for him.

---

12 The Kardomah was one of a chain of tea and coffee shops of the same name.
13 Brig. Gen. Noel Lee, GOC Manchester Brigade and former CO 6th Manchesters; Lt. Col. Gerald Graham Percival Heywood, CO 6th Manchesters; Capt. Philip Vaughan Holberton, Adjutant, 6th Manchesters. See Appendix III: Soldiers' biographies.
14 On 10 August 1914, Lord Kitchener invited the Territorial Force to volunteer for foreign service. By 12 August, the day Brig. Gen. Noel Lee addressed the 6th Manchesters, the commanders of all three infantry brigades of the division had accepted Kitchener's invitation, but it would not be until the beginning of September that the majority of the troops agreed to serve overseas.
15 Ardwick Drill Hall, Ardwick Green, Manchester. Headquarters of the 1/8th Bn, Manchester Regt. DR stands for for despatch rider.

CHAPTER 2

On Sunday, August 16th, we had a meal in an obscure café in Peter Street to escape the official rations, and at 1.30 p.m. we paraded for the Cathedral, where Bishop Welldon gave us a farewell address. The bishop, who was the Dean of Manchester, was a fat man dressed in baby clothes. We pretended to be amused. To cheer us up, he said:

'… but, there is a light shining on the distant hills!'

His address finished with these six words:

'Till we meet! Till we meet!'

I met him in Netley, two years later.[16]

I went home for tea and the night.

We knew we were leaving Manchester. On Tuesday I banked the proceeds of the war up to date, and that night was my last at home for a long time. Wednesday was our last day in Manchester.

---

16 Royal Victoria Hospital, Netley.

Figures 2 and 3. Camp of the Manchester Regiment, Hollingworth Lake.

CHAPTER 3

Hollingworth

Reveille was at 3.30 a.m. on Thursday, August 20th. At 4.45 a.m. the battalion marched to Piccadilly, the rendezvous. Pilk's orders had been so indefinite that we did not know exactly what to do. Some of us started with the battalion, and the rest came alone in ones and twos, the last man joining us just before we reached Piccadilly. Pilk was annoyed and said so; we were not at all helpful. Then he told us that we had seen Manchester for the last time. He added that wherever we went our cycles must go as well. This we interpreted literally.

At 6 a.m. we left Piccadilly for Hollingworth on the far side of Rochdale. Pilk went with his company, and Joe was in charge of us. We rode ahead of the battalion, dismounting and walking occasionally to keep within reach of it.[17] The route was by Rochdale Road to Rochdale, where in Town Hall Square women gave us drinks and asked when the battalion was due. We left the square before it arrived, and in due course pulled up at a public house at a convenient time for all concerned. We were not feeling at our best. Pilk had stirred up a mutinous spirit. We reached Hollingworth soon after nine o'clock. The camp and reservoir were about a mile and half from Littleborough and near Smithy Bridge Station. The brigade camp was in a large field near and below the reservoir. Our tents were near the brigade marquees. Our kit-bags had been left in Manchester, so we had to depend on such

---

17 The 6th Manchesters were followed by the 7th and 8th Manchesters with a 30 minute interval between each of the three battalions. Eventually all four battalions of the Manchester Brigade would be camped at Hollingworth Lake.

necessaries as could be carried in our haversacks and on our cycles. The 6th Manchesters' lines were near brigade headquarters. We felt better when the battalion arrived, and we heard the usual cheerful noise of a camp.[18]

The small amount of work we did at Hollingworth was easy and pleasant, if not of much value; and was, of course, all visual signalling. And there were more or less ambitious schemes.

We discovered Rochdale. I had stayed there often enough, but had never been on such really intimate terms with it as we were in two or three days. Off duty at 4 p.m., we could reach the town in time for a good tea. At first we were content with Duckworth's in Drake Street. We discovered Rochdale Baths, where we could both swim and dawdle in unlimited hot water. We bought a Primus stove, coffee, tinned milk and sugar for our tent. The field was damp, and we were glad of hot drinks when we got back to the tent at night. We were still without our kit-bags.

On Sunday I went to see the 6th Manchesters' doctor instead of church parade, but made up for it after dinner when we had orders to strike camp and pack up. This was done, and in two hours we were reported as being ready to move. Our division told us it was only a test, and that we could put the camp back again. We were not amused; but while we sat on such kit as we had, and waited, we had a sweep on probable destinations. It was a dull, dreary Sunday, but we were soon cheerful again when we discovered a good tea in the White Swan, in Yorkshire Street. This was the first of many good teas in the White Swan.

Prudence Blackhurst, the waitress, was a very pretty girl, who made our lives worth living. With the teas came great dishes of stewed plums and other fruit. And the bills were so small that we wondered what profit there could have been. Mrs Ormesher and Edward met us there one Sunday. S.H. came too, carrying on just enough to be amusing without being vulgar.

More money was handed out. This time it was 26/-.[19]

---

18 Civilians had been discouraged from visiting the troops and camp lines were closed to the public. However, Hollingworth Lake had long been a tourist attraction and over the weekend 51,000 people travelled by train to the nearby station at Littleborough.

19 One pound and six shillings in pre-decimal coinage.

CHAPTER 3

Once again Pilk asked for names for active service. Mallalieu and Tommy gave theirs.[20] Tommy, of course, had already signed on. Mall went to see the MO, and was rejected temporarily.

We were given four-hour duties as telephone orderlies in one of the brigade marquees. Two men to be on duty together. On these duties we discovered that the staff were living very much as we were—in the plainest style.

We talked mostly about volunteering. Men in the 8th Manchesters said they would not volunteer unless they could go as 'a unity.' On August 27th, Noel Lee spoke to us again about this matter, and it must have done some good, or perhaps we had reached a time when we could not hold out any longer, for, with a few temporary exceptions, we signed Army Form E.624, admitting our liability to serve in any place outside the UK in event of national emergency. All No. 4 went overseas.

Loud cheers came from the lines of the 8th Manchesters. We asked what the noise was about, and they told us:

'We're going as a unity.'

Most of that battalion had volunteered. There is a monument to a large part of that 'unity' in Ardwick Green today.

There was a bit of excitement when a suspicious character was caught in the 6th horse lines. After that, a sentry was posted.

There were rumours. We were going to Wellingborough and into billets. On the 28th this was cancelled. Williamson, the 7th Manchesters signals officer, hovered about us.[21] He told me he would most likely be in charge of our section, and on August 31st he came to us officially. On Tuesday, September 1st, our kit-bags arrived. We had managed very well without them, and we did not like the idea of luggage. One day, early in September, Captain Collins, the adjutant of the 8th Manchesters, appeared wearing a khaki helmet with a big red bob on one side of it.[22] This helmet attracted general admiration, and Knight,

---

20 Spr 617 John Mallalieu. See Appendix III: Soldiers' biographies.
21 Capt. Charles Harry 'Tim' Williamson. See Appendix III: Soldiers' biographies.
22 Capt. C.H.G. Collins, Duke of Cornwall's Light Infantry, attached 1/8th Manchesters.

our brigade major,[23] sent Hague,[24] who was on duty in the marquee, to Collins with his compliments, to ask where he had bought the helmet. We had Williamson's 'five-minute lectures,' which we did not enjoy, until Pilk said they would be just the thing for a long voyage. Egypt was in the wind.

We were given a half-day's leave on Friday, September 4th. Parents, friends, and girls had come to the camp to see many of their boys; but most of us had not seen any of our friends since leaving Manchester. We were very excited about this holiday. Our section was to go in two parts: one in the morning and the other in the afternoon. The evening before, we arranged our parties. The first was to leave camp at 6 a.m., but as there was a train at 5.30 a.m., the party crept out of camp, and off to Smith Bridge Station. Times of return were uncertain. Haworth was several hours late. I was on the afternoon party, with leave from noon until 10.30 p.m. I met M—— in Deansgate, did a bit of banking, and then went home for the last time.

For years it had seemed a very ordinary thing to go home but now it was strange, and I felt strange in my own home for the first time. I went up to my old bedroom. I should not be sleeping there again. I looked round the familiar rooms. When we had tea I felt as if I was saying goodbye to the patterns on the plates and cups. I was. And to those I had lived with for so long. I noticed how clean the tablecloth looked, and how nice the bread and butter tasted. I dreaded the time when I must say goodbye to Mother, Father and M——. There was a goodbye atmosphere everywhere. I had said it to my brother and family,[25] but this was worse. M—— took me to the tram for Manchester. Poole,[26] with his mother and girl, were waiting for it as well. M—— and I said goodbye. That was the end of all things. As Poole and his friends went inside the tram I went on top. The tram started. An old life seemed to be slipping away.

---

23 Maj. Henry Lewkenor Knight. See Appendix III: Soldiers' biographies.
24 Pnr 3614 Ernest Houghton 'Claude' Hague. See Appendix III: Soldiers' biographies.
25 Thomas Alfred Riley, half-brother and 16 years Riley's senior.
26 Pte 1112 Arthur Poole, killed in action at Gallipoli, 5 July 1915. See Appendix III: Soldiers' biographies.

CHAPTER 3

I joined Poole at Victoria Station. In the dingy carriage neither of us had much to say, but we were glad of company. When we got back to our tents that night there was none of the usual eloquence.

Our section left Hollingworth on Monday September 7 for Chesham Camp, Bury, where we joined the main part of the East Lancs Div. Signal Coy.

Chesham Camp was a poor place compared with Hollingworth, and what made it worse was part of the scenery—a black and gloomy-looking church with an uninspiring spire.

We were drilled, graded as signallers, and made suspicious, generally, by an increase of regimentation.

At roll call, on Tuesday night, Lieutenant G.H. Broad read out the list of names of those who would 'proceed to Southampton on the 10th.'[27] On Wednesday we packed our kits, packed equipment in the skips, loaded the wagons, and generally got ready to leave. By midday it was raining hard.

In Bury, we bought some cheap novels, and odds and ends we thought might be useful. Some of them, such as chlorodyne, were. When we reached camp again blankets had been rolled and returned to store. Our homes were no longer furnished.

At 11 p.m. we had a potato-pie supper in a cottage on our field. Some of us adjourned to the cook-house to stand round the fire, warm on one side and cold on the other. The cheerful blaze brought out songs and choruses. We were very excited. At last we went back to our tents for what sleep or rest we could get.

We paraded at 2.15 on the morning of Thursday, September 10th, and marched to Knowsley Street Station, Bury. Our cycles had been crated. Cable carts, wagons and crates had to be loaded on the train. By the time the train started, for Southampton, at 5 a.m., we were tired and uncomfortable, but settled ourselves for the long journey.

---

27 Lieut. Gordon Leslie Broad, RE (TF). Later awarded the Military Cross and Mentioned in Despatches for his service at Gallipoli. See Appendix III: Soldiers' biographies.

As daylight came we pulled ourselves together, and noticed that we passed through Rochdale, Huddersfield, Penistone and Sheffield. Most of us had fat heads, and there were no songsters in our compartment. Our previous journeys in khaki had been to camps; this was something new, and it was taking us away from our old haunts and friends. A brighter outlook came later on.

Reaching Leicester, we saw squads of recruits, for the new Kitchener's Army, being drilled. At level-crossings, near villages, women and children had gathered to wave, and shout something we could not hear, as our train passed them. Here and there flags hung from windows. We passed through Willesden, the Aldershot country, Woking and Winchester. Near Southampton, the line was guarded by territorials; nearer still, sentries were posted at short intervals. Red Cross trains were waiting near the docks. We had been in the train for thirteen hours when we pulled up alongside a quay with tall cranes and a large shed, and the Donaldson liner SS *Saturnia*, our transport to Alexandria. We left the train and saw our wagons and crates being swung on board. A Boy Scout came to us asking if he could post any letters for us. I scribbled a postcard home, and handed it to him just as our turn came to embark.

The *Saturnia* carried Brigadier General Frith,[28] the staff of the Lancashire Fusiliers Brigade, the 6th and 7th battalions of the Lancashire Fusiliers, and the East Lancs Divisional Signal Company. The strength of the latter was five officers and one hundred and thirty other ranks.

The East Lancashires were the first territorials to volunteer and go overseas as a division.

---

28 Brigadier General Herbert Cokayne Frith, GOC Lancashire Fusilier Brigade. See Appendix III: Soldiers' biographies.

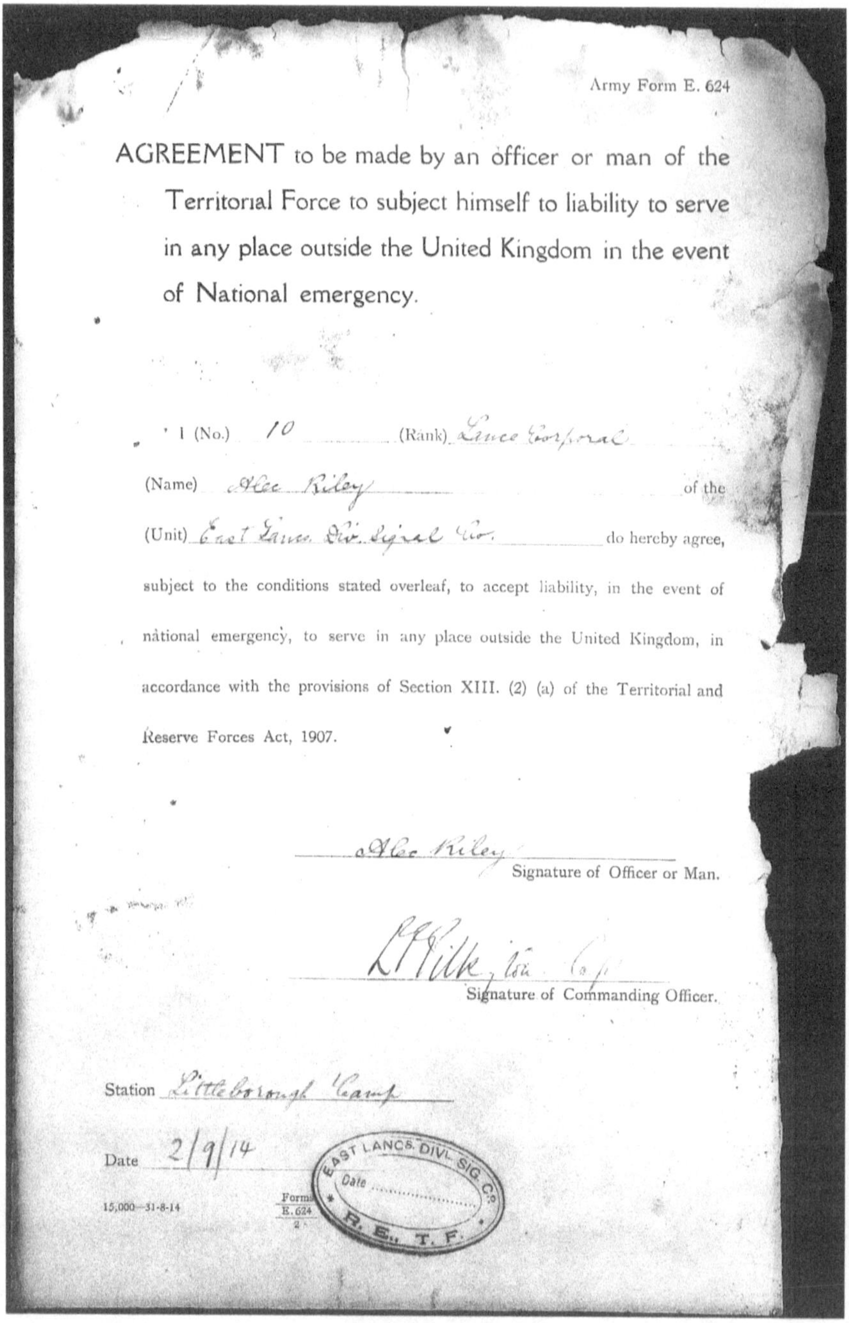

Army Form E. 624

AGREEMENT to be made by an officer or man of the Territorial Force to subject himself to liability to serve in any place outside the United Kingdom in the event of National emergency.

I (No.) 10 (Rank) Lance Corporal

(Name) Alec Riley of the

(Unit) East Lancs. Div. Signal Co. do hereby agree, subject to the conditions stated overleaf, to accept liability, in the event of national emergency, to serve in any place outside the United Kingdom, in accordance with the provisions of Section XIII. (2) (a) of the Territorial and Reserve Forces Act, 1907.

Alec Riley
Signature of Officer or Man.

E. Pilkington Capt.
Signature of Commanding Officer.

Station Littleborough Camp

Date 2/9/14

Figure 4. Army Form E.624, signed by L/Cpl Alec Riley and his OC, Capt. Edward Fielden Pilkington, on 2 September 1914 at Littleborough Camp.

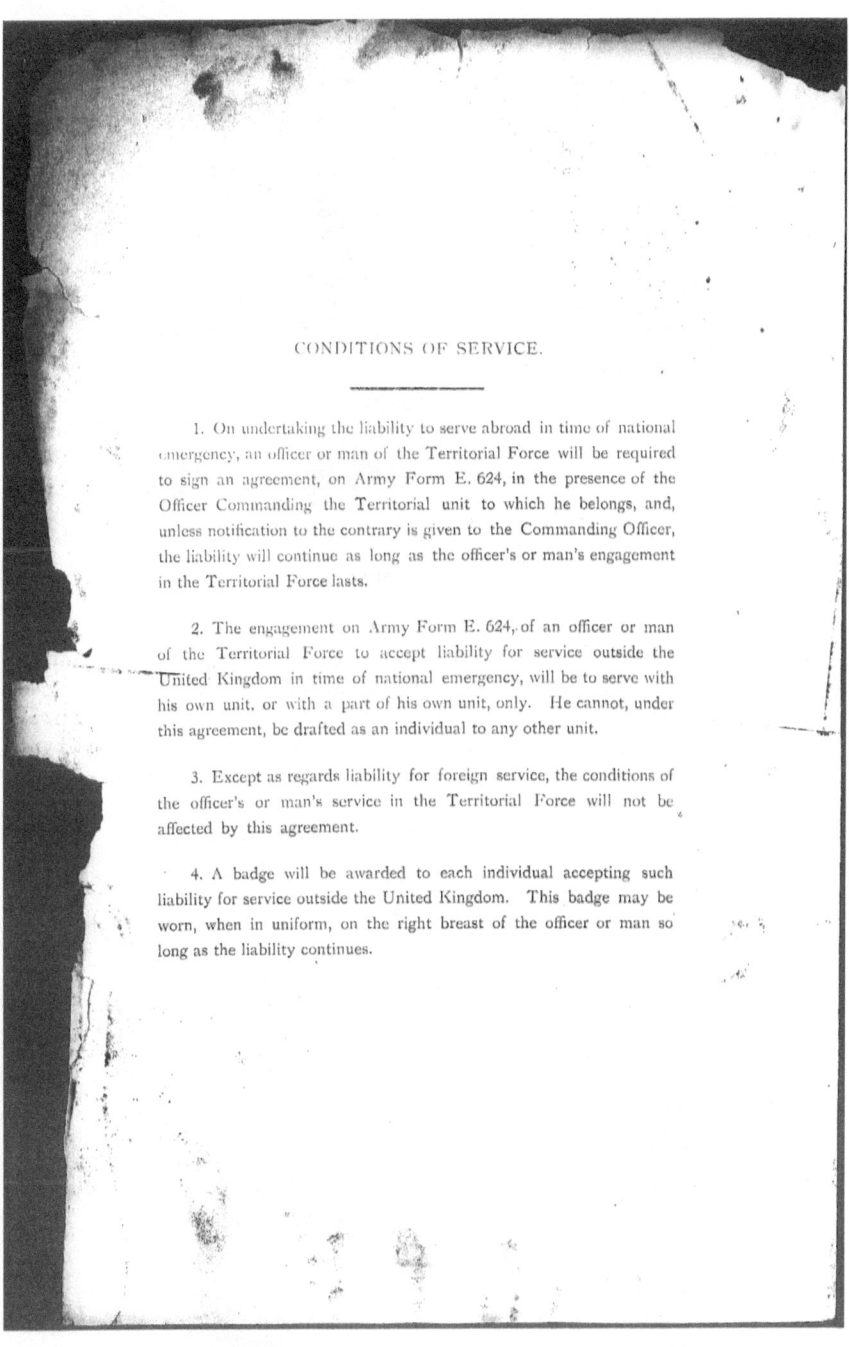

Figure 5. Conditions of service, Army Form E.624. Riley has assented to overseas service, but cannot be compelled to join another unit.

Figure 6. HM Transport *Saturnia*.

Launched 1910 for the Donaldson Line to carry passengers between Glasgow and Canada. Served during the Gallipoli Campaign. In a notorious episode, *Saturnia* appeared at Mudros after the Battle of Gully Ravine with 700 wounded suffering from filthy conditions on board, the transport having previously been used to carry horses and mules. The lack of hospital ships had forced *Saturnia* to act in this capacity. Scrapped 1929.

CHAPTER 4

On the 'Saturnia'

We were soon up the gangway and on a deck where men were crowding and pushing. We felt lost. My head ached. NCOs were paraded, and someone gave me a scrap of paper torn from a notebook. On it was scribbled 'Mess 127 Main Deck 2, 20 men.' I was in charge of Mess 127; and when I found it I saw that it consisted of five cabins, with four berths in each, and a place for meals. My duties were to see that the meals were decently managed, and that the cabins were clean. In my cabin I had three lads, Allen, Yates and C. Ridings.[29] We were fortunate to be in cabins; most of the Lancs Fusiliers were crowded on the lower decks, where they slept in hammocks. We drew tea-buckets and bread-tins from stores. We had plenty of blankets. Mine smelt as if somebody had been sick on them. Our kit-bags were stored for the voyage; we had taken out what we thought we should need. Our portion of No. 2 Main Deck was near a companionway leading up to the Main Deck—our parade ground. A variety of noises reached us, for our ship was still alongside the quay. We were all very tired, and as soon as we were settled I went to bed.

Waking in the early morning I could hear the sea lapping against the ship's side. We had left Southampton about 11 p.m., and the *Saturnia* was the last of our divisional transports to sail.

---

29 Spr 838 Charles William Ridings. See Appendix III: Soldiers' biographies.

Figure 7. The East Lancs Divisional Signal Company aboard HMT *Saturnia* in the Bay of Biscay.

We felt strange and out of sorts when we turned out on Friday morning. There was no early parade, but later on there was a general parade and inspection by the brigadier. We did not know our way about; the sea and sky were grey, and it did us no good to look at them. For most of that day the ship rolled about, a few miles off Rame Head near Plymouth, where we joined the other transports. There were fourteen of them, carrying our division of about 15,500 men, and about 1,000 of the Herts Yeomanry and the City of Westminster Yeomanry. Our escorts were the *Ocean*, a battleship, and the *Minerva*, a cruiser. There was also an ammunition boat, the *Chevington*. The names of the transports were *Aragon*, *Caledonian*, *Avon*, *Grantully Castle*, *Saturnia*, *Mesaba*, *Deseado*, *Corsican*, *Ionian*, *Atlantian*, *Indian*, *Californian*, *Norseman* and *Neuralia*.

A job was found for our section; we were posted on a deck over the galley, and we were told to look out for messages signalled from the other transports. GHQ was the *Deseado*.

CHAPTER 4

In the distance we could see the Devon coast and Start Point. On this gloomy afternoon the land looked as dull and grey as the sea and sky. The swaying of the ship made us feel very uneasy. When we sailed that evening, we saw the Eddystone lighthouse, small in the distance, against a dull red sunset.

The ship went on rolling, and by Saturday most of us felt ill, and many were sick. I escaped being sick, but had all the symptoms. When we rolled I had a kind of dark green feeling; but my bunk was comfortable and I had plenty of blankets. I used my life-belt for a pillow. Looking about me, I thought the cabin needed washing and painting, and the brass-work round the porthole wanted polishing. My cabin companions were quiet and subdued—like most of the other passengers.

The ship rolled more, as we approached the Bay of Biscay. Men from the lower decks came up our stairs, going to the deck to be sick. Some of them were sick before they reached the deck, and our landing and passages were used as vomitoriums. The latrines on the upper deck were hopeless.

'Hell-faced Bill' looked very holy;[30] and I felt very saint-like, living on dry bread and biscuits.

All the parts of the ship that I saw were filthy. The sea was rough all day, and worse at night.

On the morning of Sunday, September 13th, however, I felt better, and when the wireless news was posted up we were so cheered by the news from France that we wondered why we were going to Egypt at all. It was predicted, officially, that we should all eat our Christmas dinners in England, although the Kaiser was said to have sworn that he would dine in Buckingham Palace on Christmas Day. If everything was going so well, why did not our transports turnabout and go back to England? But they did not.

---

30 Probably the brigade postal orderly. 'Hell-faced Bill' is referred to in Riley's Gallipoli diary as 'the postman.' He was the source of news in more ways than one, as Riley points out: 'Hell-face was always ready to discuss the situation in general, and rumours and the goings on at YDB in particular.'

Our ships were now in four lines, something like this:

	Ocean		
Chevington	*Avon*	*Deseado*	*Californian*
	Grantully Castle	*Corsican*	*Norseman*
Caledonian	*Aragon*	*Ionian*	*Indian*
	Saturnia	*Minerva*	*Neuralia*
	Mesaba	*Atlantian*	

At other times they were in two lines; at others, three.

We steamed at nine knots by day, this being the speed of the *Chevington*, the slowest boat. At night the *Minerva* bustled the *Chevington* to the front, but she was usually astern again by morning. Only navigation lights were shown by night.

Routine was established. Reveille was at 6 a.m., breakfast at 7.15 a.m., dinner at noon, and tea at 4 p.m. Between ten and eleven o'clock, each morning, we paraded on our deck, while the brigadier and staff, preceded by the ship's captain, made a round of inspection. Their approach was heralded by Gs on a bugle. After the first inspection, complaints about our cabins reached us through the usual channels.

Boat-parties were detailed. I was in charge of one of them; but when an alarm was sounded that afternoon for boat-parties to assemble at their stations, it took me half an hour to push my way through the crowded decks to ours. Nobody said anything about it, so I did not either.

According to the custom at sea, our Sunday dinners were excellent, particularly the plum puddings. After dinner we went to the Promenade Deck to listen to the Fusiliers' band. We had tea on deck. The cruiser signalled 'two horses dead.'

One of my cabin companions, Private Charles Allen, a youth with an unfascinating exterior, and a wearer of spectacles, found his voice. His song was about a man called 'William Hall,' and it consisted of several repetitions of the statement that 'His name was William Hall,' followed by his deficiencies, and ended by telling us what to do with the drummers. Pte Allen offended me by tying my life-belt to my mattress, and I told him so.

CHAPTER 4

We began to understand that the Donaldson Line was feeding us very well indeed. I had to issue or divide, more or less equally, whatever came to Mess 127. At breakfast, porridge and syrup, mixed, could only be served with a cup, and the ration worked out at a cup and a half per man. Jam or marmalade were issued, and we could buy tinned things from the dry canteen. Occasionally, we had coffee instead of tea.

By Monday, September 14th, the sun was strong, and as few of us had been out of England before, we began to feel it. In the heat of the morning we had physical drill in bare feet, on the Boat Deck. We looked upon it as an outrage. More nasty things were said about our cabins and bunks, and at dinner Mess 127 was very noisy. The weather was delightful, and the sea blue and calm. More good news was posted up.

Some of the men in Mess 127 had been vaccinated three weeks earlier. Most of their arms were red and swollen, and very painful. It took us all our time to keep reasonably clean, and very little could be done to keep down the results of vaccination. I had some lint and bandages, and used most of it on those who needed it. The MO said he had no bandages. We could not get hot water. Naturally, there was a lot of grumbling.

That night at 8 p.m. an order was given: 'All below, and Lights Out in ten minutes.' Humphries heard firing, or thought he did.

Next morning the cabins were hot and stuffy. At 11.30 we paraded for our first half-doses of inoculation. Our RAMC men painted iodine patches on our arms, and then we filed past the MO who gave us the needle. He gave me a stiff and sore left arm, slight headache and giddiness. I spent the afternoon resting on the Boat Deck. We were promised another half-dose in ten days. At night we were feverish, but were left in peace.

About twenty men in our company held out against inoculation. Claude said that he and the two Ridings had refused it.[31] Claude had no particular reasons for this; and later on, while he was lounging on the deck, he heard the MO arguing with some obstinate Lancs Fusiliers. As there was no response, Claude offered himself and the Lancs Fusiliers followed like sheep. Each of us appeared to feel slightly different effects from the others.

---

31 Pnr 3614 Ernest Houghton 'Claude' Hague. See Appendix III: Soldiers' biographies.

Some of the Lancs Fusiliers objected very strongly to inoculation—it was such an unknown quantity. Their reasons were various: one man had a brother who was inoculated in South Africa, and then had scarlet fever twice; another said that a woman in his street had sores after being vaccinated. Others would not argue about it, even when we pointed out that the army was not doing it for fun, or at no expense.

I had an old pair of grey trousers, a felt sun hat and canvas shoes. With these and a shirt I was comfortably dressed. The Promenade Deck was the pleasantest part of the ship available to other ranks. We spent a lot of time on it, lying about, lounging and watching the sea go past. I could not settle to reading, and did not want to. Life was full of real interests.

The Lancs Fusiliers sergeants and staff NCOs didn't like us at all. They tried, but failed, to have us moved from our cabins. One of them made Tommy take off his Imperial Service badge, saying, quite rightly, that we were all on imperial service.

One night we spread a rumour that one of my cabin-companions had a phosphorescent face. We turned the light off and invited people to step in and have a look at it. Noble accepted the invitation,[32] came to the door and stepped in a can of water.

We were heavy and tired after inoculation, but roused ourselves to look at Cape St Vincent, about five miles off, through our telescopes.

With increasing heat we got very thirsty. Drinking water in the tanks was warm and brown, but we drank it. We could buy beer, ginger beer and lemonade, but they were expensive. Some of the Lancs Fusiliers sergeants bought sweets and cigarettes, and retailed them to the men, saving them the trouble of queuing up at the small canteen. There came the voice of one crying:

'Oo sez a Bombay kewler? Oo sez another? Bombay kewlers—penny a cup! Oo sez one?'

In one hand he carried a cup, in the other a bucket of water in which he had mixed a tin of salts. These merchants, who had been charging double prices, were found out, and then the market became easier. The crew were fond of money, too.

We saw few ships, apart from our transports; not a dozen in a week.

---

32 Pnr 1392 George Richard Noble. See Appendix III: Soldiers' biographies.

CHAPTER 4

Figure 8. The Rock of Gibraltar seen from a troopship carrying the East Lancashire Division to Egypt, September 1914. The lighthouse on Europa Point can be seen just right of centre in the foreground.

We watched the black porpoises, their wet skins flashing in the sunlight as they dived and turned. Our boat was on the level now, but we saw other transports being tossed about. Evenings were delightful, and the sunsets wonderful to us. In our bunks, however, we were very hot— sometimes too hot to sleep.

When we went on deck, on the morning of Thursday, September 17th, we were approaching the Straits of Gibraltar. To our left was the Spanish coast, brown-baked and barren, until it was relieved by the white, flat-roofed buildings of Tarifa, and its lighthouse. We ran into a sea-mist, and were in it until 11 a.m., nearly colliding with another boat. We should have met it mid-on and at right angles; but we were steaming so slowly that there was time for both ships to clear. Then, out of the mist came the Rock of Gibraltar. The mist lifted.

From a route guide father had lent me, we located the points of interest on the Rock as we approached it. We anchored in the bay, about three-quarters of a mile from shore, and nearly opposite Rosia. Few of us had seen the Rock before, and it looked very attractive in the sunlight.

Figure 9. HMT *Saturnia*. Warm weather in the Mediterranean. 'Hose-pipings kept us fresh.'

We wanted to go on shore and explore the Moorish Castle, the walls, the pink-brown houses on the lower slopes and the great rocky peak and ridge. Some captured German vessels were anchored in the bay. We had written letters, but the naval people who came out to us would not take our mails. Small boats brought hopeful traders, but no business was allowed. With small flags we called up some Middlesex territorial signallers who were sitting on a balcony of their barracks near Rosia.

After dinner we were squirted with sea water from hose-pipes. We queued up, naked, and ran into the cool, refreshing water, and we took all we could get, feeling better for it. The *Ocean* and the *Chevington* left us at Gibraltar.

We sailed at 5 p.m. As we drew away from the Rock we had our first glimpse of its precipitous side. Entering the Mediterranean, we looked back at a fine spectacle of the Rock and the Spanish mountains—black against the dull red glow of sunset. The night air was damp and chilly, but we stayed on deck watching the searchlight on Europa Point, whose beam followed us for many miles. We approached the coast of Morocco, where high mountain peaks were outlined against bright lightning flashes. Over the ship's side we looked down to the bright phosphorescence of the water.

The days passed easily and pleasantly. We sat on the large hatches, dozing, when we were not eating. The sun was warmer now, and we began to take it seriously.

In obscure and mysterious corners, there were schools of thought dealing with 'Housy-Housy' or 'Crown and Anchor.' It amused us to hear the cries of 'Kelly's Eye,' 'Legs eleven,' 'Top of the bunk,' 'Clickety-click,' 'Blind Thirty.'

Parading on our deck one morning, General Frith addressed us from the end of the Promenade Deck above us. What he said surprised us, for he used a lot of bad words, and when some of us squinted up at him, he said:

'Yes. Some of you look surprised, but that's what I hear passing my cabin all day long.'

We noticed how bright the stars shone at night and went on deck to look at them, and, in particular the reflection of the Milky Way on the calm dark water.

On the morning of Sunday, September 20th, Shoeing-smith A. Turner, DOYIY, fell through a hatchway on the *Atlantia* and was killed.[33] We paraded at 4 p.m. for the funeral. The fleet slowed down, and we stood at attention until 4.15. The boat was rolling and it made me feel rather giddy and sick. We faced the side of the ship. Ormy dashed from the ranks and reached the side just in time, hanging over it until he had quite finished being very sick indeed.

Lawford, our OC,[34] gave us some notes on health in hot countries. He knew little about it, and the notes were scanty. We saw land to port, but did not know what it was. Next morning we saw Pantelleria, and, in the evening we passed south of Gozo and Malta, where powerful searchlights played. We saw the glow from the lights of Valletta. A ship's concert, followed by a visit to the deck to watch some lightning, ended the day.

---

33 Shoeing Smith 3315 Alfred Turner, Duke of Lancaster's Own Yeomanry. Commemorated Chatby Memorial, Alexandria, Egypt.

34 Maj. Arthur Niven Lawford. See Appendix III: Soldiers' biographies.

One of our despatch riders, Flatters, who wore a long string of ribbons, had been to Egypt and Cairo some years before. We were curious about it, but all he seemed able to tell us was that there were some barracks on a hill in Cairo.

About 4 p.m. on Tuesday, September 22nd, our fleet met the Lahore Contingent of Indian troops going to France.[35] Including warships there were about 39 vessels, all stopped for an hour while messages and compliments were exchanged. Our *Minerva* went back with the Indians, and their *Weymouth* came with us.

Hose-pipings were keeping us fresh, and we found a new game with sea water: dropping empty bottles from the bows, and watching the rainbows in the fine spray from the splashes.

Private Bridge of the 9th Manchesters, having died from pneumonia, there was a funeral on the *Aragon* at 10 a.m. on Thursday, the 24th.[36]

As we approached Egypt, kit-bags were brought up and stacked on deck, and a guard mounted over them. The night was very hot indeed. We were up at 4 a.m. on Friday morning. Dawn and sunrise were beautiful in their delicate colours. At last we saw the low coast of Egypt—sandy shores, odd white buildings and a few green palm trees. We ran into a lot of brown water. This was from the Nile, and the sea and river waters had not yet blended. Then, in the distance, we saw the forts, buildings and minarets of Alexandria. Steaming slowly, we approached the quays, and by 9 o'clock we were moored to one of the coal-quays. The sun was very hot. A procession of labourers was coaling a boat, carrying the coal in buckets. Then came a crowd of natives, barefooted, wearing dirty white, blue or black 'night-gowns,' scrambling for the coins our men threw down to them, until Soudanese policemen chased them away with the help of long canes, belts, stones—most of which were effective.

---

35 The 3rd (Lahore) Division, Indian Army.

36 Pte 1705 John Bridge, 9th Manchesters. Commemorated on the Chatby Memorial, Alexandria, Egypt.

CHAPTER 4

The US warship *North Carolina* came in, her latticed masts attracting our interest.[37] On our waterside, boats came alongside with fruit and cigarettes. Business was done by basket—the money being sent down first. Bottles of supposed whisky came through the port-holes. That evening we each drew a suit of khaki drill and a helmet. At night we heard noise, and shouting from an officer on deck. Two small boats were alongside, and the officer was threatening to fire his revolver. I was glad to leave the crowded boat at ten o'clock on the morning of Saturday, September 26th. As I put my foot on the setts of the quay, I remember thinking that my first step in a foreign country was on a very dirty place.

Our train to Cairo was close by. While we waited to enter it we saw our cycle-crates slung out of the hold and crashing against the *Saturnia*'s side as they were lowered. We marched to the train, found places in third class coaches, and stored ourselves and our equipment in them. The wooden seats were hard, and their cracks and corners were full of dust. The rest of the train carried Lancs Fusiliers. While we waited for the train to start we heard strange cries outside. From the wilderness of coal and dust came shouts of 'Bē'ar' sheeling,' or 'Bē'ra' sheeling,' meaning bottles of beer for a shilling. There was fruit as well, and a large melon came from somewhere. The change was very dirty and very damp. It came from somewhere near the armpits of dirty men wearing dirty clothes.

At last the train steamed slowly out of the quay-sidings and on to the main line, passing coal-stacks and shabby huts. Then came the suburbs of Alexandria, rather European-looking, except for the vegetation and palms. At last the train began to move more quickly, on the journey of 130 miles. The railway crosses a canal, runs along the side of Lake Mareotis, and enters the Delta country, 17 miles from Alexandria, at Kafr el-Dawar. Then comes Damanhour, a large town; then a bridge over the Rosetta arm of the Nile, then Tanta, Benha, and Cairo.

---

37 The North Carolina's band welcomed the convoy with a rendition of 'God save the King' to which the band of the 8th Manchesters, unsure as to the national anthem of the United States, responded by playing 'Marching through Georgia.' As the 42nd Division's history states, 'All too late came the reflection that possibly the cruiser's complement had been drawn from States that might not appreciate this air.'

Figure 10. A woman carrying water.

Figure 11. Tall-masted rivercraft on the Nile near Cairo.

The landscapes and life of the Delta, as seen from the train, include cotton fields, fresh green cultivation, palms, cactus, prickly pear. Along the *gisrs*, or raised canal-banks, are camels loaded with green fodder or vegetables held by rope nets; donkeys, carrying men or women on their rears; small family groups; women in dark blue robes carrying water pots on their heads. The villages are built of mud-bricks, easily repairable, dirty, quaint and curious to us; the slender, pointed minarets of the mosques reminding us how far away are our own churches; small cafés with chairs outside, little circles of old men puffing the water pipe and passing it round. We pass houses old and new, painted in various colours—yellow, white, red, blue; cemeteries, small white domes of tombs peeping through green vegetation. By the canal sides, water is being raised by *shadoofs*, with their tall, slender poles, or by *sakiehs*, horizontal wooden wheels interlocked with vertical wheels, the former being driven round by camels or water buffalo, usually blindfolded. There are houses with white walls decorated with rough paintings of trains, palms, lions, ships, indicating the home of a Mecca pilgrim. Men and boys are bathing in dirty ditches, and women are washing clothes at every available spot of water.

We were interested in our first glimpse of the Nile, with its tall-masted *gyassas* and smaller rivercraft; and again, when we crossed the Damietta branch, near Benha. We were very hot and tired, when, just at dusk, we saw the Pyramids of Gizeh, pink in the evening light, far away to the south-west over the palms. Then came the Libyan hills, the Mokattams and the Citadel close by, with the two slender minarets of the mosque of Mohamet Ali. Then came gardens and villas and the suburbs of Cairo. Behind railings and palms the high buildings looked mysterious. Leaving the main line, the train went on slowly until it reached Abbassia sidings, where we got out.

We had spent six and a half hours in the train. It was quite dark. No. 4 Section was alone. We did not know where either the Lancs Fusiliers or the rest of the Signal Company were. What we wanted was something to drink. We waited in the darkness until someone came to tell us where to go to; then we crossed a stretch of dusty sand, kicking it up, covering ourselves with dust and swallowing a lot of it. We saw some lights and buildings ahead. These were barracks. From a ground-floor room at the end of one block shone a light. It came from a canteen. I saw the others were busy while I was lowering a pint of shandy. I was so dry that I could not taste it—I could only just feel it. We felt better. Where there was beer there was hope. Two of our party had lost us but found the Westminster Dragoons canteen. Then, over more sand to the old Camel Corps School—a long, single-storey building on the edge of nothing. This was our home for the next few months. We were hungry. We dumped everything on the sand against the wall and went to look for food. The canteens, at the far end of the building, were closed, but a Camel Corps sergeant soon had them opened for us, and before long we were having sausage and mashed, bread and tea. Behind the counter was a dark Egyptian, known to us as Moursi (phonetically). After our meal, we went outside and laid down on the sand along the wall, and were soon sleeping our first Egyptian night.

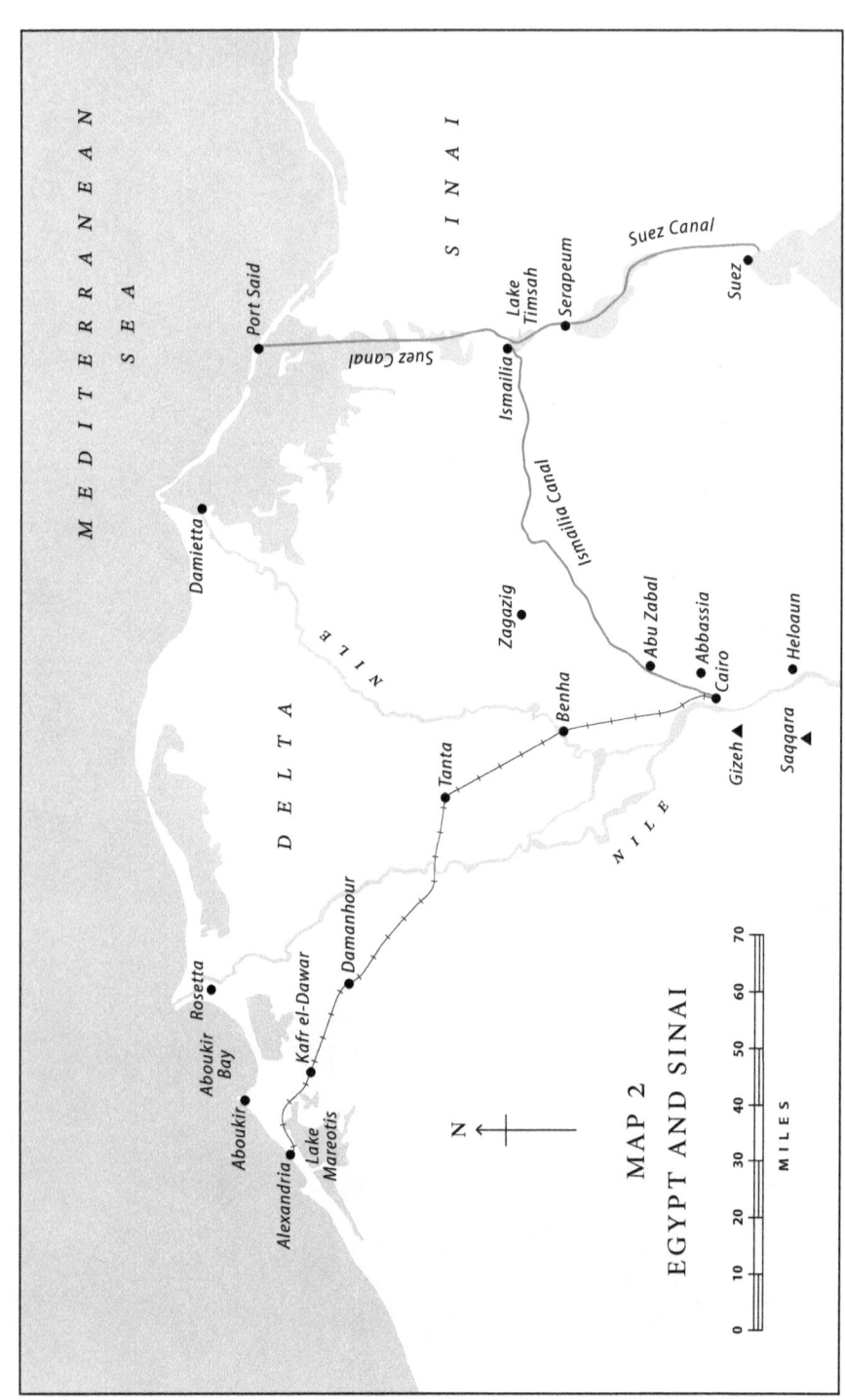

CHAPTER 5

Cairo — Polygon Barracks

Next morning, we shook the sand from our clothes, found the washhouse, bathed, bought our breakfasts in the dry canteen; the rest of the day was spent in drawing bedding, stores, biscuits, or sacks of straw for our beds. We were posted to our rooms. To my disgust I was in charge of No. 11, and twelve men. Letters from home were handed out. This day, Sunday, September 27th, the regulars left for France. We needed and had many drinks. At night we found the Soldiers' Home, where there were English papers and where Reuters' news for the day was posted up. Several of us were bitten by mosquitoes. I found it hard to get to sleep.

The state of our company on September 27, 1914, was five officers and 131 other ranks. The OC was Captain A.N. Lawford. Lieutenant G. Broad was I/C Cables. Lieutenant R.S. Newton had the Lancs Fusiliers Brigade Section,[38] Lieutenant N. Robinson the East Lancs Brigade section,[39] and Captain C. Williamson was in charge of ours—No. 4, the Manchester Brigade section. Our CSM was Nuttall and our CQMS was Campbell.[40] Between these two a gulf was fixed, although they shared the same quarters. No. 4 Section was in rooms 1 and 11, all my particular friends being in No. 1.

---

38 Lieut. Robert Saunders Newton, 1/6th Lancs Fusiliers. Later awarded the Military Cross and Mentioned in Despatches in France in 1917. See Appendix III: Soldiers' biographies.

39 Lieut. Nicolas Robinson, 1/4th East Lancs Regt. See Appendix III: Soldiers' biographies.

40 CSM 240 Roland Harry Nuttall, RE, and Sergeant (A/CQMS) 4492 James Edward Campbell. At this time, Nuttall, although senior in rank, was a territorial with just eight years' service, while Campbell was a regular with over 18 years' service. Campbell had been posted to the East Lancs Sig. Coy in 1908 as Instructor Sergeant when Nuttall was still a sapper, and Nuttall's rapid promotion above Campbell to CSM may have caused the 'gulf' that existed between the two men. See Appendix III: Soldiers' biographies.

Our hours were reveille 5 a.m., rouse parade 5.30–6.15, parade 7.30–10.30, and then, during the remainder of the hot season, nothing more until 4–5.15 p.m. Breakfast was at 6.30 a.m., dinner 12.30 p.m., tea 5.30 p.m. and lights out 9.30 p.m.

It was illegal to go out of doors without a helmet. The local Indian tailor fixed puggarees on our helmets at a small cost. We ordered khaki drill shorts, for which 15 piastres were given to us. We wore khaki drill suits, the issue being two suits per man. Excellent health rules were posted on the notice board. I made a copy of them—they seemed so useful.

Our building was of a pink-brown colour outside; the rooms were whitewashed, and painted where necessary. The wash-house had shower-baths, and we used an old circular camel trough on the parade ground for a plunge-bath. With its thick walls, the building was cool by day. By night, we had candles and later on oil-lamps.

The dry canteen was run by Liptons. Here we could buy teetotal drinks, and lime juice which was kept in a large glass barrel where we

Figure 12. Entrance to the military barracks, Abbassia.

CHAPTER 5

Figure 13. Troops of the 1/5th East Lancs Regt mounting the guard at Heliopolis.

Figure 14. A gharry with officers of the 1/5th Bn, East Lancs Regt.
From left to right are Second Lieut. Jack Baron, Second Lieut. James Thornber and Capt. Cyril Robinson.

could see the limes floating. For two piastres (five pence) we could have sausage and mashed, liver and bacon, fish and chips, eggs, tea, coffee, bread—half a piastre extra.

The native servants did all the cleaning and dirty work.

The heat was dry and shrivelling. It seemed to hit us hard when we went outside from the cool shade. Dusty sand made us dry and thirsty.

We soon got used to the coinage. Piastres (Egyptian) were 97½ to the English pound, one piastre being two and a half pence approximately. Then there were half-piastres and milliemes—ten milliemes to the piastre and 1,000 to the pound (Egyptian). Piastres were commonly known as 'disasters.' The half piastre piece had the old Sultan's monogram on one side. This design was known as the 'perambulator' from its shape. The half piastre was used for tossing-up as well as business. We discovered 'backshiesh' which became 'buckshee' meaning 'for nothing.' Tea was 'shai' and 'shai up' meant that tea was ready. Rations were mostly on English standards. Breakfasts were often very good. Meat at dinner was usually scraggly. Teas, helped by the daily sixpence allowed for each man, were good. I had to divide the rations at my table, solving such problems as dividing three tins of herrings— four in each—among thirteen men. At breakfast time newsboys came round shouting 'Gypsum Mail,' 'Gazette,' both printed in English. We heard that one newsboy shouted 'Bloody good news for English soldiers. Lord Roberts dead,' on the morning after that event.

Just before our reveille we heard the trumpets of the Egyptian cavalry. Clear and pure, over the sand, came the calls. We were not pleased, when ours sounded, to have to get up and turn out in the chilly air, just as the sky was grey in the dawn. As we fell in and numbered, we saw the sun rise over the edge of the desert, and at once the sand changed from grey to pink, and then warm brown, while the red and pink of the sky changed to pale green, then yellow, then blue. The acacia trees were green now, or golden as the horizontal beams of early light flashed through the leaves, while the hoopoes or 'kite-hawks' gave us a song or two. By this time we couldn't help being awake, and our parade seemed very insignificant, in the warm light and colour of an Egyptian sunrise.

On our free evenings we began to discover Cairo. We were about four miles from the central station. From the main guard on the Heliopolis Road, the tram fare to the city was four milliemes. It was late afternoon, except on Sundays and half-holidays, when we were free. On the road, we passed mysterious looking shops and hovels. There were innumerable cafes, often at street corners, where chairs were placed on the pavement, and where men sat, smoking water pipes or 'hubble-bubbles' as we called them.

There were plenty of cycles and motors on the roads. The gharry was the usual conveyance, and from the main guard we could hire a gharry to Polygon for a piastre each passenger. Camels were commoner than horses, and donkeys commoner still. Often enough we returned by donkey. For some time we were amused by the sight of fat Egyptians on small donkeys. Other donkeys carried *bersim* (clover).

The varieties of colour and dress in the streets pleased us—blue *galabiehs*, flowing white robes, baggy breeches, turbans, tarbouches, European and native clothes mixed.

Figure 15. A street in Cairo.

Figure 16. Drink vendor, Cairo.

On the wall is pasted a proclamation in the name of General Sir John Maxwell, commander of the British Force in Egypt. (Martial Law was declared on 2 November 1914, and Egypt made a British protectorate on 18 December 1914.)

The vendor appears to be wearing British Army boots.

CHAPTER 5

The cries of the street-hawkers amused us:

'Orangees! Very good, very nice! Oranges soo-ib in usher (sweet as sugar)!'

Others were selling buttons, matches, studs, bootlaces, dirty-looking sweets; others sold very red strawberries on very green leaves, or 'quoits' of bread, or cakes on large wooden trays carried on the hawker's head, while he carried the trestle in his hand. There were palms, fountains, large earthenware jars full of water—for any passer-by to drink from— by the edge of the pavement. There were gardens, public and private; and there were pestering boot-blacks:

'Clean it boots, mister. Very good, very nice. No good, no money.'

We discovered Oriental cakes in cafes and patisseries. We did not know anything about cakes before we found these. Most of them were liberally soused in honey.

The native police wore black uniforms, leather belts, red tarbouches, and carried batons.

By night, we thought Cairo was more fascinating than by day, when we passed the cafes and shops brightly lit inside, or dimly-lit and mysterious-looking little dens where men moved as shadows. We enjoyed it most when riding on the toast-rack trams back to Abbassia, for the evening breeze—if any—made them pleasantly cool for us. Trams had one or two trailers or coaches. From the toast-rack seats we could see what was going on in the streets. The conductor blew a squeaker—a little brass horn about six inches long—when he wanted the driver to start or stop. He came for his fares along the outside footboard, and usually found great difficulty in giving us small change.

The tram centre was Ataba el-Khadra. Here there was plenty of life. Lemonade and sherbet sellers, in their curious costumes and their peculiar brass or glass vessels with long spouts. By tilting them, the liquid flowed into the glass or cup held a short distance from the end of the spout. The man carried two little brass trays in one hand, and these he clinked together to advertise his presence. A good deal of street-watering was done from skins slung on the waterer's back, and the flow controlled by a hand on the narrow opening of the skin. Much of the water came from the Nile, and there was a never ending procession to

Figure 17. 'Scouts Class' run by officers and men of the Gurkha Rifles, Abbassia, 1915.

Officers sitting, left to right: Second Lieut. John Bolton, 1/5th East Lancs; Second Lieut. Walter James Ablitt, 1/9th Manchesters; Second Lieut. William Lillie, 1/9th Manchesters; Second Lieut. I.L. Simpson, 1/4th East Lancs; Lieut. N.V. Holden, 1/6th Lancs Fus.; Second Lieut. A.C. Middleton, 1/8th Lancs Fus.; Hocking, Gurkha Rifles; Brown, Gurkha Rifles; Lieut. R.W. Wilde, 1/10th Manchesters; Lieut. W. Kelly, 1/7th Lancs Fus.; either Lieut. G.S. James or F.A. James, 1/5th Manchesters; Second Lieut. H.K. Hoyle, 1/5th Lancs Fus.; Second Lieut. W.N. Molesworth, 1/6th Manchesters.

and from certain popular watering places on the river banks. There was the usual cry of 'Oranges good and beeg! Three fil half,' or 'Gib it Mister,' or 'See, Mister, gib it backshiesh.'

Before long, No. 4 Section had few members who were not specially employed; so many that when we had paraded in the early morning, and numbered, it was necessary to give the order:

'Fall out, the specially employed!'

We went so far as to create special employments, or to use old jobs for the same ends. Sometimes, when a dozen or so had no legitimate reasons for falling out, we had short walks. At first we did real walks, but they soon degenerated into a short march to the Old Battery on the Suez Road, where we played duck-stone. Or, after a lot of noise, we marched round the end of the building, in at a door on the far side, and back to bed.

CHAPTER 5

There was nocturnal card playing and gambling by candlelight in No. 11, and there was practical joking. Beds would collapse—until we made a habit of inspecting them before we got in, to see if any pins had been removed. Occasionally pyjama legs or arms were stitched up. Not even the lance corporal in charge escaped, but, as a rule 'countermeasures' were effective.

Some little birds, rather like sparrows, stayed with us for two days, living on a piece of cable, stretched between two pegs, for hanging our equipment on. They were very tame and would sit on our fingers. The mother would sit on Slater's pipe while he smoked it. We caught a lizard and kept it in a mess-tin, feeding it on flies. One night something with many legs walked over my face. One man kept a chameleon, which changed its colour according to its surroundings. It lived on a broad window ledge in the thick wall. We never tired of watching it shoot out its long tongue to catch flies on the window glass. The eyes protruded and we saw them turn upwards or sideways, as it watched the flies. When it had taken slow and careful aim it rarely missed its mark, unless the fly happened to be on the wrong side of the glass. At times we were tormented by sand-flies and mosquitos, for we had no curtains. On Sunday mornings we took our beds to pieces, to clear the nicks and joints of bugs, by dipping them in paraffin. All the iron-work was wiped over with a paraffin rag.

Our work, in the early days, consisted of flag-drill, buzzer practice, short lectures, lamps—twice weekly, rifle inspections, kit inspections on Saturday mornings. Later, we had an hour's drill on Saturday mornings, and cycle inspections. At first we kept our cycles in the corridors, but later on, a store was found for them.

In the early days, when there were no afternoon parades, and the weather was hot, it was popular to undress completely, and lie on our beds with only a sheet over us. Our most popular songs were 'I'll sing these songs in Arabic,' and 'Til the sands of the desert grow cold.' The latter being most favoured when we were sweaty and tired, after a long day on the desert.

Although our company was so small, each section kept much to itself, and it was some time before we mixed ourselves. The brigade section never mixed very much with 'the cables' at any time.

Lance corporals had several duties: they were in charge of the nightly guard over our wagons, and canteen corporals. These duties came round about once a week each. The canteen corporal carried a big stick. There was more trouble in the 'dry' than the 'wet,' for we kept an eye on both. We could close the canteens at any time, but such action would have needed a lot of explaining. We had to make customers queue outside the 'dry,' allowing our own men inside, and making outsiders wait until there was room for them at the counter or tables. We closed the canteens by banging the big stick on the counters, and shouting 'Time!' Canteen corporals were given a free supper for services rendered. Occasionally strange visitors were seen. One was a very large Soudanese, with a knife strapped to his arm.

We increased our vocabularies. At first our only words were *imshi, yalla, sa'ida*.[41] Then came *nahârak sa-id, lêltak sa'id, bōkra, kattar khêrak, ma'lehsh, ta'âla hena, shawish, okilombasha*;[42] and the more advanced *yalla, enta abne kalb*.[43] On our morning walks, a native woman we frequently passed was greeted by 'sa'ida Nellie.'

* * *

I went to the Gizeh Pyramids several times, usually in congenial company. From the tram-centre in Ataba el-Khadra, the fare for the ten miles journey is one piastre (two and a half pence) for men in uniform. The journey takes an hour. The road runs through Bûlak, and crosses Bûlak bridge over the Nile to the island of Gezireh, which it crosses to the Pont Zamalek, then along the small west arm of the river, and on to Gizeh village, passing the Zoological Gardens. (There is a variation of route, via the Old Cairo line and the island of Rôda.) From Gizeh village the road crosses a canal and a railway line, and then it leads straight towards the Pyramids, still nearly five miles distant, which we see on the edge of the desert plateau, gradually growing in apparent size as we draw closer. On either side of the road are fields, a few scattered houses, and the road crosses canals here and there. The road

---

41 Go away; go on or hurry up; nice to meet you.
42 Good day; good night; tomorrow; many thanks; never mind or don't worry about it; come here; sergeant or perhaps policeman; lance corporal.
43 Get away you dog!

Figure 18. 'Hossack and his pyramids.'

Pnr (later Spr) 2119 Ernest Frank Hossack, RE (TF), later 444256, RE. Served with Alec Riley in No. 4 Section, and features regularly in Riley's Gallipoli diary.

is on an embankment to allow for the annual inundation. Men, calling themselves guides, board the trams, pestering us, producing letters of recommendation, and offering their services at a price. The tram terminus is at the foot of the Pyramids plateau, which is ascended by a gradually sloping and dusty road, and which bends left after passing some tourist shops on the left, and Mena House Hotel on the right. At the foot of the slope, we were the centre of a human swarm, offering camels, donkeys. Until we became used to them and found out how to deal with them, we engaged a guide for the sake of peace. He kept off fortune-tellers, beggars, and men selling 'Roman' coins—from the tombs—so they said. Having gained the plateau, Cheops was before us with his height, mass and jagged edges, and the entrance—a hole in the north face, about 55 feet above ground level, and easily reached. Along a rough passage, we reached the top of a ramp, where we were grabbed and snatched at by fifteen men, yelling and jabbering for prey. We were pulled and shoved down a polished slope, using slight depressions in the surface for footholds. We had to stoop. Then up an incline, climbing to a place where the two guides placed our hands and feet. One guide pulled us from the front and the other pushed us from behind. Then along a square-ended passage to the 'Queen's Chamber,' where we made exclamations of wonder, to which the guides suitably responded... In the 'King's Chamber' the granite blocks look freshly cut. There are ventilation shafts. The guide said 'You pleased?' or 'Me please you?'

'Yes.'

'Then you please me after. That business.'

The ascent of Cheops is made at the northeast corner. We had a guide the first time; after that we used to do it alone. The steps are about three feet high, and several rests are needed. The platform at the top is about 12 yards square, and is at a perpendicular height of 450 feet. There was a pleasant breeze on the platform and we had coffee there, while we watched men climbing up the smooth overhanging cap of the Second Pyramid. One or two Australians were killed, later on, at this dangerous game. The view may be good or bad, according to the amount of haze. We discovered that we had to be either on top of, or inside Cheops, to appreciate him. The view is one of life and death, fertility and desolation. To the west we look down on acres and streets of mastabas,[44] excavated by Dr Reisner; to the east lies the flat cultivated, and green, land of the Delta. The Sphinx looks insignificant. The landscape is at its best just before sunset, when the features of the desert are thrown into relief, and when the long, dark shadows of the two large pyramids stretch over the Delta towards Cairo; when the sun no longer scorches, and the sky goes through its colour changes, until the sun sinks below the desert horizon. From the top, the angle of Cheops looks very steep...

We explored the precincts of the Sphinx, then unexcavated, and the sphinx himself. Tommy and I were on his back when a policeman chased us off. We visited various tombs and temples, the Third Pyramid, of Mykerinos, with its granite facings, rough and smooth, at the base.

---

44 An ancient Egyptian tomb consisting of an underground burial chamber with rooms at ground level to store offerings.

CHAPTER 5

Figure 19. The Sphinx and the Great Pyramid of Cheops at Gizeh.

Near the Second Pyramid we could hardly see sand for people, when we looked towards the Sphinx. We had camel rides, but refused to be photographed with the Sphinx as a background. When we were hot and tired, we were jostled by Gyppos competing for the honour (and price) of pouring water on our hands from their earthenware jugs. We noticed several deep, wide and square shafts in the sand. There were several bars in wooden sheds on the sands. Australians and New Zealanders had a large camp close by, and they were round Cheops and the Sphinx in hundreds. The photographer's shop, the postcard shop and the post office, near Mena House, were doing plenty of business. The trams ran every quarter of an hour. They were crowded. Men climbed to the tram-tops and sat back-to-back, and it was one of our joys to watch the conductors climb up to collect the fares.

(This account of our visits to the Pyramids has nothing whatever to do with archaeological details or measurements. It is, mainly, what we did and what we saw, in our spare time.)

* * *

From the early days of October, 1914, it was part of our work to maintain visual communication between our barracks, where the helio and limelight station was known as GN, and Abu Zabal,[45] a large wireless station known as AZ, via a transmitting station on Gebel Ahmar (Red Hill), one and a half miles from the barracks, known as GA.

To protect AZ, detachments of infantry from our brigades were posted there.

I was on the GA duty several times, and at AZ three times.

Our section worked both GA and AZ for some weeks. Duties on GA were by the day; on AZ for a fortnight or longer. We cycled to the post of GA, taking rations for the day, and then climbed the ruddy and rocky hill to our station, taking our cycles up as well. In hot weather, the sun made us feel sick, and we had to endure the smell of several acres of Cairo's refuse dumped near the foot of the hill. Near the refuse dump

---

[45] Abu Zabal (or Zaabal) is situated on the Ismailia Canal about 12 miles NNE of Abbassia. It is now the site of an extensive chemical and military-industrial complex.

was a cemetery, and these two features of the landscape were always before us. There was little shade, and there were no half-holidays until we complained and were relieved of GA altogether.

AZ was a different matter. I was one of the first party to go there, early in October. Loaded with full marching order, rifles and ammunition, helios,[46] telescopes, and one kit-bag for each two men, we went by tram to Pont Limoun Station. Newton was in charge and in a hurry. Before long we were muttering mutinously. We travelled third class, changing trains at El Marg.

---

46 The heliograph (or helio) uses sunlight to flash signals in Morse Code. The British Army's Mark V heliograph came as a sturdy wooden tripod with a leather case for the mirror assembly and spares. In good conditions, the helio could transmit messages to a receiving station more than 70 miles away.

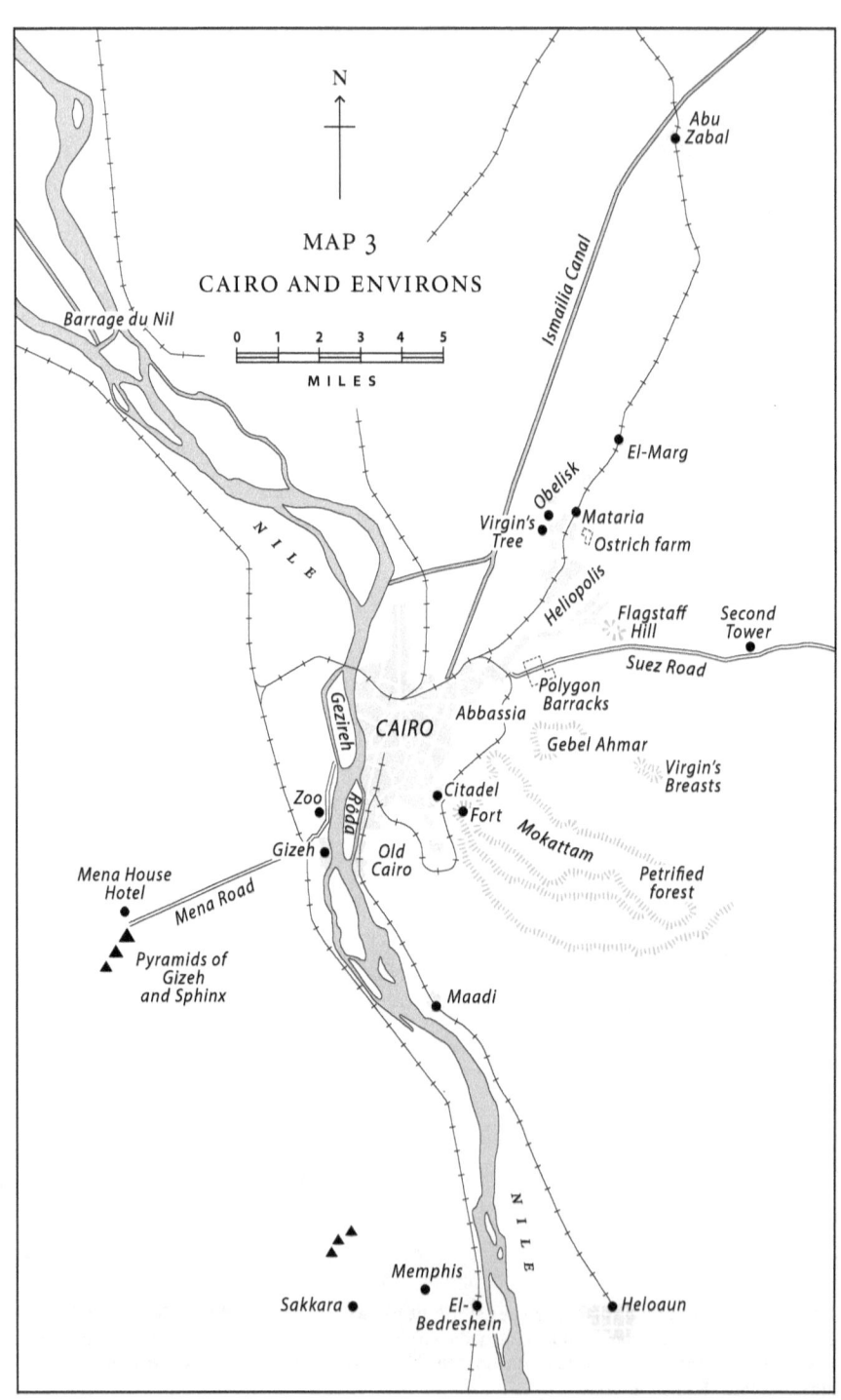

CHAPTER 6

Abu Zabal

We saw that the village of El Marg was a picturesquely dirty collection of mud houses among large palm trees. The crowds on the platform, with their many-coloured garments and turbans, their red tarbouches, the young and swarthy men, the white-bearded and benevolent-looking old gentlemen, the trays and baskets of oranges, the cornucopias of dates, the supercilious young bloods in European dress, the boot-blacks, the few men in khaki—ourselves—all these against the tall green palms, made up a fascinating picture. Later, we saw the palms against a lovely evening sky—pale blue, with pink fluffy clouds.

Including Lieutenant Newton, there were ten of us in the party. We reached the small station of Abu Zabal, and set off for the wireless station, about one and a half miles over the sand. Water pipes were being laid, and we walked on these wherever possible. Reaching the Ismailia Canal, we crossed to the east bank by a wire-rope ferryboat.[47] On the east bank was the engine-house, and beyond, on level land, the eleven masts, 300 feet high and about six feet in diameter at the base. Later on we were told by one of the Marconi men that there would be 14 new masts, 350 feet high. Only six of the present ones were in use. This Marconi station was in touch with Poldhu, Cornwall, with India, South Africa, and Nikolief on the Black Sea.[48] Completion was due in

---

47 The Ismailia Canal, also known as the Sweet Water Canal or Fresh Water Canal, was built to facilitate the construction of the Suez Canal. It originally ran from a point just north of Cairo city centre to the city of Ismailia where it joins the Suez Canal.

48 Nikolayev is the modern-day city of Mykolaiv in southern Ukraine.

Figure 20. The wireless station at Abu Zabal photographed sometime before March 1923. Riley described a tennis court being prepared, perhaps the one seen on the right. Beyond the tennis court is the 'power-house.'

about three years. The new masts would be on the west side of the canal. In addition to the masts and power-house, there was the engineers house where the Marconi men lived, and on the roof of which we had our visual station, and where we slept, Indian-pattern marquees for the troops, the land agent's house, rough huts and a canteen for the native labourers, and a mud-built village (*esba* in dialect), self-contained and without suburbs.

My first visit only lasted two days, and on this first look round we sized up the place and its possibilities. I was thirsty, hot, irritated by sand; and my mouth was sore. Food had small appeal. A dose of chlorodyne was helpful. Our marquee was full of flies and sand-flies.

CHAPTER 6

On the second night, a sentry posted among the masts fired two shots.[49] We turned out with rifles, bayonets, bandoliers, and ten rounds each, but had no chance of firing them. By night, also, the wild and noisy dogs of the village prowled about, barking; and, getting in the marquees under the curtain, sniffed us. We could taste the dust in the marquee. One uninteresting meal consisted of rice and jam and tea. Tommy and I explored the various buildings. I did one duty on the visual station, thinking more of a dry throat and a sore tongue than of the duty. I spent a piastre on a bottle of some foul stuff at the canteen; this being followed by a drink of water from the pump. Two of our party had returned to Abbassia, and Newton had left us the first evening. Somebody stood us a canteen parade, with a choice of beer, cigarettes or soap.

We saw tall columns of dust—'sand devils'—moving over the desert surface. Some of them were three or four hundred feet high. A native was arrested for assaulting one of the engineers,[50] and Lieutenant Lilley,[51] in charge of the detachment of fifty men of the 9th Manchesters, sent a message to General Douglas asking for instructions on what to do with the prisoner.[52] After dinner a message came, ordering the return of two lance corporals; so Forrester and I returned, leaving Abu Zabal on the 6.30 p.m. train, and having our bags carried to the station by a native. In Cairo, our first duty was to call at a convenient patisserie. We must have been sugar-starved. The others followed, leaving Ormesher and Thomas,[53] only, at AZ.

---

49 The threat to security was real as there was a great deal of unrest among nationalist elements. A few days earlier a sentry at Kasr-el-Nil Barracks, Pte 1637 Herbert Fish of the 9th Manchesters, had shot and wounded an 'Arab' intruder armed with a revolver.

50 The arrested man was a German national and the episode was described by one of his captors, Pte 1497 James Chatburn: 'I had the pleasure of capturing a German Spy, and escorting him to the consul in Cairo. He was a fine man, about six foot. When I first saw him, he was drawing the plans of the wireless station, which I found on him. When searched he also had with him a khaki suit and a soft black hat. He said he was looking for work. They knew him in Cairo, and he was wanted on another case of importance.' ('Captured Spy', *Ashton Reporter*, 24 October 1914)

51 Second Lieut. William Hampson Lillie, C Company, 1/9th Manchesters.

52 Maj. Gen. Sir William Douglas, KCMG, CB, DSO. GOC East Lancashire Division. See Appendix III: Soldiers' biographies.

53 Probably Pte 2391 Richard Thomas. See Appendix III: Soldiers' biographies.

On November 2, Haworth and I were detailed for AZ. We bought some groceries—jam, syrup, tinned fruit, Nestle's milk. I had to look for a railway warrant. The Garrison Adjutant would not give me one, nor would divisional headquarters, and Nick Robinson had to find one—and did. Claude Hague and four men escorted us to the station— calling at the 'Khedivial' on the way. This time we carried 50 rounds of ammunition each. At Abu Zabal station we found a carrier for our kit-bag, paying him one and a half piasters for one and half miles. I reported to Lieutenant Wolfe, the officer in charge.[54] He told me that martial law had been declared in Egypt and the Sudan. All men leaving the wireless station must be escorted, and none could leave camp. There was haze, so we could not get GA on the helio. The *Egyptian Mail* rumoured that Russia and Turkey were at war.

Our home, now, was on the flat roof of the engineers' house, which was surrounded by a parapet about four feet in height. We reached it by a wobbly ladder standing on an old Tate's sugar box. From the roof we saw plenty of desert in the Cairo direction and to the left. Behind us was the canal. Near the *esba* were monkey-nut plantations; dotted about were the water-raising wheels—the *sakiehs*—usually in small clumps of trees. We were soon used to the ceaseless creaking of these *sakiehs*—a kind of country noise and not unpleasant to hear. That was by day; by night we heard familiar music on a piano in the house below. Or, the croaking of the canal frogs, while from the power-house came the whirr of the engines, bright green flashes from the windows, and the loud, buzzing '····–, ····–.' After a time we ceased to notice the latter. Occasionally, we heard shots. And we could hear the weird cries of the *gaff'eers* (night-watchmen).

Mosquitoes plagued us, and our handkerchiefs dangling over our faces were small protection.

When we awoke, we sometimes found everything wet with dew. One morning, feeling hungry, I found ants busy on the bread of my previous day's ration. For a time the detachment was short of rations, and there was a lot of grumbling. Someone fired a shot near the canal, so Wolfe

---

54 Probably Lieut. Percy Wolf, 1/4th East Lancs Regt, KIA Gallipoli 4 June 1915. See Appendix III: Soldiers' biographies.

CHAPTER 6

Figure 21. Scoops on the vertical wheel of a *sakieh*.
A drive shaft connects it to a horizontal wheel that powers the device.

Figure 22. *Gamoose* (water buffalo) driving the horizontal wheel of a *sakieh*.

Figure 23. 'Rural scene' with *sakieh*.

Figure 24. The millennias-old *shadoof* in operation.

took a small party to see what was going on. Food became shorter, grumbling increased, and a deputation went to see what Wolfe was going to do about it. Haworth and I, however, were far from starving. From our roof we watched long strings of camels carrying rope nets of mud bricks slung on each side. I was well bitten, and my face was covered with red spots.

The sand was hot, scorching our feet through our boots. By day, we had no shade, only heat and flies. By night we had cold, and the noise of barking dogs, croaking frogs, and biting mosquitoes wherever they could find any parts of us to bite. Beer was short as well as rations. Through our telescopes and binoculars, we watched such life as there was on the desert—distant caravans, and the convicts from Abu Zabal prison, long strings of them with their armed guards. They were dressed in blue and worked in the local quarries. They were on the far side of the canal. When days were cloudy the helio was useless; when there was sun, there were few messages to send or receive. In some trees to our right was the white dome of a tomb, and far beyond it, against the pale green, pink and yellow evening sky, were the slender minarets of Mahomet Ali on the Citadel hill. On cold evenings we went to the power-house for a warm, and a talk with the Marconi men who gave us hints on how to treat troublesome natives. We were soon friendly with the two sergeants of the East Lancashire detachment on duty. My legs were scorched and very sore. I read and re-read all my letters.

Lieutenant Wolfe was suspicious about a distant caravan he had spotted. He came up to our roof, but by then the camels were out of sight—even through the telescope. I spent many hours with Wolfe, in his tent. He kept his revolver at hand. He asked me many questions about his method of doing things. I wondered what his men would have said if they had known how much more work he would have found for them if I had not persuaded him that sentry duty at AZ was quite enough. He said he could not understand his men or their ways and bits of horse-play, and I had to explain that it was only their way of relieving the monotony of sitting in their dark tents from 5.30 p.m. to bed-time.

When Wolfe and his men left us, their place was taken by 2nd Lieutenant Bolton and men of the 5th East Lancs.[55] We messed with his sergeants in a shed we called 'Denver Dan's Saloon' where flies were thick. We gave attention to the dogs which came to the rubbish tubs near our walls. We took stones up to the roof and dropped them on the dogs. On our parapet we propped a helio-mirror for our shaving-glass. Our eyes tired with looking through the telescope, watching for the GA helio. Food was plentiful now, and we began to grow, and feel, fat and lazy. We read such books as we had brought, took and sent odd messages; but our main interest was in the general life of AZ, making friends in the detachments, watching camels, riding one, now and then, wandering along the canal, watching natives make mud bricks and drying them in the sun, and raiding the monkey-nut plantations. (The nuts grow on roots—20 or more on each.) We explored the sheik's tomb in the trees. The native who came to us said 'sheik quois'—a good man in life. We drew tins of water at the *sakiehs* and sluiced our naked bodies, emptying the tin five or six times over our heads. We watched the *gamooses* (water buffalo) driving round the horizontal wheels. The Marconi men fired their revolvers at the dogs. The dog-war never ceased. The natives called us by our ranks. A sergeant was *shawish*; with one stripe, I was *okilombasha*. Most of our exploring was done in the mornings before the clouds and haze had lifted, usually about noon.

Near our house a gang of labourers was making a tennis court. The ground was first ploughed and then levelled; then hardened by being pounded with heavy wood—lifted and dropped, end on. The men walked in line, their boss facing them. As they worked they sang their work-song 'Al-Mindala.' The boss sang the first 'line' and the men the next and the chorus. We called it the Al-Mindala Chorus, and this is what I made of it.

---

55 Second Lieut. John Bolton, 1/5th Bn, East Lancs Regt. Died of wounds, Gallipoli, 4 June 1915. Originally buried above Y Beach, he is now commemorated by a Special Memorial in Twelve Tree Copse Cemetery. See Appendix III: Soldiers' biographies.

CHAPTER 6

Al-Mindala.	Anna Wulla.
Al-Mindala.	Allah Hay.
Al-Mindala.	Ruha Wuha Halli.
Al-Mindala.	Bokra Muorto.
Allah Hallah.	Ragtīmēna.
Yaha Baby.	Raha Wittahalli.
Mēna Hō.	Will-you-me.
Yalla Lĕvi.	Tansicumellac.
Al-Mindala.	Yaree Talla.
Elli Halli.	Bērno Bērno.
Amen Gari.	Ello Hello.
Amun Dali.	Yari Vēgi.
Tari-Tari.	Al-Mindala ... etc.

'Al-Mindala' followed each expression. While the hammering went on, buckets of water were thrown over the surface. We called out to them 'Al-Mindala,' and they sang it all over again. A stone surface was added by the same method, and to the same music.

A message came from Newton saying that we should continue on duty for the next week, and asking if we wanted any pay. We had enough to last for the rest of the period, but we sent a private message to Joe asking for groceries and letters. These came the following day, with papers from home and films. We had found an extra blanket each, and a barrel of beer had arrived. As it was a cold evening and we had nothing to do, we went to bed at 6.30 p.m.

We were never tired of the *sakiehs*, and inspected them in detail. The vertical wheel is either hollowed in short sections, or has earthen pots fastened along the edge. These dip in the water, and empty themselves, as the wheel turns, into a trough leading to irrigation channels. We spent many hours wandering along these channels and watching the water spread over the cultivated patches. There were *shadoofs* on the canal side—long pivoted poles with a large lump of mud as counterbalance. On the Nile banks are *shadoofs* in series—each raising the water higher, until the top is reached. They are, of course, worked by men.

November 12th was a day of rumours. Poole sent them to us. General Maxwell was reported to have said that our division was going to Palestine.[56] There had been fighting on the east side of the Suez Canal; the *Emden* had been sunk by the *Sydney*; there were letters waiting for us. On November 13th, England declared war on Turkey. All we did was to eat and rest—the day was cloudy and dusty. The flies pestered us. I was covered with flies while I wrote my letters. We saw nothing of GA, but heard distant artillery practice. The Marconi men told us that the Turks were getting busy to have a shot at Egypt; that the Germans had taken Dixmude; and that an English submarine had been sunk off Dover. It was windy and cold at night, and I found it hard to keep my blankets on, and slept badly. There was shooting during the night. Claude and Pindar relieved us the next day, which was cold, windy, bleak and wintry. Near AZ station we passed a string of convicts. The warders kept us back until the procession had passed, saying the convicts might try to rush us to get hold of our rifles. We called at the Khedivial, in Cairo, and reached barracks tired and dirty. I dropped on my bed and stayed on it.

Limelight apparatus arrived.[57] We were to work it to and from AZ. Lawford said that nobody would touch it, and that he had come to No. 4 Section for help. Ormisher and Claude took it to the QM's stores, got the apparatus out, fixed it up, made oxygen in the retort—all by the book of words. The lamp was set up on one table and the gas-bag placed on another table. The bag filled and light came, but pressure was needed to improve the light, so they persuaded Lawford to sit on the bag, his head near the ceiling, and at once the light was brilliant. Officers and NCOs came to see the fun, laughing at Lawford who got off his perch. The light went down, so they persuaded him to get back on the bag.

On December 4th, I was detailed for AZ again, this time with Pearson as companion,[58] the following day. I spent the Saturday morning

---

56 General Sir John Maxwell, GCB, KCMG, CVO, DSO. Commander in Chief, British Forces in Egypt. He later served as Military Governor in Ireland and played a key part in the military response to the 1916 Easter Rising, ordering the executions of the leaders of the rising.

57 The Lime Light signalling lamp could transmit a focussed beam of brilliant white light to a receiving station ten to fifteen miles away. A jet of oxygen gas was forced through the flame of a spirit lamp onto a thin 'pencil' made of quicklime, raising it to a white heat.

58 Dvr 1121 Edward Pearson. See Appendix III: Soldiers' biographies.

learning how to make the limelight work, Abie Williams instructing me.⁵⁹ We took some manganese with us, and I was given five piastres to buy a bottle of methylated spirit in Cairo. We caught the 7.30 p.m. train from Pont Limoun. At AZ we found Challinor feeling ill.⁶⁰ The blankets had been returned, so we had to borrow one each. We slept in the canteen with our feet in a piece of sacking, and a piece of tent canvas thrown over us. Nine of us messed in the canteen.

By now, I was quite at home at AZ, and ready to continue explorations. Next day we explored the mud village (or *esba*)—a filthy place. Most doors had wooden locks and keys, on the falling-pin principle. We saw many domed structures made of mud and straw, and full of holes. These were *ma'mal katakeets*—incubators, used mostly in winter.⁶¹ We discovered Morri, an intelligent youth, who increased our vocabulary, phonetically, and we took down the idioms and memorised them, a few at a time. We played with the limelight apparatus, made some washers from bits of composition padding we found in the power-house, and made plenty of oxygen. GA told us to have our limelight working at 5.30 p.m. next day. Ours worked all right, but GA's was poor and hard to read. I sent a message to Lawford complaining about defective tubing and other faults in the apparatus.

We explored some attractive palms, watched the process of maize-drying, crossed the canal, had a walk through the prison yard, and chased dogs with mallets, waiting for them round the corners of the *esba* walls. Boxing gloves and a football had arrived for the detachment, and a boxing match was arranged, with two 10 piastre prizes, refereed by a Marconi man.

There were two swing-bridges over the canal, and these we used as turning points on our canal rambles. Near the second one were many camels and Bedouin camps with their brown goat-hair tents. The families sat round fires with large black pots on them. These people were heavily covered. They were feeling winter more than we were. Returning through the prison, we saw native troops standing on their

59   Spr (later L/Cpl) 664 Richard 'Abe' Williams. See Appendix III: Soldiers' biographies.
60   Spr (later Sgt 426906) 1247 James William Challinor, formerly 1/4th East Lancs Regt.
61   An Egyptian egg oven that dates to ancient times. Large quantities of eggs are hatched by incubation using artificial heat.

Figure 25. *Shadoofs* at a village well.

beds in the barracks for inspection. A Greek came to our canteen and offered to show me and Pearson an Arabic–English book he thought would interest us, if we would go to his room. There, we found a girl and a high-smelling native. After a look at the book, the Greek invited us to sit on the floor. Shortly, the native brought in a basket-tray holding a large enamelled bowl of white creamy stuff. The three of them sat down, broke off pieces of flatbread, dipped them in the bowl and ate them. We were pressed to join them. We said we had just had a good tea, but we did our best. I was given a spoon and Pearson a fork. We dipped. We were told that the stuff was butter. It tasted like very lumpy buttermilk. I felt rather sick after mine. We talked about the war. The Greek expressed shooting by putting up his hand saying 'bom-bom.' He said, also, 'Russa good.' Two natives came in. The Greek said 'gaff'eer.' We nodded recognition. Then he continued bom-boming and we saw he was pointing to one of the natives. He was the *esba gaff'eer* and wanted cigarettes from the native canteen, but a sentry had stopped him. We took him to our canteen but there were no cigarettes. On the way, our *gaff'eer* showed us what he did when challenged by a sentry: he clapped his hands, held them above his head, and said 'ana' (friend). The canteen was lively: a barrel of beer had arrived. Sentimental songs were in full throat. Several men were tight, and were troublesome to clear out at 8 p.m. When he had got rid of them, Sergeant A—— had another little drink and kept us bright for an hour, by telling us what he thought of Corporal Hales, and trying to light his pipe but missing it with the match. At last we got to bed.

We visited the sheik's tomb, reaching it by crossing the canal bridge and going through fields where there were *shadoofs* and *sakiehs*. We were allowed to keep our boots on to enter the tomb. The interior was plain. The tomb itself had a tarbouche on it and a bit of green cloth. Round it were texts from the Koran. Returning over the sand, we passed the Greek's house, where a woman on a mat was teaching a child to count. *Wa'hid* (one), *etnain* (two), in monotonous voice. When the child rebelled, he was smacked. Then the woman made him place forearm on forearm, tied them together with a piece of white cloth, and sent him inside. Presently he came out with the cloth in his hand, so she tied his wrists, after crossing them, and sent him in again. We did not see him get out of that. In spite of good light, GA was not available, so we had a walk with Sergeant Harrop which ended in camel rides.⁶² Mine seemed to be on very rough country. The Greek and a native arrived, complaining that our men had been taking monkey-nuts and had knocked a native down. The Marconi men said that planks had been stolen for firewood. Very likely they had. An enquiry was promised—and postponed.

No extras having come with the rations, we had to fall back on 'Sunshine Salmon' on dry bread. Papers and letters were welcome. A boatload of Nile mud was being unloaded for the cultivation near the canal. When we were in bed, a dog got inside the tent and we found it jumping up the curtains, but it was out again before we could reach it.

Another AZ character was 'Gazelle'—a big, fat, greasy fellow, but amusing. He was trying to improve the *esba*, and had made a plan of it. Old homes were being pulled down. We went to the *esba* with Gazelle and saw that the poor mud bricks soon crumbled in a few showers. Other characters were Sadek Basta, a friendly and intelligent youth; and Sūkri, who lent us an English-Arabic grammar book; and 'Joe Etnain,' a native, who became far too familiar and had to be put in his place. One of our men was sick, and the doctor (*hakim*) from the prison was sent for. He was a fat little man with a short grey beard. He wore a frock-coat and a tarbouche. He arrived on a donkey, carrying a large basket of medicine bottles over one arm.

The canal, like all water in Egypt, was a place where women washed clothes. We watched their sloppy ways, and how they squatted while they washed. A more pleasing little picture was a young boy on the canal bank, holding a rope with a young *gamoose* at the other end, up to his knees in the water.

We speculated as to who would have to spend Christmas at AZ, and we had an evening of cards and card-tricks, varied with some experimental first aid on my leg and finger, and more on the crushed finger of one of the guards. Our time at AZ finished on December 19.

We were glad to be going back to Cairo, but we had enjoyed ourselves at AZ. Sadek Basta said goodbye to us at the ferry, and at the station we saw once again the long string of passing convicts.

---

62   Sgt 1126 James (Joseph) Cox Harrop, C Company, 1/9th Manchesters. See Appendix III: Soldiers' biographies.

Figure 26. Portraits of local people by Pte George Harrison, 6th Manchesters.

Figure 27. Church parade, Abbassia.
Troops are from the 1/5th Bn, East Lancs Regt.

Figure 28. Return of the Church Parade, led by Capt. Cyril Robinson.
The barracks in the background are the officers' quarters.

CHAPTER 7

Polygon Barracks again

Early on Sunday mornings we laid our bedding out in the sun and air. Our Gyppo washed the floor of No. 11 and cleaned our beds and boxes. We each paid him one and a half piastres (four pence or so). At 9 a.m. we had church parade; in the Garrison Church, Main Barracks, for C of E. Later on, I became a nonconformist, and so was free long before the Church of England parade was over. Church parades were unpopular, but they made a change and filled up our Sunday mornings. On Sunday, October 18th, the Dead March was played in the Garrison Church for two officers of the —— Yeomanry, now in Cairo; both were killed on the Western Front.

There were rumours. Those of October 23rd said that we were to go home in December for a fortnight and then to France; that each man on foreign service was to get £10 on his return; that we were to go home on December 8th, as rations were only indented for to that date. We knew that flies in the wintertime went to Egypt, but where did the rumours come from?

On Saturday, October 17th, 1914, I was on the mat—after the usual and appropriate ceremonial. On the table was a pipe and a box of matches, and behind the table sat Captain Lawford, the OC, pursuing a crime on AF 252.[63] It seems that on the previous night I had reported No. 11 all present; yet, when Newton, the orderly officer, was crossing the parade ground, he heard a voice in the empty camel trough observing

---

63 Army Form 252 was the charge sheet used when soldiers were brought in front of the OC for a minor breach of discipline.

that 'It's all right in the open air,' and 'It's too hot to sleep inside.' The voice was that of Noble, who could not have been in No. 11 and in the camel trough at the same time. What had I to say? I had not prepared a speech, but as Lawford was anxious to have a conversation I obliged him and said that Noble slept out with my permission, after reporting in No. 11. Newton said that if men slept out, there was nothing to stop them from going to Cairo. I said that I had slept out myself often enough. Newton said 'We can't have it.' The OC said he wanted to have confidence in his NCOs, and it mustn't happen again. The sergeant-major and I understood Lawford to be saying goodbye, and under the sergeant-major's directions, I left the orderly room in the regulation way. What Newton did not know was that there was another man in the camel trough, also from No. 11; but he had enough sense to keep his mouth shut.

On another October night, when I was on wagon guard, there was a wonderful show of shooting stars when I awoke, aching and shivering with some temporary ailment, at 1 a.m. Dean was missing.[64] At last I found him with the stable guard looking after the camel trough, where the water had overflowed and couldn't be stopped.

We noticed that no natives were working in Gebel Ahmar quarries on October 30th, as it was one of the Moslem festivals, Kurban Beiram, when faithful Moslems eat a piece of meat in memory of Abraham's sacrifice, and the poor are given meat by their richer co-religionists. On some waste ground near Abbassia was a fair, with tents and booths for the festivities. We heard guns at intervals. We were not allowed to leave the barrack area, guards were given ball ammunition, and three extra men were put on duty as the ammunition guard.

On October 31st, I was on duty at GN when our company took part in a divisional route march through Cairo. Those on duty at GN and GA helio stations were given 15 rounds per man of ball ammunition. On the same day Lawford and a cable party went to Ismailia on the Suez Canal.

In November a rumour came along that our section was to go to Alexandria. However that might be, I had to go to see a dentist at once, selecting Zuckerman who put me right for 15 piastres and passed

---

64 Dvr 1568 William Dean. See Appendix III: Soldiers' biographies.

unfavorable remarks on the workmanship of my dentist in Manchester. I agreed with Zuckerman. We spoke in French. In the waiting room his assistant was flirting with a girl, and I was a witness to unlimited hand-kissing.

The Cairo Museum was the place to learn a little about ancient Egypt, for Mr Quibell, the director,[65] took parties of troops round on Wednesday and Sunday afternoons. I attended three times. We were told a lot about the evil eye, and how it still holds good; that mothers don't like their children to be kissed or fussed, as they might be envied and so have the evil eye cast on them. That is one reason why so many of the children we saw were filthy, their eyes covered with flies. When a child is shown, the proper thing to do is to spit, and say how ugly it is. Near the museum entrance was a statue of Ramses II. When it was found, the natives worshipped it. One made a sacrifice to it, another wanted to make a shirt for it, and a woman mocked it, saying 'Why didn't you heed Moses?' Mr Quibell said that he could not account for such effects on the minds of ignorant *fellahin*. One of our party asked if fraud was common in ancient Egypt. Yes, and an example was a jerry-built wall with imitation pointing. And it was a common trick of undertakers to seal tombs correctly, which, when opened, were found to have been robbed. We were told how dust gets into the museum cases. During the warm day, the air inside the case expands; when it contracts at night dust is drawn in. We were shown a piece of restored flooring. A native labourer broke it when he found it, to make trouble for the local headman. We had a lecture on mummification and its varieties, and were shown the embalming slit in the left side of a mummy, covered with a leaf-shaped gold plate. We were told that Flinders Petrie had permission to search the rubbish heaps of an inefficient French excavator, and found more in the rubbish than the Frenchman had found in his excavations.[66] Mr Quibell explained that the mummy wrappings we saw were not the original ones—the latter were replaced periodically every few hundred years, by special officials, and the event recorded. He said he thought the mummies would be reburied in the pyramids in a few years. Our attention was drawn to models, from tombs, showing daily work of all

---

65 James Edward Quibbell, keeper of the Egyptian Museum, 1913–1925.
66 Sir William Matthew Flinders Petrie, pioneer archaeologist and Egyptologist.

Figure 29. Houseboats on the Nile.

Figure 30. Kasr el-Nil bridge, Cairo.
Note the New Zealander with his camera on the near corner.

kinds in ancient Egypt, and in particular, to a company of light infantry. The figures are about 18 inches high, marching four abreast, with their left feet forward, and showing quaint ideas of sizing.[67] Wigs amused us. They had curly black hair, and were roughly 18 inches by 10 inches. A silver-covered sarcophagus, now black and tarnished, showed only very slight discolouration when the tomb was opened. When it had been opened for two days the discolouration was twice that of the first day. It was deduced, therefore, that at some time in the past the tomb had been opened for one day only, for purposes of robbery. The museum galleries were carefully guarded by attendants at every few yards.

In our early days the Nile was a great attraction. We enjoyed many rambles along the palm-shaded banks watching the brown, swirling river. The daily papers gave notice of the closing and opening of Kasr el-Nil, Boulac and other bridges. Bathing in the river was forbidden as there is risk of 'bilharzia,' caught by a mud insect burrowing through the skin of the feet. Many boats were moored to the banks—*dahabiehs*, *feluccas*, houseboats on the Gezireh bank, and Cook's river-steamers, idle now that there were no tourists. There is a story that Cooks used to keep a small crocodile chained up in a tank, to show tourists. There are no crocodiles for some hundreds of miles south of Cairo.

We visited many cinemas. Salle Kleber was a favourite, calling itself 'Cinéma des chefs d'oeuvre.' The descriptions were in English, French and Arabic, and they were shown at the side of the pictures. We saw *In the bottom of the seas*, described as 'documental views;' *Tata could not do it* ('comical scene'); *By the Kaiser's Orders*—'great patriotic drama in three parts'; and 'A Complete Set of England's War Films.' Sometimes I went to the Cinéma Palace-Dahur; and here I saw 1,500 metres of *Black Jack*, a 'film of detective showing the capacity of English detectives in tracing criminals,' and *Saved by the telegraph*, an 'Australian drama in two parts of hard life. It is a modern film indicating the anguish of the soul when leading a hard life of labour.' The Third Grand Film was *For the Harem*; 'soldiers in particular likes to see it tho times instead of one.' *A Horrible Vision* was a 'drama of love in two parts, very interesting and sentimental—it is an opportunity for the soldiers to hasen and see this

---

67 Riley probably means 'sizing' in the sense of 'sizing' a body of men before they form up in ranks. For example, shortest to the left, tallest to the right.

horrible vision, and tell their friends to come with them.' At the Cinema Belle-Vue Daher we saw 1,700 metres of *Mortal Love*, 'a pathetic tragedy in three parts marvellously played by the best artists of Rome.' (The spelling in this paragraph is copied from the handbills.)

We enjoyed the zoo, near Gizeh. The vegetation is luxuriant. In the lion house, seven large lions were roaring. On the stone-work round a giraffe cage nearly twenty large and beautiful lizards were playing. The giraffe's cages are large, and open at the top. The giraffes stretched out their long necks, trying to reach trees from which they had already stripped the bark. Palms, botanical specimens, water, bright colours, made the zoo very attractive to us. There are African and Egyptian insects, reptiles, chameleons, lizards, vultures, and monkeys with black and white ringed tails. The attendants carry revolvers.

Figure 31. Cairo zoo.

The giraffes were a popular subject for soldiers' cameras. This portrait was taken by an officer of the 1/5th Bn, East Lancs Regt, either Second Lieut. John Bolton or Captain H. Hargreaves Bolton.

CHAPTER 7

Figure 32. The Citadel of Cairo and the Mosque of Mahomet Ali with its 'two slender minarets.'

The Citadel accommodated troops of the East Lancashire Division including the 1/4th East Lancs Regt who spent six months in its barracks. Beyond the Citadel are the Mokattam Hills. The old fort explored by Riley and C.W. Ridings can be seen on the skyline (left of centre).

We explored the Citadel; looked down on the city with its domes and minarets and noise, and beyond to the long thin streak of the Nile with its boats, and their tall, graceful masts and immense white sails. Further still was the desert, and the Pyramids small in the distance. In Mohamet Ali mosque a clock struck eleven. It was 4 p.m. We were told that the Moslem day starts at 6 a.m. (one in our time) and therefore 4 p.m. is their eleven o'clock. We inspected the 'curios'—red carpets, Koran texts, stonework, coloured glass, suspended globes, Mohamet Ali's tomb and the Khedive's *mihrab* (niche).

We explored Heliopolis (known as 'Nearly opposite'), a modern, residential suburb of Cairo. We had tea at the Amphytrion. Advertised as 'Blackpool South Shore from home' was Luna Park. Here we spent some evenings, wandering round the sideshows, spending a lot of time and money on the scenic railway; and there was a roller skating rink. We sat in an open-air café-cinema, where the films were shown on a white wall.

Figure 33. Musician with Nubian lyre.

CHAPTER 7

Meanwhile, life went on at Abbassia. We got to know our Royal Engineer companions better; a reading-room was opened; a piano arrived; the kite-hawks went on squawking; the old and patient native sat under our acacia trees with his basket of dates and Turkish Delight, and we did a lot of business with him, although we had to wash the dates thoroughly before we dared to eat them. We made our nicely polished boots very dusty as we walked down to the main guard. In No. 11, our vocalists sang 'Why do you keep looking at me with your bright blue eyes?' or 'Down in Alabama where the bad men are' or 'Rag-time Cowboy Joe' or 'Ten little fingers, ten little toes, two little eyes and one little nose.'

In November we worked the 'Defence of Cairo' scheme—an old, Regular Army practice. I was on the Citadel Station, in touch with Abbassia. Other stations were Flagstaff Hill, near Heliopolis, Police and Fire station, Abdin Barracks, Kasr el-Nil Barracks,[68] Egyptian State Telegraphs, Telephone Exchange, Military Police Station, and the British Agency. We went on our cycles to the Citadel, passing the Tombs of the Khalifs and along a road through the 'Dead City,' where there are streets of small brick houses containing family tombs. The houses have doors, and the window-frames are boarded up.

We started on small brigade signalling schemes, and on these we discovered the Second Water Tower on the Suez Road, two miles past the Heliopolis tram-sheds. The road is over open desert.

One night, as corporal of the guard, I was told to turn off the water when the camel-trough was full. Next morning, taking the guard in half-an-hour before time, we found the trough overflowing. I had turned the tap the wrong way.

In Cairo, we listened to Arab music on gramophones in the native cafes, and to native musicians playing their six-foot long bamboo pipes, as they sat, cross-legged, on shelves. We heard an orchestra doing its best with 'Tipperary.' A black Soudanese with fuzzy and feathered hair, a thin neck and a black dress, nodded his head, lifted his knees, and played five notes on a strange, stringed instrument, repeating the notes, time after time, in the same order. He gave us (and the street) a treat.

---

68 The Kasr-el-Nil barracks stood on the eastern end of the bridge by the same name and was at the time home to the 1/9th Manchesters. Demolished in 1948 after the British left Egypt, the buildings which replaced it formed the western boundary of Tahrir Square, the epicentre of the January 2011 uprising.

Figure 34. Bristol Hotel, Cairo.

Figure 35. The entrance to Shepheard's Hotel, Cairo.

In Ezbekiyeh Gardens we walked under the great banyan trees, whose branches take root when they reach the ground.[69] We enjoyed the palms, the water, but thought the cacti were repulsive. We saw men wearing frock-coats, pill-box caps, revolvers in their sashes. I discovered the Bristol Hotel, where my father had stayed, years before.[70] We wandered along the arcaded footpaths, bought picture postcards and tried to write something original on them. We had rows with gharry-drivers over fares; we entered all kinds of shops, drank all kinds of drinks, ate all kinds of Oriental cakes. We saw snake-charmers—one of them quite drunk, a long strip of snake twined round his fingers, and a large leather bag of snakes slung over his shoulder. Another man wore a conical horn on his head. He was covered by a many-coloured patchwork cloak. Cairo shop names were mostly Yussuffs or Ali Mahomads. A triangular bit of Cairo, with its apex at Midan el-Khazindar, is full of small streets. Known as the Fish Market this is the area of 'disrepute.' One of the boundary streets, Wagh el-Birket was known as Red Blind Street. The other name for the Fish Market is el-Waz'a. In Red Blind Street were 'hotels' with pretentious names, bars, and a few shops. In this street we were accosted by prostitutes of many nationalities. In early days we heard of men having their caps snatched off in Wagh el-Birket, or even their bayonets, the prostitutes running inside the houses to induce the men to follow. The Waz'a was a name known to all who served in Cairo. At the doors of tiny houses in the back streets sat wretched hags. Most of the girls were inside, or shouting from the balconies overlooking Wagh el-Birket. We heard many strange stories of the Waz'a. What we saw was too poor to be worth recording.

In Sharia Kamel we listened to Shepheard's Hotel band, playing on the garden terrace. Sometimes it was a military band.[71] We saw the waiters and pageboys, dressed in scarlet pantaloons, busy amongst innumerable British and colonial officers of all ranks. In the street

69 Set in central Cairo, the gardens were a popular recreational area for British and Anzac soldiers. There was a roller-skating rink and the New Zealand YMCA established a canteen there. The area was also popular with prostitutes.

70 The Bristol and Nil Hotel was a mid-range hotel close to the Esbekia Gardens. It was open all year round and in 1911 its tariff for a single room started at 20 piastres per day (about four shillings sterling).

71 Riley would have listened to the band from a distance as higher-end hotels like Shepheard's were out of bounds to non-commissioned ranks.

were motors, camels, donkeys, gharries, and on the pavement were the Egyptians in their clothes of many colours, and their red tarbouches with black tassels. A good tarbouche costs about 4/– to 5/–. I bought one, and had it properly fitted, complete with tassel. Modern buildings, banks, hotels, stores, houses, mosque architecture, light and shade, palms, crowded streets, many coloured clothes, and an Egyptian evening sky: these were our backgrounds to such mental pictures as we composed for ourselves.

We watched street money-changers and their ways, and we watched a fat tram conductor with a barrel waist, a busy face and a pimple on his nose. He told me:

'Me, France. Yes.'

'Germans' (spat).

'Turks' (spat).

'Engleesh good.'

Three milliemes change was for him—*backshiesh*.

I said: 'No. Backshiesh for me,' and got it.

We were often told *Ingleze, quois* (good); French, *quois*; German, *mush quois* (no good); Turk, *mush quois*. We used to start them on this line for a bit of fun. In Place Ramses, near the Central Station, a Red Cap told us that the military police barracks there had strong steel plates behind the windows, loopholed for rifles and machine-guns, commanding the square.

In Old Cairo we visited the Mosque of Amru, the oldest in Cairo. In 1914 it was said to be 1,280 years old, and is used only once a year, at Ramadan. The exterior, like other mosques (but not all) is decorated with alternate broad and horizontal stripes of red and yellow ochre wash. We rambled about the inside, saw the famous pair of columns, far enough apart for the 'saved' only to get through, and were told by our guide that the mosque has 366 columns, the number of days in the Moslem year. Within a double-railed enclosure was the tomb of Sheik Abdulla, son of Amru. On one end of it was a green turban, and there were Koran texts on the sides. On a house-wall near the mosque was a representation of the holy carpet procession.

We wandered through narrow and dirty lanes in the Coptic quarter, passing ancient doorways where beggars sat holding out their hands and saying 'Gib,' while children pestered us for *backshiesh*. We called at the

Coptic church of Mari Georges, with its dim and dirty interior, where a woman brought three tallow candles and showed us three altars, in dim recesses, to Father, Son and Holy Ghost. (We found that all Coptic churches have three such altars.) The wooden fronts and doorways are beautifully carved and inlaid. There were ancient paintings on wooden panels, one of them showing St George and the Dragon, and various saints. Then we visited another Coptic church, that of St George, where the main point of interest is the crypt, the traditional place where Joseph, Jesus and Mary rested on the flight to Egypt. In October, the Nile rises three feet in this crypt, and we saw traces of ooze round the columns. The crypt was reputed to be 1,950 years old—a very convenient calculation.

Returning to the healthier open air we were ferried over to Roda, to see the Nileometer in its pit about 16 feet square. The pit has a stone stairway. Two arches cross the middle, and a shaft below them has measurement marks in Arabic and Cufic. A new Nileometer is on a wall on the side of the island. Of course, we had to see the place where Moses was found in the bulrushes, near an old *sakieh*, and where a tamarisk tree grows. The guide told us to take a sprig of tamarisk. Everyone does so!

Another excursion was to the site of the City of On (Old Heliopolis), near Mataria, to see the famous obelisk in a railed pit, and to the garden where the 'Virgin's Tree' can be seen for a small tip. It is certainly a very old tree, and shoots from it have been planted close by. The trunk, in several pieces, has names cut in it in several languages, and the guide invited us to add C.W. Ridings and A. Riley, but we would not. He insisted on giving us bits of wood and leaves from a shoot. We drank cold, fresh water from the well. The garden is another legendary resting place of the Holy Family; in fact, the water was brackish until Mary had had a drink! On the far side of Mataria Station, a walled and shabby enclosure was the ostrich farm. We had a look at these curious birds, passed a few remarks about them, and reckoned there must be about 200 of them. Rambling round, we noticed scratchings in the sand, and a lot of bones. A boy, seeing our interest, showed us a place where blue beads could be scratched up; and a man who was superintending more scientific excavation showed us the unearthing of a brown-boned skeleton, bit by bit...

Figure 36. The obelisk at Mataria, the only surviving element of a great temple built by Pharaoh Senusret I (1971–1926 BCE) in ancient Heliopolis. The red granite obelisk is 68 ft (20.73 m) tall.

Figure 37. The holy well at Mataria. The Virgin Mary and Saint Joseph are said to have rested here on their flight to Egypt.

CHAPTER 7

The Museum of Arab Art, in Cairo, has a large collection of objects out of their natural settings, and while I could admire the fine workmanship, metal-work and carving, pottery and so on, it seemed that there would be more pleasure to be got from a single object in, say, a mosque, than from the whole lot in this museum.

Behind the Citadel is the high ground of Gebel Mokattam. Here we had a signal station, now and then, reaching it through the Citadel which we left by the Mokattam gate, and by a rough and dusty track, crossing a railway line, great masses of rock, and up a steep road to the top of the first Mokattam level and an old fort at the end of an offshoot of the hill. When C.W. Ridings and I were detailed for the Mokattam station, we went with the idea of seeing all we could and doing no more work than we could help. Our duty was to explore the fort. By candle-light we rambled through all the dark passages we could find. In the central area are two well-like holes, with hand and foot-holds on the sides. At the bottom of one of these holes we found ourselves in a crypt with a groined roof. We explored galleries and old barrack-quarters, noting that most of them would be safe from artillery in the period when they were built. The masonry was strong and well-preserved. Outside the fort are small ruined houses. From the top of the tower the view of the Citadel and Cairo made it seem the best view-point we had found. Another view-point is the Giyushi Mosque, on the west edge of the plateau. The Mokattam sides are precipitous in most places. They have been quarried for centuries, and parts of the Pyramids were built of this brown-tinted limestone.

* * *

Figure 38. NCOs of the East Lancs Divisional Signal Company, Abbassia, 1914. One man sports a despatch rider's goggles on his cap.

Christmas Eve, 1914, was a warm day. The evening was the most unpleasant one of all our time in Cairo. We had a meal of our own in No. 11, to which I contributed 20 piastres, giving it to two men I could trust, to lay out on eatables. We brought in our two tables from the corridor, and these were soon covered with canteen medals.[72] As Tim said, when he came in, there was plenty of tipple.[73] N—— got very drunk on a bottle of local poison he had bought.[74] He shouted 'I'm going mad. I know I'm going mad!' so we fastened him to his bed with two belts. Joe and a bottle of whisky came in, so did another sergeant with another bottle. Campbell, the CQMS, sat at the table, a happy, childish grin on his face. M—— was full of drink and song.[75] Noise and the smell of stale drink kept us from sleeping much that night. Next morning, our native cleaner demanded extra money for cleaning up certain parts of No. 11. I agreed with him, and in spite of grumbling, those who had made beasts of themselves paid up. I think many of us were home-sick,

---

72 Vernacular term for spilled food and drink stains.
73 Capt. Charles Harry 'Tim' Williamson. See Appendix III: Soldiers' biographies.
74 Probably Spr 1392 George Richard Noble. See Appendix III: Soldiers' biographies.
75 Probably Spr 617 John 'Mall' Mallalieu. See Appendix III: Soldiers' biographies.

and took the easiest way of forgetting what they were most used to at Christmas. Letters and cards from home helped me considerably. I needed them, badly.

The corridor-walls were bright with flags, festoons, streamers and a few military badges and Xmas mottoes (which amused some of us). I heard that N—— had been brought in from the camel-trough at 3 a.m. When I went into the corridor on Xmas morning, I saw him riding a bicycle between forms and tables, in a shirt and no trousers, the shirt-tail dangling over the saddle—until he fell off with a crash. He said he was trying to ride up a wall. There was church parade at 9.30. For dinner, which was good, suitable and plentiful, white cloths had been nailed on the tables. I helped the carver at mine. When the others had been served, we did what we could for ourselves. The officers came in. Lawford read a message from the King, Newton and Nick made speeches, and Tim was told, by a driver, that he was the best little lad we had. Broad was greeted by:

> Sapper Duffy, saddle hup the b'y! (bay-horse)
>   (repeated thrice)
> All pull your chin-straps down.
> Bandoliers—off! Bandoliers—on! QUIETLY!

... until Campbell stopped it. Broad's face lengthened when N—— sang 'The German Clock-maker.'[76]

> A German clock maker to Manchester once came
> Any old clocks or watches he'd mend.
> He'd put them to right nine times out of ten
> With his too-re-lum, toodle-um, too-re-lum-day.

> Chorus (after each verse):

> With his too-re-lum, toodle-um, too-re-lum-day
> Too-re-lum, toodle-um, too-re-lum-day

> He met a young lady in Stephenson Square,
> She told him her clock was in want of repair.

---

76 A ribald English folk song. The lyrics have been added to the text by the editors.

He followed her home to the lady's delight,
In about five minutes he had her clock right.

They sat down to tea and to loving they got,
All of a sudden to hear a loud knock.
In walked her husband with a hell of a shock
To see this young German winding up his wife's clock.

He got him hold by the back of his neck,
He shaked him about till his teeth fall out.
He made him promise no more in his life
He'd wind up the clock of another man's wife.

After dinner I got out of it for the rest of the day. I heard that Driver Harbour had been seen on the floor, searching for a turkey's leg.[77]

* * *

On Boxing Day, five of us went to Memphis and the Sakkara necropolis. I went again, later on. We went by train to El-Bedreshein, 20 miles from Cairo, and then by donkeys. There was plenty of country life to interest us—the *fellahin*, the water buffalo, the children, men raising water by the Archimedean screw, quaint-looking goats, one of them standing on the back of a donkey as it rested; the wooden plough, and the *nôrag*, or threshing-sledge, like an armchair on timbers, between which are semi-circular knives fastened to a roller. The sledge is drawn by oxen or buffaloes, guided by a man sitting on the sledge. The *gamooses*,[78] mouse-coloured, are fine fat animals, quiet and tame. Palms cover the site of Memphis. The ride through these palms is delightful, but there is little to indicate what was once such a famous city.

We saw the two fallen statues of Ramses II, and a large sphinx. We sat on Ramses, but not in peace—for the donkey-boys were worrying because they said they had no candles:

'Me show you tomb of Ptah-Hotep, Tomb of Ti, Tomb of Mera and Serapeum. Four tomb. No candle. Buy candle at Sakkara. Mahomet's brother live Sakkara.'

---

77 Dvr 1884 Robert Harbour. See Appendix III: Soldiers' biographies.
78 Water buffaloes.

Figure 39. The red granite Sphinx of Memphis at El-Bedreshein.

I said 'Yes. But we're going to the Pyramid of Unas and one of the Persian Shafts, first.'

'All right. Six tomb. Sheik he only say five tomb, but I take you six. After, you pay backshiesh.'

My donkey cantered most of the way. Beyond the palms came a large area full of *shadoofs* drawing water from wells. The long, slender and curving poles, going up and down, made a curious effect against the sky. We reach Sakkara village, pretty, dirty, picturesque, with an open-air market, and palms here and there. Through more palms to the foot of the desert plateau, which we climbed, had a look at Unas, descended about 100 feet of a Persian shaft, where we went through passages and rooms with reliefs on the walls. The sarcophagus was lowered long before the owner wanted it, and then the lid which was temporarily rested on supports. After these preparations, the shaft was filled up. When the owner died, the mummy was lowered down another shaft, connected with the sarcophagus chamber by a passage. When

Figure 40. New Zealanders on the colossal statue of Ramses II at Memphis.

Figure 41. The Step Pyramid of Zozer at Sakkara.

the mummy was in the sarcophagus the lid was lowered. There was an arrangement by which sand would fall on anyone who got inside the other shaft. We ate our lunches as we sat on the verandah of Mariette's house. After a drink of muddy water, a small cup of coffee and a rest, we went to the Tomb of Ti. The Nile is prominent in the reliefs. There are representations of fish, crocodiles resting on the river-bed, country life and work in many forms, dancing. In Ptah-Hotep's tomb, we saw a large, dark-red relief of Ptah-Hotep at table, drinking; a doctor giving medicine; a lion catching a bull by the head; a fight between boatmen. The Serapeum was close and stuffy. We each had a candle. We passed along the large sarcophagi of the sacred bulls, noting the points of interest. One sarcophagus has a large hole in one corner. Another has its lid raised on supports so that the interior can be seen. All are of granite.

The Step Pyramid is in six stages, the outside being so loose and crumbling that it is dangerous to climb. It is about 200 feet high and is one of the oldest stone buildings in Egypt. It is of poor, clayey limestone, quarried locally, and is the tomb of King Zozer. Close by are the ruins of its temple—pillars etc. with reliefs.

Returning to Bedreshein along a narrow path two feet wide, we noticed a large amount of broken pottery. We passed a Bedouin encampment. Brown naked children played near it. In one part of the tent were hens and goats. In front sat an old woman wearing her yashmak, working a quern. In front of the other part of the tent sat three men, one of them looking as ancient as King Zozer. They stared at us, moving their heads very slowly. Outwardly, their faces were expressionless, but their eyes turned in all directions, missing nothing. Mud walls, distorted and grotesque in the red evening light, were repulsive. It was pleasanter to look higher, at the green palms. That was my recollection of ancient Memphis.

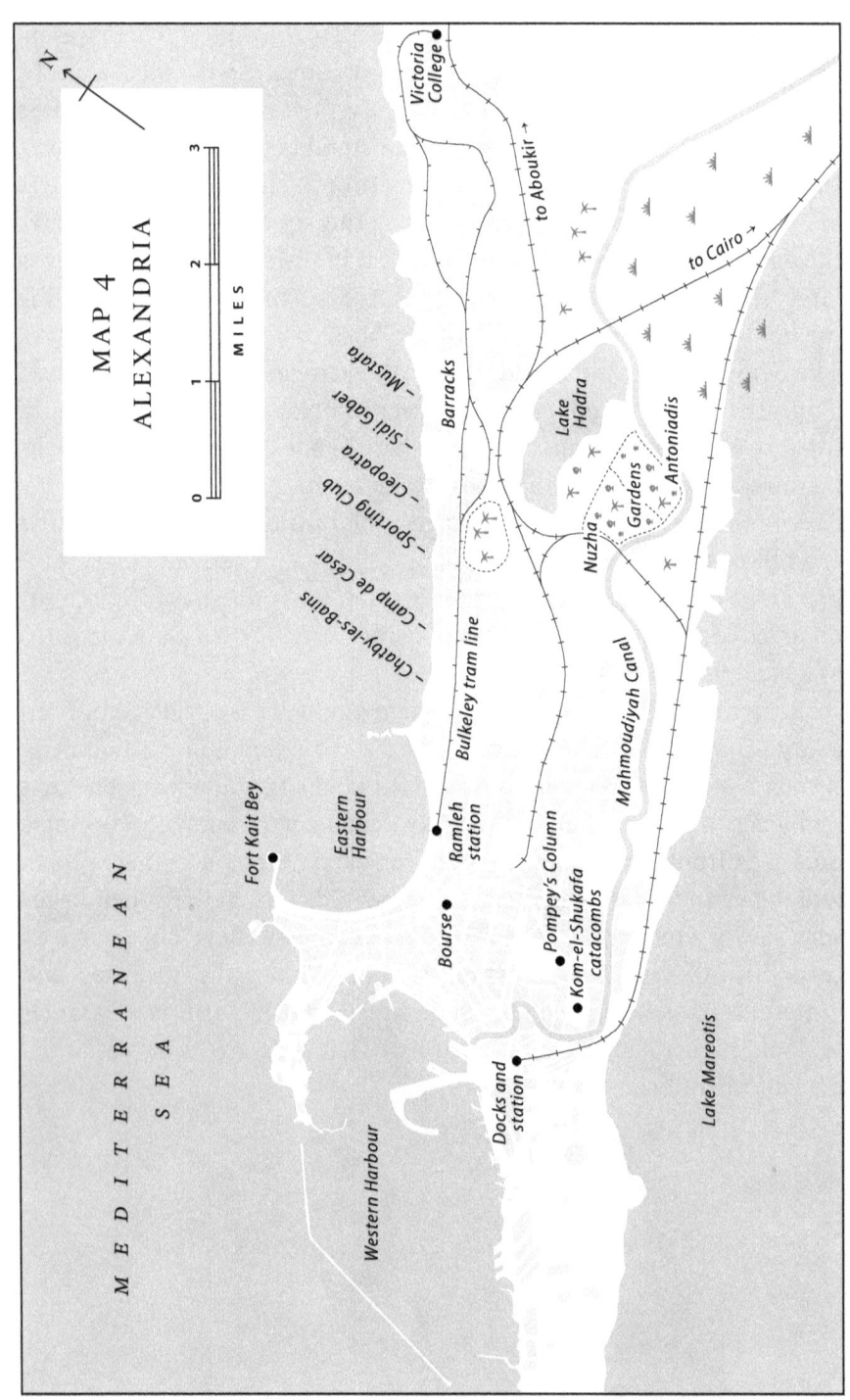

Figure 42. Mustafa Barracks, Alexandria.

Figure 43. Men of the 6th Manchesters at Mustafa Barracks, Alexandria. The group comprises one corporal, one lance corporal and 14 privates, probably a rifle section.

Figure 44. Nuzha Garden, Alexandria.

The park once formed part of a grand estate owned by an Alexandrian Greek born on Lemnos, Sir John Antoniadis (1818–1895).

Figure 45. Kait Bey.

A 15th-century fort that stands at the entrance to the eastern harbour of Alexandria. It was once the site of the Lighthouse of Alexandria, one of the Seven Wonders of the Ancient World.

CHAPTER 8

Alexandria

Our section (the Manchester Brigade) went to join the brigade at Alexandria at the end of December 1914. All the brigade was there, excepting the 7th Battalion which was still at Khartoum, with a detachment in Cyprus.[79] We were to live with our old battalion, the 6th Manchesters. Our quarters were in a large marquee, and we had meals with D Company, in a hut. The windows were covered with light matting to keep the flies out. This battalion was at Mustafa, near the sea, and near Sidi Gaber Station. We had been sent there for brigade training with the battalions of the Manchester Brigade. We had, of course, many old friends in the 6th Battalion, and this made our stay in Alexandria very pleasant. Apart from that, our chief interest was in exploring a new town and district. The routine of training is not sufficiently interesting for much to be said about it.

We cycled along the bank of the Mahmoudiyah Canal, where native houses, life, and trees are reflected in the still water, to Nuzha Garden, a public park well laid out, and having a small zoo. A short way along the road we came to the Garden of Antoniadis, to see the tropical plants and the garden statuary.

There is a wide promenade along the side of the Port East, with large modern buildings across the road. The bay was beautiful when the sun shone, and the sea was blue. The western arm of the land ends in a

---

79 Half of B Company, 7th Manchesters, under Capt. E. Townson, remained on Cyprus until its annexation by Britain on 5 November 1914. The rest of the battalion was stationed in the Sudan until April 1915 when it moved to Cairo.

Figure 46. Fort Kait Bey. 'We saw old guns sawn horizontally through their muzzles.'

hook with Fort Kait Bey at the tip, on the site of the ancient Pharos. The fort is dilapidated. An Egyptian artilleryman showed me round. On the ramparts are the old mortars, bits of iron, cannon balls, and we saw old guns sawn horizontally through their muzzles. Some marked 'dangerous' were still loaded. These, of course, were not sawn. A few natives were living inside the old buildings in the fort. Outside, a breakwater was being built, and divers were at work on it.

Church parades were held in St George's Garrison Chapel in the East Block of Mustafa. Here we were entertained by Kerby, the Brigade Chaplain.[80] He was a little man, with a lot to say. This is what I wrote about it: '...every Sunday Kerby has something to say to the 6th Manchesters, never credible to them, and never said tactfully. Today, he got on to his usual line in the sermon, and there was quite a little discussion in the congregation. This set him off again—"There's somebody talking over there..." Most of the battalion is against him. Men send him notes about the hymns. He gave out "I choose the hymns" and that if they only knew four hymns, "Fight the good fight," "Rock of Ages," and two others, he would see that they got one each Sunday. And so on.'

---

80 Rev. Edwin Thomas Kerby, Chaplain 4th Class. Later Chaplain to the 7th Manchesters at Gallipoli. See Appendix III: Soldiers' biographies.

Figure 47. Pompey's Pillar, probably erected to honour the emperor Diocletion (297–300 CE). Pompey was a Roman general and statesman who was assassinated in Alexandria in 48 BCE. The sphinx is a Roman copy of that at Gizeh.

Figure 48. Men of the Manchester Regiment explore a village near Sidi Gaber, Alexandria, 1914.

We explored the district of 'Pompey's Column,' which had nothing to do with Pompey. Including the pedestal and Corinthian capital, this monument is 88 feet high. The shaft, which is solid, and the other parts are of red Assonan granite. Close by are the Catacombs of Kom-el-Shukafa (hill of potsherds). Tommy and I were out to see all we could so we descended the large, circular and well-lit shaft, by the winding staircase to the two storeys of catacombs, entering various passages, recesses and chambers. Burials date from the Roman period and are in family groups. There are reliefs of the Egyptian Apis.[81] Some recesses held as many as ten burials. There were bones in some of them—many bones being laid out. In the main part of these catacombs most of the holes are 3 feet high, each holding from four to ten bodies. Many are still intact but most are open and contain plenty of bones. The whole place was lit by electric light. One grave had a corner of the lid removed, and by putting an eye to the little hole we saw three skulls when our

---

81 Sacred bulls.

guide switched on a light inside the grave. After rambling round some adjoining ruins, and enduring some rude remarks from local children, we were glad to leave the place for a cheerful and tasteful tea at a popular restaurant.

Letters from home, re-addressed from Cairo, were very welcome. I was always well supplied with letters. Without them, life would have been hard, so far away from home and friends.

A parcel came for our section from the ladies of the battalion. In it were 12 body-belts, 12 pairs of socks, 12 bars of chocolate, 12 tins of toffee, 13 packets of cigarettes. Some of the latter held little cards with the names and addresses of their senders, and some small message. Tommy answered his at once. As I had most of the things I needed, my share was a pair of socks, chocolate and toffee. I had received parcels from home but this official one was also appreciated.

We had an exercise in an area new to us, where our surroundings were palms, yellow sands and blue sea, while overhead was a blue sky. Few of us had seen anything like it before.

It was winter now: windy nights and flying sand; but we had occasional bathes. There was rain, too, and this led us to shelter and interest in one of the local windmills, creaking and groaning as it ground corn.

Figure 49. Tram at the terminus at Ramleh.

CHAPTER 8

Figure 50. The 6th Manchesters on parade at Mustafa Barracks, Alexandria.

One evening a few of us were guests of Mr and Mrs Samson. They had asked an elderly Frenchwoman to meet us—a nice old dame—and they gave us a good dinner, with plum-pudding, as well. Mr Samson told a naughty story and said he was a Mason. Mrs Samson had had the pleasure of meeting A——, who told her a lot about his accomplishments, and to avoid men of certain battalions. She said he was fishing for an invitation, but didn't get one. And while we are talking about food, a plum pudding from home had reached me and was eaten with pleasure, and appreciation from those who shared it.

A letter came from Cairo about our transfers from the Manchester Regiment to the Royal Engineers. It was presumed that in view of the 'increased emoluments' we should have no conscientious reasons against it, and on January 18th we said we had none.[82] This was an occasion for M—— to make one of his short but official speeches, beginning:

'I propose...'

By the end of three weeks we knew the chief points of Alexandria which concerned us: the Gare de Ramleh, our tram terminus, Sharia

---

82 As Royal Engineers, the transferees would have qualified for 'trade pay.'

Figure 51. The Mediterranean shore near Aboukir Bay, looking towards the old fort.

Figure 52. The drawbridge to the fort at Aboukir Bay.

Cherif Pasha, the Bourse, Kursaal, Sister Street;[83] and we knew all the tram stops on the Bulkeley line: Sidi Gaber, Mustafa, Cleopatra, Sporting Club, Camp de César, Chatby-les-Bains; and we were amused by the conductors' squeakers. If we returned to Mustafa late at night, we left the tram before it reached Sidi Gaber, and we crawled home by various and devious back ways. In town we patronised boot-cleaning saloons, where customers sit on thrones in rows while their boots are cleaned and highly polished, or we had them cleaned by the street boys whose boxes had a footrest on the top. When one boot was finished, or he wanted to let the polish dry, the boy gave the boot two light taps with his brush. We paid half a piastre. We met Australians, New Zealanders, Americans. One American sailor, a pleasant man who attracted me because he wore patent leather shoes, told me that he was one of the crew of the *Tennessee*, which, with the *North Carolina*, was knocking about in the eastern Mediterranean. He talked a lot about 'Brinsily' and 'Amurcsul,' which, after a time, I discovered to mean 'Brindisi, Italy,' and 'American consul.' An Australian officer treated us to a drink and 250 cigarettes.

On brigade training we used our helios to represent artillery for infantry exercises. It was a fine sight to see our old battalion, the 6th Manchesters, on parade. They were fine men and looked smart in their khaki drill and helmets.

We were reminded of an older war by the white monument to General Abercrombie,[84] in some trees on the tramway side of our barracks, and by a visit to Aboukir.[85] The shore there is low, like all the north coast of Egypt, and the landscape apparently uninteresting.

I spent my time exploring an old fort at the top of an easy slope, below ground level and surrounded by a wide fosse about 20 feet deep,

---

83 Cherif Pasha was one of the principal commercial streets in the centre of town. The bourse, or stock exchange, was an imposing building and landmark. Kursaal may refer to a theatre or music hall. Sister Street was found in the red-light district.

84 General Sir Ralph Abercrombie died of wounds sustained during the Battle of Alexandria on 21 March 1801. The battle was a decisive victory for the British Expeditionary Force leading to the surrender of Alexandria and so to the expulsion of the French from Egypt. Major General John Moore said of Abercrombie that he was 'the best man, and the best soldier, who has appeared amongst us this war.'

85 The Battle of the Nile was fought in Aboukir Bay between the Royal Navy, commanded by Rear-Admiral Sir Horatio Nelson, and a French fleet, from 1–3 August 1798. Nelson won a decisive victory.

Figure 53. Dismantled guns in the fort at Aboukir Bay.

with smooth plastered walls. There were a few guns on the ramparts, which gave a good view of the famous Aboukir Bay. The fort is entered by a drawbridge. Inside the gateway is a grating, hinged at the top, made of one-foot-square wooden beams, and held up by chains. Wooden props had been added. I explored chambers, galleries, magazines, barrack-rooms; rooms with curiously shaped walls. Below ground a loop-holed circular gallery commands the fosse—in which were a few goats. In the galleries were some jumping cats. The quietness of desertion was the prevailing atmosphere.

Walking along the railway line to catch a train back from Mamoura, I met a native who told me he had served with the English in one of the old wars. Very proudly, he showed me some wound scars on his leg.

We left Alexandria on January 19th, after a very pleasant change and holiday with our old brigade. Our return to Cairo marked the end of our age of innocence in Egypt. From then, onwards, our training was on the divisional scale.

Figure 54. The 6th Manchesters rehearsing an attack on the Virgin's Breasts.

CHAPTER 9

Cairo again

January 20th, 1915, saw the start of a new order of things. It was a misty and very cold morning, to begin with. Then, for the first time, we had field telephones of obsolete pattern issued to our section, and we drew also boots, socks, shirts, white overalls, hair-brushes and helmet covers. We did what we could with the field telephones, the day after, and we were lectured on elementary electricity.

On January 22nd we were up at 4.30 a.m., and paraded at 5.30 for our first divisional field day. The Heliopolis side of the Suez Road represented the sea, and the division was an invading army marching on a desert hill of a shape suggesting its official name, the Virgin's Breasts. Unofficially, a suitable abbreviated title was given to it.

Next morning we were divided into small parties for telephone work, one NCO and five men in each: two operators, two linesmen, and a driver to look after the pack-horse which carried mattocks, earth-pins, and four drums of telephone line, two on each side. Each drum held half a mile of thin cable. There was a double-handled spindle by which two men could carry a drum between them, unreeling it as they walked. Long before 1914 we had been used to reading Morse by double clicks; now we had to read it by long and short buzzes.

We had our second doses of inoculation, and, as before, certain men found good reasons for not being needled. The Manchester Brigade had come to Abbassia. Our Divisional Signal Company was to be reorganized, increased and further equipped; while we who had transferred to the Royal Engineers would shortly receive extra pay. The Australians

Figure 55. Entrance to a mosque in Cairo.

and New Zealanders, drawing 6/- per day as compared with our 1/-, were spoiling Cairo, and there was some high if not really bad feeling about it.

Our daily work was much the same. It was usually about 5 p.m. before we were free, and then we were tired and stayed in our rooms or called on friends in other rooms. My chief place of call was No. 1, where the rest of No. 4 lived. I continued my explorations on Saturdays and Sundays.

The mosques, I found, had each their own special points of interest. With a guide I visited the Moslem University, el-Azhar, and was surprised when the porter said:

'No backshiesh. Ingleez soldiers no pay. Tourist pay sheeling.'

With the large and sloppy shoes of yellow leather over my boots, taped round the ankles, I watched the university at work. In 1914 there were more than 14,000 students, and more than 500 professors or sheiks. We saw them in little groups, nationalities keeping together, scattered over the court or *salun*, and in the *liwan* (the covered and columned portions adjoining the *salun*). From 8 to 9 a.m. the sheiks talk about the Koran, and for the rest of the day the students sit in their groups, learning it from the yellow pages of their books. Many students were so short-sighted that they could only read if they held their books a few inches from their eyes—for flies had spread ophthalmia when the students were very young. The noise of audible reading was like the buzzing of bees. The complete curriculum at el-Azhar lasts 17 years. The *liwan* had matting on the floor. We looked in the Algerian, Soudanese and Turkish rooms, with their students' lockers by the walls. In the dormitories, the students sleep on matting. The sheiks' chairs were chained to columns in the *liwan*.

We had visited the famous Sultan Hassan Mosque. Across the road is the Mosque of Rifaiyeh, built over the tomb of Ismail (who got Egypt into debt). The artistic and decorative effects surprised us. We had not imagined anything like the magnificence and grand proportions of the interiors of some of these mosques.

We visited the bazaars in Khan el-Khaleli several times. These are near el-Azhar, and are reached from Ataba el-Khadra by a long street with three names, the first and shortest stretch being known as the Muski. (The bazaars were wrongly called 'the Muski,' sometimes.) For the first visit we needed a guide, as the place is hard to find at first. Through a narrow opening, little more than a doorway, we were in a maze of narrow lanes, where our steps made no sound in the soft dust, and where there was a peculiar 'scent'—a kind of mixture of spice and dust and who knows what else. Some of the alleys are paved. There is a dimmed light effect as there is usually some kind of cover high overhead. Our guide was, of course, in league with the merchants, saying to them in English (which gave him away at once):

'This not ordinary tourist'—a piece of good business flattery, if of small value.

We saw brass, copper, gold, silver, slipper and other bazaars. Some of us bought things to send home. We watched men ironing, working a wooden-coated iron with a hand and a foot. We smelt scent and spices. We saw boys pounding spices in mortars:

'Arab woman. Eat it. Make fat,' we were told.

We wanted to see the inside of a house.

'Arab house. Show it!' we said, but the guide would not do so.

I spent 3 piastres. When he found we were not buying—not even a carpet at 3 pounds—he got anxious, and kept saying 'Where you go now—home?'

When we parted from him he said 'May God give you long life.'

Once while we were in the bazaar, a flight of locusts passed overhead. They had been hanging about for an hour or more, for we were then in the locust season. Ours were brown, and roughly three inches long. Many dead locusts lay about on the desert. We had known flights of them large enough to darken our room in barracks when they were near the windows. Outside, if we held our caps up, several would fly into them. Recruiting for the Egyptian Army was stopped temporarily and the Egyptian troops were used in getting rid of the pests and their eggs in the cultivated areas. In the country we saw and heard tins being banged by the *fellahin* children to scare the locusts from vegetation, for they eat all they can find very quickly. Tons of locusts were destroyed, and special rules for their destruction, during their raids, were printed in the *Egyptian Mail*.

Figure 56. A view from the Citadel's Bab al-Azab gate.
In the foreground is the minaret of the Mosque of Mahmud Pasha. Beyond it is the Mosque of Rifaiyeh. On the left is Sultan Hassan Mosque.

Figure 57. A street in Old Cairo, 1915.

We wandered through dirty alleys in Old Cairo. In one area, Roman columns and capitals were lying about in dust and debris. We revisited Roda, this time to see a large, wonder-working tree of the saint Mandûra (a nebk tree), hung with bits of tape, cloth and rags. The superstition is that one who has been ill or injured must offer to the saint the cloth which covered the affected part, and to the latter he must tie two leaves plucked from the tree. When Arab women go there to pray, they hang a bit of rag on the tree. It is in a garden-grove at the north end of the island.

One of my duties was to draw and sign for a man held in the mounted military police barracks in Cairo. When I had drawn him, I took him to a café for light refreshment before going back to Abbassia, where I had to remain in charge of him until I managed to get out of it.

Tommy and I met a man called Simmonds who gave us his card and invitation to spend an evening with him and his wife. In due course we called at Maison Sobki, Bey Hussein, Zeitoun, where we heard how they escaped from a burning house and village in the Balkans when Simmonds was a railway engineer there. 'Mrs Simmond's hair streamed wildly as they made for safety.' She played the piano for us—mostly music I knew and liked.

On our field days we might or might not reach the rendezvous before we were parched. As it rose, the hot air quivered over the desert surface, and mirages were numerous. There was, apparently, water on the sand a mile or so ahead, and the white buildings of Heliopolis seemed to have a lake in front of them, the dithering light of the buildings reflected in it. Two dogs came to us. We poured water in our hands for them to lap, then they laid down in our shadows and rested. One of them, seeing a cast snake skin, rolled on it. Under a bit of low desert shrub we found a fat lizard eating a locust. Locusts bumped against us on their flights. After such field days we had long, leisurely tramps back across the sand to Abbassia. We carried full marching order, usually, our telephones, and sometimes flags and helios as well. We were very tired, but we were also very strong, and the only effect was weariness. Sometimes we were too tired to put our cycles in their proper place. This was unfortunate for those who left them in the corridor when the orderly officer took their numbers one night, and their owners had each to dig two holes through a foot of concrete for stable alterations. I had had enough sense to take my cycle into the barrack-room for the night. Harrison, a RAMC friend of ours, told us that his CO, Colonel Coates, had paraded the objectors to vaccination, and told them:

'We don't care a damn whether you live or whether you die. What we care about is whether you're a nuisance to everybody else.'

No. 11 called me a 'bully of n——s,' [epithet deleted] when I had said all I could think of to a couple of them, the first for washing our tables with water in a tea-dixie, and the other for mauling our butter with filthy hands.

There came a field day when the rendezvous was ten miles out, by the Suez Road. We had our cycles. By the road side, at long intervals, are ruined towers with the remains of ancient caravanserais close by. On this day we were at the Third Tower for a time. It stands on a small ridge from which we had a survey of local and distant scenery—'naked' ridges, more or less level desert, with its purple patches and many shades of khaki, brown and yellow, while the sun and cloud played with light and shade on the landscape. One of my tyres was punctured and I was captured, and so saved from any further work.

Most of our field days, however, were near the Virgin's Breasts. Starting in the early mornings, we were all right for an hour or so. Then we dripped sweat, and watched patches of it grow larger and darker on the drill tunics of our companions. We could only drink from our water bottles when official permission was given, and there was always some fool who had not bothered to bring any water, and who had to depend on our charity. Gyppo lemonade and chocolate hawkers followed us to the rendezvous. More than once I was glad to buy stale chocolate from them. We saw some of our more uncouth men upset a hawker's tray on the sand, but we did not admire them for doing it. On one field day we were so moved to compassion at the sight of our pack-horse that we gave him a drink from a water bottle. I opened his mouth while Hopkinson poured the water in. Flies were with us always, and there were plenty of lizards, odd snakes, and things with flattish bodies, frog's heads and rat's tails. Our work took us, also, to the Black Hills at the east end of the Mokattams—wild desert country, and we crossed the Small Petrified Forest, a large area full of pieces of petrified wood, all sizes and shapes, from chippings to gnarled and knotted parts of branches and trunks. As we kicked them, the stones gave out a metallic ring.

On one field day, the General said to our OC: 'Work man; don't dream!' On another, Ormesher and I were the last two men of the whole division to return. We thought we were, as we wandered slowly over miles of sand towards Abbassia, carrying our full marching order, a drum of wire and other equipment, until we rounded the base of a desert hill, to find an infantryman lying there exhausted. We lifted him up, divided his heavier equipment between us and supported him, one on each side, making for Heliopolis. There we stopped a wagon, told the driver to take the man home, and feeling like a rest and a drink, we had both. We had our desert nights, or days and nights combined, when we wandered on neck-breaking rocky hills in the dark, or made fires and tea. When we bivouacked we scratched hollow holes, long enough to lie in and broad enough for two of us, covering ourselves with our overcoats. Close by, large fires were burning. Daylight followed dawn very quick, and then we saw the fine and quickly-changing colours of the sky.

CHAPTER 9

One morning, when we paraded at 4 a.m., there was a cold wind, and candles outside were blown out while our horse was being loaded. It was taken into our store room. The nag mistook the store for a stable, and only Ormesher's quick action with a bucket saved the situation.

In early March, the 6th Manchesters concert party gave a show in the Surtees Hall, Abbassia. General Douglas and staff officers of meaner magnitude sat at the back of the hall. In due course the General made a speech. Most of it referred to unrest in the division because it was not on active service, and he ended by saying:

'Unless I'm very much mistaken, you'll all have your bellies full of active service before long.'

The concert items were the popular songs of the day: 'Gilbert the Filbert,' 'A Sergeant of the Line,' 'Love and Wine,' 'Do they all go to see the sea?' (From what Private Lomas told us, they want to see a good deal more.) Then there was 'The Matrimonial Handicap,' and

> Toddling home, in early morning,
> Toddling

> Toddling home, when day is dawning...
> I got hold of Johnson's hand,
> And he got hold of Brown,
> And we played at ring o' roses

> Till we all fell down.

* * *

Figure 58. Barrage du Nil, or Nile Barrage.
A soldier is seated on a rail trolley beside two men wearing *galabiehs*.

A favourite excursion was to Barrage du Nil, to see the dams on the Rosetta and Damietta branches of the river, and the island where they divide. The dam sluices were worked by winches carried by trucks on rails. From the station, it is usual to go by trolley to whatever part you want—dams, gardens, or right over to the village of El-Manashi. Each trolley holds four passengers, and it is pushed by a native. The gardens are beautifully laid out in lawns, with palms, subtropical vegetation, pleasant paths, and there is plenty of shade. In the gardens are conjurers and acrobats, who work at the rate of half a piastre a trick.

In the village, Tommy and I called at a school, a small and dirty room, where a teacher was busy with sixteen boys—one of them 'in the corner.' The teacher and one boy squatted on a small form, one at each end of it. This was in another corner. The other boys mumbled and swayed as they learned their lesson. We went to a better school where there were desks. Here the boys used a kind of celluloid 'slate' and ink. We heard their curious monotones as they read. Outside, someone was rash enough to throw a half-piastre to some boys playing in the village.

CHAPTER 9

Figure 59. 'Gib it backshiesh.'

This brought the whole population of children round us, shouting for *backshiesh*. They crowded us, some with stones, following us, crying, screaming, shouting, until a man came and chased them off.

March weather in Egypt was varied. One morning it was hot and close, then came cold wind, then rain which wet us through in two minutes, and then the sun scorched us. All in a few hours. A hot north wind, the *Khamâsîn*, often blows for two or three days at a time in March, April and May. It blows from the hot deserts and is often strong, carrying sand and dust until there is a thick yellow fog, dense enough to hide the sun. Dust and depression are everywhere, when the *Khamâsîn* blows.

The papers published notices about the shooting of wild dogs in various districts:

> Shooting of stray dogs. Marg, April 13th. Back of Citadel, April 14th. Heliopolis, April 17th.

We read notices of local crime:

> Benjoumin Affifi Nehd got a month's hard labour 'for misappropriating a tin of butter.'

> Taker Ahmed and Ibrahim Soliman stole seven eggs. One month's hard labour.

> Mohamed Ahmed Hajon got three months for throwing with intent to steal.

> Ibrahim Ali stole a demijohn of medicine at Shebin el Kom Station; a man stole a melon at Benha, others stole salted fish, coal, soap, tobacco, figs, dates, and Ibrahim Mansour stole 14 kilos of cotton at Gabbary.

We noted the names of local people:

> Ali Hassan, Amin Idris, Abbas Khalil, Ali Gad Allah, Morsi Shaaban, Mahmed El-Ganini, Ibrahim Ahmed Nasr, Dissonki Abdallah, Sayed Ali Sayed, Hassan Abdel-Fattah El-Zanali, Mukhtar Mahomed, Mohamed Ali, and so on.

The hawkers shouted:

> 'Or-an-gers 3 fil half; Tomadies, Flag cee-garettes; Flag cee-garettes and box of matchesh; Very good, very nice; Or-an-gees good and big; Half-piastre. Gib it backshiesh. Clean boots—no good, no money.'

CHAPTER 9

We watched native funerals—Moslem, Copt and other Christians. At the head of a Copt procession a cross was carried. Then came a black velvet cloth with symbols in gold, then the hearse and coffin. We were told that a white coffin indicated youth; a black one, age.

Inside a rail, in front of a native cinema, an orchestra of five Egyptians were making a noise like tins, pans and whistles—all going at once.

In Mahomet Ali Street we watched the grinding of corn in a quern; and in 'O be joyful's' bed, a chocolate-coloured centipede was found.

* * *

On March 19th our company was made up to full strength by the arrival of men from Southport, who had much to tell us, both about their voyage, and of what was going on in England.

The *Egyptian Mail* and the *Gazette* rarely failed to inform or entertain us. There were articles in them helpful to those of us who wanted to get all they could out of their time in Egypt; and such things as the doctoring of drinks in the low bars of Cairo, or silly-season letters on the quest 'Do camels croon?' We followed the correspondence on this matter, not because we cared whether camels crooned or not, but for what fun we could get out of it, adding our own comments on the mangy, slobbering animals.

One afternoon, all our NCOs went with Lawford and the other officers to Gebel Ahmar to discuss strategy and tactics and cable-wagons. We sat on the slope of the rear valley, looking down and eastwards to our manoeuvring grounds.

Said Lawford: 'What do you see in the valley?'

'A n——, sir.' [Epithet deleted]

Lawford: 'If you were bring cable-carts up the gully and the enemy opened fire on you with 5″ guns, what would you do?'

'Open on them with 9″ guns, sir.'

And so the farce went on.

Figure 60. Motorcycle despatch riders of the Divisional Signal Company, East Lancashire Division, in General Sir Ian Hamilton's review of British troops on 28 March 1915 in Cairo.

On March 28th we had a divisional route march in Cairo. Sir Ian Hamilton—who seemed to be eyeing details closely—with other English and French generals, took the salute.[86] The saluting base was in Opera Square, at a corner of the Continental Hotel. Rumours increased so much that I sent home for money and ten spools of film, in case there was an accident and we were sent somewhere or other.

When Good Friday came we had half an hour longer in bed than usual, but we did not get much out of it—we were all so used to getting

---

86 General Sir Ian Hamilton, GOC MEF. See Appendix IV: Biography of Ian Hamilton. The general sent a message to the East Lancashire Division complementing it on its 'turn-out and soldierly bearing.' Hamilton had a long-standing regard for the Manchester Regiment stretching back to his Boer War service when the 1st Manchesters had been under his command. Hamilton's diary entry went even further: 'How I envied Maxwell these beautiful troops. They will only be eating their heads off here, with summer coming and the desert as dry as a bone. The Lancashire men especially are eye openers. How on earth have they managed to pick up the swank and devil may care airs of crack regulars, only they are bigger, more effective specimens than Manchester mills or East Lancashire mines can spare us for the Regular Service in peacetime. Anyway, no soldier need wish to see a finer lot. On them has descended the mantle of my old comrades of Elandslaagte and Caesars Camp, and worthily beyond doubt they will wear it.'

up at 5.30 a.m.—strange as it may seem. In the afternoon Tommy and I went to the Pyramids. Returning to Cairo, we found the streets full of troops: Red Caps, Mounted Police, Yeomanry, pickets. Particularly in Sharia Kamel and round Ezbekiyeh. A Red Cap stopped us and told us to return to barracks. We decided to find out what was happening. The Australians had been making and finding trouble in what the papers called the 'notorious quarters'—the Waz'a. Houses had been set on fire, furniture thrown out, revolvers fired, Red Caps, police and Australians hurt. These incidents became so famous that an Australian paper published some verses about them.[87] The New Zealanders do not seem to have been concerned. The General had a paragraph in our orders, that 'as was expected, no territorials were implicated in last Friday's riots.' But it would have needed only a minor incident to make serious trouble between the Australians and ourselves. Later on, when we knew them better, we altered our opinions, finding that what they wanted was action and not so much discipline and routine, even if they needed discipline. Early in April the Australians decided to raid our canteens, and on the night of April 6th, when I was canteen corporal, the company was warned to be ready to turn out at a moment's notice, with bayonets. I was told to round up all men confined to barracks, about six in number, and post them at our doors with rifles and ammunition. Major Lawford and CQMS Campbell sat at a table in the corridor, and Lawford had his revolver on the table. The Australians had announced their intention of wrecking as well as raiding our canteens, and we heard that our infantry battalions were waiting to receive them. But nothing happened.

---

87 On 2 April 1915, drunken Anzac troops rioted in the area, an event which became known as the Battle of the Wazzir.

Figure 61. Cairo's main railway station.

Returning to our Easter holiday, we were allowed out on condition that we went 'as bonafide parties to places outside Cairo.' I joined a party for Ismailia while others went to Port Said. A *khamâsîn* was blowing when we went outside at 5 a.m. on Easter Monday. We felt blasts of hot air, while fine dust filled our eyes, ears and mouths—and the railway carriages when we started our journey from Cairo Station. In open country we could not see far because of the fog of dust. This Monday was the festival of Sham el-Nessim, a national holiday. At Ismailia, on the Suez Canal, we met some men of our company who were stationed there. They showed us round. We drove to the Canal ferry, passing the northern portion of Lake Timsah, through which the canal passes. When the air cleared slightly, we could see two of the river gun-boats for the defence of the Canal.

The ferry was a big, clumsy affair, and very slowly pulled across the Canal by a native crew squatting on both sides of the boat and hauling on the fixed chains. It took us nearly a quarter of an hour to cross the narrow Canal. On board also were some sheep, and about fifty Indian soldiers who gathered round us in a friendly way, but their bright eyes could change from a twinkle to a glint in an instant.[88] They were delighted by our efforts to talk to them. Some of them knew a few English words, but all most of them and ourselves could manage was

---

[88] These men probably belonged to either the 22nd or 29th Indian Brigades which at the time were manning the Canal defences around Ismailia.

CHAPTER 9

Figures 62 and 63. Ferry Post, Ismailia.

primitive sign language. One of them tried to relieve me of my stick. There had been shelling at Ismailia.

On the far side, we explored the trenches, but saw only two guns, with their heaps of shells close by. The other guns had been removed, as danger was considered over, but we saw plenty of barbed wire. On the shore of Lake Timsah were six Turkish pontoons riddled by bullets and shell fragments. Later on we saw a few Turkish prisoners of war in Cairo. A poor, weary lot—after the hardships of their desert march to the Suez.

On our return, we saw Red Cross trains, and an armoured train; and by the rail-side were mounds of stores and fodder, and plenty of camels for transport. The railway engines were fitted with cow-catchers. Drifting sand had blocked the line since the morning, and our train was an hour late in reaching Cairo.

On the morning of April 12th, we were told to get ready to go to Helouan with the Manchester Brigade—a route march of about twenty miles—in marching order, with our pack animal and full equipment. We fell in at 3.15 p.m., and moved off from the main guard at 4.15 p.m. We had a halt near Cairo Station, another near Old Cairo, with further halts every fifty minutes until we reached Maadi. By then it was nine o'clock and, of course, dark. After a meal in a group of palms we lay down and rested for two and a half hours, starting again at 11.30 p.m. The road was rough. For several weeks we had been on the desert and had become used to it; but now we were on a rutty and bad road, and our feet felt the difference. At times we saw the lights from boats and banks reflected from the dark water of the Nile. The marching pace was quick. Our feet were tired and sore. We began to walk mechanically. The only remarks I heard were about 'this bloody route march.' We knew it could not last forever, but we wondered how long we could last. It became a matter of will-power. We could beat the distance if we could—and we did. But in the early hours of the morning we were not marching, we were staggering. We had to help Tommy to keep going. I was in charge of the animal and his load of tackle, although he had a driver to look after him. We had to watch for fragments of tackle falling off the pack, and fasten them on again; but we lost eight earth-pins, shaken loose from their leather carrier. Language grew stronger. What one did not say, another did. While we were wondering if we could stick it out, we had taken another hundred paces; and so it went on until 5.30 a.m. when we reached an open space near a large hotel in Helouan. Our wagon was missing but turned up later. Early morning was cold when I lay down on the *Manchester City News*. At 8 a.m., when we got up and shook ourselves, we were tired, stiff and sore, walking slowly and painfully. There was nothing to do, except have a look round, so, with Ormesher, Hopkinson and Abie Williams, I went to the English Winter Hotel, a large and quite good place, for a hot bath and a shave. Later on, we had dinner there. The old man was French, and his wife English. Returning to our bivouac, we lazed all afternoon. So many of the 6th Manchesters went sick with sore feet that Jerry H., the Colonel and Acting Brigadier started to arrange for a train to take these men back to Cairo.[89] A divisional order stated that only 14 men per battalion, the worst cases, should return by train. General Douglas arrived by car. There was a grand palaver of General and colonels. Our hearing was good, and we heard Douglas shouting at Jerry for letting the MO have so much influence.

'I tell you H...!' shouted Douglas.

We thought he was hard-hearted. Really, however, we wanted to stick out anything we were told to stick. Somebody had 'exclusive information' about a letter asking if the division was fit for service or not, and the Manchester Brigade had been selected for the test.

An order came that we were not to march back until the night of the following day. We lay down very early that night. Next morning we went to the baths and sulphur spring, which tasted like sugar and salt in water. We could not get towels for the baths and didn't go in. We washed and shaved in the Winter Hotel bathroom, returning to the bivouac for dinner and tea. I had to issue the rations. Part of it was a problem in spherical geometry, for I had to divide a Dutch cheese into 19 equal shares. However, I heard no grumbling about the inequalities of segments. We went back to the Winter Hotel for the evening.

The march back to Cairo started at 9 p.m. We cut off a stretch of bad road by crossing the sand. We marched slowly, in a very cold

---

89 Capt. Philip Vaughan Holberton (6th Manchesters adjutant), Lt. Col. Gerald Graham Percival Heywood, and temporary Brig. Gen. Noel Lee, respectively. See Appendix III: Soldiers' biographies.

wind. I kept nodding and dozing as we marched. We reached Maadi at 1.30 a.m., where a meal of tea, bread and meat was ready for us. At 2.15 we were off again, at a slow and awkward step. With the usual 10-minute halts every hour, we reached Abbassia at 7 a.m. So ended a march none will forget who took part in it. I was in debt when I got back. Some of us had not taken much money with us.

We thought we were going to have a good rest. Instead, our section had to move to a building across the Suez Road, known as M Block. Infantry signallers attached to our section were with us. But our four corporals had a little room to ourselves—this we appreciated. We took turns as orderly corporal for the block. I had been promoted to the RE rank of 2nd Corporal, and so had my meals in the company corporals' mess. Each of us paid five piastres (one shilling) weekly for extra messing, more variety and better cooking. The latter was done in the canteen kitchen. As orderly corporal for the week, I had to be up at 4.55 a.m., and had to see that every man was awake. At 5.10 I called 'QUARTER!' and turned them out for the 5.30 a.m. parade. At six o'clock I went round each room in both blocks with AF 256,[90] shouting 'Any sick?' There were usually five or six men who wanted to see the MO. These paraded at 6.45, when I marched them to the RAMC where the MO saw them. Returning from the 'sick parade' about 7.45, I handed in AF 256 at our orderly room, and then went to the kitchen where breakfast had been kept warm for me. Then, slowly and luxuriously, I breakfasted, reading the newspapers. For the rest of the day the orderly corporal of M Block did what he pleased—looking busy, of course, if there was any danger of being wanted for other jobs. As orderly corporal I was given an order to meet the sweep at 5.30 a.m. on the morning of Thursday, April 29th, 'to note the number and kind of chimneys swept. If stone or iron.' Somehow or other I failed to meet the sweep, but as nobody else said anything, I did not. Another job was to distribute the bundles of clean washing to their owners.

---

90 Army Form B.256, Morning Sick Reports.

CHAPTER 9

By this time, we knew we were going to move. Saturday, May 1st, was a day of preparation at all times. The Lancashire Fusiliers were ready to move at night. The usual Sunday orders were cancelled, and a notice was posted on the board that our address would be

> East Lancs Div'l Signal Company, RE,
> Mediterranean Expeditionary Force.

We had an idea what that meant for, on Friday, April 30th, I met A.H. who told me that we were going to the Dardanelles,[91] but that he did not know the date. He told me, also, that as the ASC officer responsible, he had had a rotten time with the Australians, apparently in the matters of bread and meat. On this day also, we had drawn our active service pay books. What was more useful to me was drawing 735 piastres back pay.

We had enjoyed Egypt, but now we were excited at the prospect of a new adventure. We were not kept waiting for long, only until the night of Sunday, May 2nd. By the morning of Monday, May 3rd, we were on the quay at Alexandria, ready to embark on a transport for the Dardanelles.

---

91 Probably Second Lieut. W.A. Halliwell, ASC (TF).

Figure 64. Soldiers of the East Lancashire Division embark for Gallipoli. The transport appears to be A.1 *Ionian*, suggesting that these are men of the 7th and 8th Manchesters.

Figure 65. The seized German transport NDL *Derfflinger* (later HMT *Huntsgreen*) in the harbour at Alexandria. The 'Dirtflinger', as she was known to the 6th Manchesters, carried Brig. Gen. Noel Lee, the Manchester Brigade headquarters staff, the 6th Manchesters and No. 4 Signal Section, with Alec Riley, to Gallipoli.

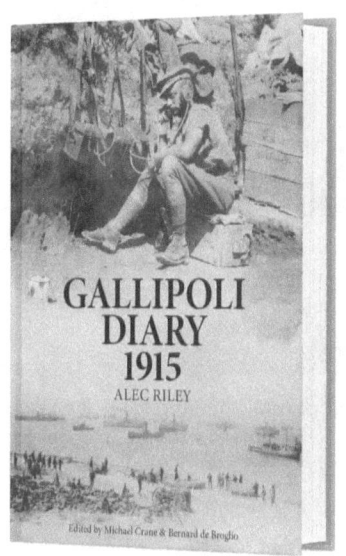

So concludes the first volume of Alec Riley's diaries.

The second, which has already been published, is entitled 'Gallipoli Diary 1915.' It follows Riley and the East Lancashire Division to Helles.

The third and final volume, 'Netley Diary 1915–1916,' is in preparation and will be published shortly.

Figure 66. The only named photograph of Alec Riley known to the editors. Riley is seen here on his return to Gallipoli Peninsula in 1930, in Krithia Nullah near the Redoubt Line.

APPENDIX I

Second Corporal 10 Alec Riley

No. 4 (Manchester Brigade) Section, 1/1st Signal Company,
42nd (East Lancs) Division, Royal Engineers (TF). Private 10, 1/6th Bn,
Manchester Regt, later Sapper 426899, Royal Engineers

Alec Riley was born in Salford, Lancashire, on 24 March 1887, son of Thomas Riley, age 50, and Mary Ann Riley (née Dobie), a former schoolteacher, age 33. He was baptised on 24 March 1888 at Manchester Cathedral.

Alec grew up with two siblings—his half-brother, Thomas Alfred, 16 years older than Alec and from his father's first marriage, and a younger sister, Margaret, who was born in 1892.[92] Riley's father owned a well-established dry salt business and was comfortably middle class. He brought up the children in a substantial detached Victorian villa, Rosthwaite, attended by two servants.

Tragedy struck in 1894 when Alec's mother died while he was seven years old. One year later, Alec's father married his third wife, 48-year-old spinster Eliza Cowley, giving the six-year-old a new stepmother. Little is known of his early years, but it is probable that Alec received his secondary education at Eccles Grammar School.

---

92 The 1881 census shows two other children by Thomas Riley and his then wife Sarah—Elizabeth, age 13, and William T., age 6. Neither of these children are present on the 1891 census, nor are there any records showing their birth, death or marriage, and it is likely that both died in childhood.

Alec joined the 2nd Volunteer Battalion of the Manchester Regiment on 16 May 1905. When the Territorial Force was formed on 1 April 1908, he re-enlisted in the retitled 6th Battalion of the Manchester Regiment. (This explains how Riley came by his very low service number of 10.) In the same year Riley served as a member of the Honour Guard when Sir Ian Hamilton unveiled the Manchester Regiment's South African war memorial in St Ann's Square. His records show he was a committed amateur soldier who attended all his two-weeks-long annual training camps between 1908 and 1912.

The 1911 census of England shows the 24-year-old Riley employed as a clerk in a salt warehouse. This was probably his father's business, at No. 3 Arch, Hulme Locks, Egerton Street, Hulme, Manchester.

Riley was an enthusiastic cyclist and was on a bicycle tour in the south-west of England when war was declared. Cutting his tour short, he returned to Manchester on 5 August 1914 and reported to battalion headquarters at 3, Stretford Road, Old Trafford, in the afternoon to be embodied.

On 20 August, Riley moved with the battalion to Hollingworth Camp, near Littleborough, and on 2 September, by now a lance corporal, he signed Army Form E.624, volunteering for overseas service.

On 10 September 1914, the East Lancashire Division sailed from Southampton for Egypt. On the same day Riley was attached to the 1/1st East Lancs RE Signal Company which embarked, together with the Lancashire Fusiliers Brigade headquarters and the 6th and 7th Lancs Fusiliers, on the Donaldson liner SS *Saturnia*. After an uneventful passage, the fleet carrying the division arrived at Alexandria on Thursday 25 September. Riley and his company disembarked in the early hours of the following morning and, after a delay, entrained for Cairo. They arrived at Abbassia sidings after a journey of six and a half hours. 'The men, hot and tired, tramped across a stretch of sand to their barracks, where there shone a light. It came,' wrote Riley, 'from a canteen. Where there was beer there was hope.' Now a member of No. 4 Section, Riley had arrived at his new home in Polygon Barracks, Cairo.

For the next five months the East Lancs Division undertook a program of training designed to raise the men's fitness and turn the amateur soldiers into an effective fighting force. The men of No. 4 Section took part in some of this training, but the greater part of their time was occupied in operating various communications facilities in and around Cairo and on the Suez Canal. On 18 January 1915, Riley and the other members of No. 4 Section were transferred into the Royal Engineers. In April 1915, Riley's aptitude was recognised with a promotion to 2nd corporal.

By the beginning of May 1915, the East Lancashire Division had been allocated as reinforcements for the MEF. Riley embarked from Alexandria for Gallipoli with No. 4 Section on 3 May, landing at W Beach on 6 May. During his time at Helles he was attached on various occasions to the 1/5th, 1/6th, 1/7th, 1/8th and 1/9th Manchesters and briefly to the 1/4th Bn, East Lancs Regt, giving Riley the opportunity to have close personal contact with many of the key personnel within these units and to see a great deal of the Helles battlefield. He was present in the forward trenches for both the Third Battle of Krithia and the Battle of 6–7 August,[93] and later wrote vivid accounts of both battles and their aftermath.

Riley was medically evacuated on the morning of Saturday 11 September 1915 and taken from W Beach by hospital ship *Glasgow* to Mudros Harbour where he was transferred to the hospital ship *Simla*. He remained on board *Simla* for three days, during which time he was diagnosed as suffering from jaundice, enteritis and diphtheria, with nine septic wounds. On 14 September, Riley was transferred by launch and motor ambulance to 'the infectious section' of an Australian hospital. By now Riley was unable to walk, due to paralysis caused by diphtheria. He was taken to a 'battered old bell tent', which gave no protection when a great storm swept over Lemnos that night—Riley thought it the worst night he had experienced at Gallipoli. In the morning, after being examined by a 'tall, fat and pig-like' Australian doctor called Johnson, he was designated an acute case and, in a brutal form of triage, moved to an isolation tent with two other men. Riley felt the move was to allow them to 'finish our time—that is, to peg out.' One of the men died but Riley confounded Johnson by surviving the ordeal, and a few days later was moved into a large marquee where he received better treatment and began to recover.

---

93 Also known, in acknowledgement of the only ground gained during the fighting, as the Battle of the Vineyard.

By Wednesday 20 October, Riley was considered strong enough to be sent home, and he sailed for England aboard the converted passenger liner *Aquitania*. He arrived at Southampton Water on 27 October and was taken by motor ambulance to the Royal Victoria Hospital, Netley. Riley spent the next 11 months at Netley, and its auxiliary hospitals, Shirley and Shorne Hill, recovering from his various ailments.

In September 1916, his discharge was confirmed, prompting Riley to send a telegram to his family from the hospital's post office: 'Kill fatted calf. Prodigal son returns Friday.'

After a spell of home leave, a still less than fit Riley was posted on 25 November 1916 to the 71st Division Signal Company RE to be employed on clerical work (C class). On 17 July 1917, he was reduced to the rank of sapper, possibly due to his disability. Also in 1917, in common with all other territorial soldiers, Riley was issued with a new six-figure service number, 426899.

It is unclear if Riley ever served in France, but he finished his army service with the 67th Division Signal Company RE. On 17 April 1919, he was granted 28 days leave before being demobilized on 15 May 1919. On leaving the army, he returned to Rosthwaite to live with his father and stepmother. Later that year he was awarded the Territorial Efficiency Medal and in 1920 was issued with the King's Certificate and Silver War Badge with reference to King's Regulations paragraph 392 (xvia) which designated Riley as 'surplus to service requirements having suffered impairment since entry into the service.'

Although his records show reference to a pension application there are no records of its actual award. However, it does seem likely because Riley's entry in the 1939 census described him as having retired in 1919 with his last employment being the 71st Division Signal Company RE. Nonetheless, Riley began to look for a career in writing and enrolled as a student at the London School of Journalism, established by Max Pemberton in 1920.

Family tragedy struck again at the end of 1920 when Riley's 49-year-old half-brother, Thomas Alfred, went missing on 21 December and was found dead on Barton Moss on New Year's Day 1921, leaving a wife and two children. The relationship between Alec and Thomas Alfred had been close. Alec had often stayed at his home and the news must have shocked and distressed him. Until his death, Thomas Alfred had worked in their father's business and was named successor and inheritor of the business in his will. A year and a half later, on 7 August 1922, Alec's father died aged 86. It is unclear what became of the business, but he left the net sum of £21,970 in his will. Probate was granted to his three executors—his widow Eliza, Alec (recorded as having no occupation) and Robert Isherwood (Alec's brother-in-law).

The 1921 census (taken on 19 June) shows Riley attending a Ministry of Labour Training Centre in forestry held at Brockenhurst, Hants. Whether Riley volunteered for the course or it was imposed on him is unknown.

In the early 1920s, Riley began a decade-long correspondence with Sir Ian Hamilton, which included exchanges of personal recollections and several photographs. The letters are friendly and informal despite a significant difference in the rank and social position of the correspondents.

In one letter, dated 15 December 1923, Riley encloses five photographs taken during the campaign. Hamilton's reply on 17 December is wry: 'Thank you for your letter of the 15th and for your interesting photographs. I suspect you were defying my regulation when you snapped them!' Riley also informed Hamilton that he was in the honour guard when the General unveiled the Manchester Regiment's Boer War Memorial in St Ann's Square in 1908, adding 'you were exactly opposite to me when a press photographer snapped the inspection. I have a copy of the photo.'

The correspondence appears to have ended after Hamilton had written, then re-written at Riley's request, an introduction—dated 11 November 1932—for the book 'Return to Cape Helles,' a manuscript for which Riley was unable find a publisher and which is now lost.

Riley made two pilgrimages to Gallipoli, 'independently, living near Sedd-el-Bahr for several days, tramping the country systematically and alone, and photographing what I thought to be of interest and importance.' One of these pilgrimages was in carried out in late May and early June 1930 and Riley sent at least fifteen photographs taken during this trip to Hamilton.

He also sent photographs to Brigadier General Aspinall-Oglander, two of which—'The Anzac Front' and 'The View of the Dardanelles from Chunuk Bair'—were included in Volume II of his *Official History of Military Operations Gallipoli*. Riley also provided Aspinall-Oglander with 'an odd note or two made for him at the hold-up place in Krithia Nullah.' Later, he sent a copy of his manuscript to Aspinall-Oglander in the hope of enlisting his help to find either a publisher or a newspaper interested in serialising the narrative.

The pilgrimages to Gallipoli had given Riley a rare view of the battlefield 'from the Turkish and our own points of view.' These visits provided the basis for 'Return to Helles' and were also key to getting some of his work published.

Around 1935, Riley had a lengthy article published in *Twenty Years After,* a weekly magazine that recalled major events in the First World War, and featured articles written by veterans revisiting the site of battle twenty years after the event. 'From the narrative of my rambles,' wrote Riley, 'three sections have been chosen.' He added some of his recollections of 1915 for context. Riley also contributed a total of 41 photographic images for use in his own and other Gallipoli-related articles in *Twenty Years After*.

Another of Riley's articles, written to mark the 23rd anniversary of the Gallipoli Landings, was published in *The Telegraph and Morning Post* on 23 April 1938. This article included two photographs taken by Riley. A caption under one drew attention to a 'new' Gallipoli exhibition at the Imperial War Museum, recently opened and featuring photographs and artefacts donated by Riley.

Riley never married and his later life is something of an enigma. The 1939 census shows Riley, now approaching 60, staying with the Treoaskis family in Falmouth, Cornwall, where he is described as a 'traveling photographer and occasional writer dealing with the Near East' of 'private means.'

It is clear that Riley possessed a lifelong fascination with travel and had the means to indulge this passion. In 1932, he joined the Royal Geographic Society and may have travelled with the Society on a tour of Scandinavia which he described in a letter to Hamilton 'as a complete change from the Near East and Mediterranean: where most of my travels have been.'

Nor was Riley's interest in travel dimmed by age. Ocean liner passenger lists show that he visited South Africa at least three times in his later years. In 1953, he sailed on the SS *Braemar Castle* (namesake of the troop carrier which served in the Gallipoli campaign) from London to Cape Town and then on to Durban and Port Elizabeth.[94] On the return leg of the cruise, *Braemar Castle* stopped at a half dozen East African ports, going on to dock in Aden and Port Sudan, before sailing through the Suez Canal to Port Said. Both would have been familiar to Riley from his army service. In 1955, Riley's travels took him from Southampton (another port with great significance to Riley) on board RMS *Edinburgh Castle* to the South African ports of Durban, East London, Port Elizabeth and Cape Town.[95] Finally, in 1956, when he was 69 years old, Riley took another cruise around the African coast, sailing from London on board the SS *Kenya Castle*. The first part of the journey retraced that taken by Riley and the East Lancs Division in September 1914, sailing through the Mediterranean to Port Said then passing through the Suez Canal before stopping at various East African ports. The cruise continued on to Durban, Port Elizabeth and Cape Town before returning to London via St Helena and Las Palmas.

It may well be that Riley took these cruises for the same reasons as other tourists, but it seems likely he sought itineraries that would return him to where he had served in the First World War. Riley's choice of South African destinations may have been inspired by his fascination with the Boer War, to which he alluded in his correspondence with Hamilton many years earlier.

Riley died aged 71 on 17 October 1958 at the Highfield Hotel, 141 High Street, Chorlton on Medlock, Manchester.[96] It had been his home for at least five years.

* * *

---

94 On 23 March 2021, Port Elizabeth was renamed Gqeberha, the Xhosa name for the Baakens River.

95 Riley passed through Southampton at least twice during WW1, the first time on 10 September 1914 en route to Egypt and the second on 25 October 1915 on his way to the Royal Victoria Hospital, Netley.

96 Riley's death certificate gives the cause of death as (a) Coronary thrombosis, (b) Coronary arteriosclerosis and (c) Hypertension.

Riley had made his will some twenty years earlier in 1936, including legacies and bequests to various family members. The will also references the content of certain boxes held at the Midland Bank and the YMCA on his behalf. He instructs his executors—the Midland Bank, referred to as 'the Company'— 'to dispose of the contents of such boxes in accordance with the instructions contained in the written memorandum or schedule deposited by me with the Company ...'

Although it is impossible to be sure at the time of writing, it seems likely that these boxes contained the three unpublished manuscripts subsequently donated to the Imperial War Museum. Two are inscribed on their covers: 'For the Imperial War Museum (if it is of any interest).' The first diary covers the events around Riley's mobilization in August 1914, and subsequent service in Egypt from September 1914 until his embarkation for Gallipoli on 3 May 1915. The second diary recaps Riley's last few days in Egypt and his time at Gallipoli from his arrival on 6 May until his medical evacuation on 11 September 1915. The final diary describes his evacuation from the peninsula, suffering from diphtheria, jaundice, enteritis, dysentery and nine septic sores. It goes on to describe his time in hospital on the island of Lemnos, his onward evacuation aboard *Aquitania* in October 1915, and his treatment and 11-month-long convalescence in Netley Hospital.

Riley set down the arrangements for his funeral and the disposal of his remains. They indicate what a modest, self-effacing, pragmatic and perhaps lonely man Riley was in later life.

'I wish to be cremated at the Crematorium nearest to my place of death ... but I do not desire my ashes to be kept and I direct my funeral to be as simple and inexpensive as possible and that no mourning shall be worn ... '

APPENDIX II

'M' — Margaret Isherwood (née Riley)

Margaret Isherwood (née Riley) was born in Eccles, Lancashire, on 11 April 1892, daughter of Thomas Riley, salt merchant, and Mary Ann Riley (née Dobie), a former school teacher. Mary Ann was Thomas's second wife and also mother to Alec Riley. Mary Ann died within two years of Margaret's birth, leaving the six-year-old Alec and the 23-month-old Margaret motherless. Thirteen months later, Thomas, by now 58 years old, married his third wife, a 48-year-old spinster, Eliza Cowley.

Margaret grew up in Eccles, Lancashire, in the family's substantial Victorian villa, Rosthwaite, attended by two servants. On the 1911 census she is recorded as an 18-year-old 'high school girl.'

On 11 May 1920, in Eccles, Margaret married Robert Isherwood, a 'contractor', later a veterinary surgeon and university lecturer on veterinary medicine, with whom she had two daughters, Theo Margaret Isherwood and Ruth Hannah Isherwood.

Robert Isherwood, a former captain in the Army Veterinary Corps during the war, had at one time been stationed at Gibraltar, and in August 1933 he travelled back there taking Margaret and both his daughters for a month-long stay.

Alec and Margaret appear to have had a close and loving relationship both before and after the war. Alec mentions 'M' several times in this diary and she was named as the main beneficiary of his will.

For most of her married life, Margaret lived in Warrington, Cheshire. Her final family home was at 35 Grappenhall Road, Stockton Heath, a suburb of Warrington. She died in Warrington Hospital on 7 January 1964 just four days after her husband Robert, who had died in the same hospital on 3 January.

Figure 67. Officers of the 6th Manchesters, Alexandria, Egypt, 26 December 1914.

Front row, seated on the ground, left to right: Second Lieut. A.J.I. Donald; unknown; unknown; Second Lieut. W.N. Molesworth.

Middle row: Lieut. and QM W. Wynne; Capt. H.B. Pilkington; Capt. S.F. Jackson; Major C.S. Worthington; Brigadier General Noel Lee*; Lieutenant Colonel G.G.P. Heywood*; Major C.R. Pilkington; Capt. P.V. Holberton*; Capt. W.N. Bazley; Capt. A.H. Norris; RAMC; Capt. O. St L. Davies.

Back row: Capt. E. Kessler; Lieutenant F.C. Aldous; unknown; Capt. J. Holt; unknown; Lieutenant R. Killick; Capt. D.C. Bolton; Second Lieut. H.C.L. Heywood; unknown; Lieutenant Tom Blatherwick; Lieutenant A.C.B. Taylor; Lieutenant F.M. Blatherwick; Capt. R.A. Edgar; Lieutenant A.D. Thomson.

Has biography in Appendix III.

APPENDIX III

Soldiers' biographies

The rank given for each man corresponds approximately to his time in Egypt. For other ranks, these are generally derived from the 1914–15 Star Roll. Changes to rank, as well as later awards, are shown in brackets in italics.

Second Lieutenant *(later Lieutenant)* John Bolton
Platoon commander and Scout Officer, 1/5th Bn, East Lancashire Regt

Mining engineer and manager of the commercial department at the Accrington Collieries of Messrs G. Hargreaves and Company. Born into a wealthy mine owning family in Accrington, Lancashire, on 4 January 1889. Educated at Tonbridge School where he was in the Shooting VIII. Graduated with a degree in mining from Victoria University, Manchester.

Commissioned as second lieutenant into the 1/5th Bn, East Lancashire Regt, on 19 June 1913. Volunteered for foreign (imperial) service in early September 1914. Embarked for Egypt with his battalion on 10 September 1914, disembarking at Alexandria, on 24 September. While in Egypt, Second Lieut. John Bolton was appointed battalion Scout Officer and attended a scout training course under Gurkha officers at Abbassia (see figure 17). In November 1914 he commanded the guard detachment during one of Riley's stints at the Abu Zabal wireless station.

Figure 68. Second Lieut. John Bolton.
Studio portrait taken in Egypt in 1914 or 1915.

Embarked for Gallipoli on 5 May 1915, promoted en route to lieutenant on 8 May, and landed with his battalion at V Beach on 9 May. Three days later, the East Lancs (126th) Brigade took over the right of the line from the Royal Naval Division. Bolton was later awarded (posthumously) a congratulatory card by Major General Douglas for his 'gallant actions' performed during the first night his battalion spent in the firing-line on 12 May.

Bolton had two other brothers serving in the 1/5th Bn, East Lancashire Regt. The elder, Capt. H. Hargreaves Bolton, was killed on 24 May during an operation to establish a new firing-line in front of the Redoubt Line. John was present and asked permission to go out to his wounded brother, 'but was told [by his CO] that one catastrophe was enough.'[97]

On 27 May, the East Lancs 126th Brigade was attached to the 29th Division, initially for training purposes. However, John Bolton's battalion and two others were retained as reinforcements for the duration of the Third Battle of Krithia. On 4 June 1915, while his company (A Coy, attached to the 1st Inniskillings) waited to advance from the support trenches on Gully Spur, Lieut. John Bolton was mortally wounded by a large shell fragment which shattered his left arm and tore a huge hole in his side. He died after 'bearing his pain magnificently' for six hours at the 87th Field Ambulance, a forward dressing station above Y Beach.

Bolton was originally buried in a small battlefield cemetery just above Y Beach but his remains were later reinterred in Twelve Tree Copse Cemetery where he is commemorated by a Special Memorial.

---

97 John Bolton's younger brother, Second Lieut. Geoffrey Bolton, was Mentioned in Despatches and awarded the Military Cross for his service at Gallipoli. Geoffrey was later appointed Adjutant to the 1/5th Bn, East Lancs. Geoffrey survived the war and went on to command the 4th/5th Bn, East Lancs Regt, during the post war years. A fourth brother, Capt. Maurice Bolton, MC (11th Manchesters, the Reserve Bn 5th East Lancs and finally the 1/4th Bn, East Lancs Regt), was wounded and taken prisoner in fighting around Le Cateau on 24 March 1918. He died in a German hospital at Le Cateau on 26 March.

Lieutenant *(later Major/temporary Lieutenant Colonel)* Gordon Leslie Broad *(OBE, MC)*

'IC Cables,' No. 1 (Headquarters) Section, 1/1st Signal Company, 42nd (East Lancs) Division, Royal Engineers (TF)

Born Brighton, Sussex, 29 April 1885, and grew up in Lewes, Sussex. Appointed Assistant Architect and Surveyor to the HM Office of Works in 1911 and moved to lodgings in Finsbury Park, London, later moving to the Manchester area. Commissioned second lieutenant on 14 May 1912 into the 2nd East Lancashire Field Company, Royal Engineers (TF), which had its headquarters at 73, Seymour Grove, Old Trafford, Manchester. Promoted to lieutenant on 11 December 1913 and transferred in 1914 to the East Lancashire Telegraph Company (TF).

Married Ethel Margaret Forrest Mill in Hackney, London, in April 1913. Their first child, Gordon Hepburn Forrest Broad (later a lieutenant colonel in the Education Corps during the Second World War), was born in Chorlton, Lancashire, on 21 June 1914.

Volunteered for foreign (Imperial) service sometime after 10 August 1914. Embarked for Egypt on 10 September 1914 with the headquarters (No. 1 Section) of the recently renamed Signal Company. Disembarked at Alexandria, on 24 September and remained in Egypt until No. 1 Section embarked for Gallipoli on 5 May 1915, landing at V Beach (with divisional headquarters) on 9 May. Promoted to acting captain on 14 August 1915 (substantive in May 1916). Awarded the Military Cross and Mentioned in Despatches (Hamilton's second despatch) with both being gazetted on 5 November 1915. Although known to have been admitted to hospital around the end of August, it is likely that he remained at Helles until No. 1 Section left for Mudros on 3 January 1916. (Riley mentions Broad several times in his Egypt diary, but makes no reference to him in his Gallipoli diary.)

Broad served with the Signal Company in Egypt from early January 1916 until the 42nd (East Lancs) Division moved to the Western Front on 2 March 1917. Promoted to major sometime afterwards. Later posted to the Home Army and was awarded the OBE on 7 June 1918 while holding the temporary rank of lieutenant colonel in the post of Assistant Director of Army Signals, Home Forces.

Broad re-joined the civil service after he left the army and is shown on the 1939 register working as a superintendent estate surveyor to HM Department of Works. He died on 22 December 1964 in Tunbridge Wells, Kent.

Sergeant (A/CQMS) 4492 James Edward Campbell

CQMS, 1/1st Signal Company, 42nd (East Lancs) Division, Royal Engineers (TF). Later CSM

Cartridge maker and regular soldier. Born in Aldershot, Hants, on 18 March 1877. Enlisted in the Royal Engineers on a Short Service agreement (7 years with the Colours and 5 years with the Reserve) in Aldershot on 13 January 1897. Served in Malta from March 1897 to December 1898 and in Ceylon from December 1898 to March 1900. Married Ruth Alice Spreadbury in Plumstead, London, on 15 June 1905. On 10 February 1906, by then a sergeant, he re-engaged to complete 21 years' service with the Colours. Appointed Sergeant Instructor and posted to the newly formed East Lancashire Division, Signal Company (TF) on 7 June 1908. The 1911 census confirms his occupation as Sergeant Instructor and shows him living with his wife and two-year-old son Malcolm at 30 Cromwell Avenue, Whalley Range, Manchester (within walking distance of company headquarters at 73, Seymour Grove, Old Trafford, Manchester).

Embarked with the Signal Company for Egypt on 10 September 1914 and disembarked at Alexandria on 24 September. Appointed acting CQMS on 14 January 1915 (although he was already carrying out the role when the Signal Company arrived in Egypt). Embarked for Gallipoli with company headquarters on 5 May 1915 and landed at V Beach (with divisional headquarters) on 9 May 1915.

Riley describes him in his Gallipoli diary as 'short and shirty'. Campbell's service records give his height as 5 feet 5 inches, which was not much shorter than most men in the division, which suggests that Riley was of above average height. Riley goes on to mention a surprising change in attitude when Campbell began selling comestibles to the rank and file. As Riley recalled in his usual dry wit: 'When I called at Campbell's for more eggs and milk, on the morning of Thursday, August 19, I received such politeness that I felt overcome with emotion.'

Campbell was still at Gallipoli when Riley was evacuated on 11 September, but his records show that on 17 October 1915 he followed Riley off the peninsula (probably also due to illness). Like Riley, Campbell continued to serve in the Royal Engineers, remaining in England for the remainder of the war. Awarded the Long Service and Good Conduct Medal (with gratuity) in 1916. Appointed acting CSM on 31 July 1916 while attached to the 3/1st East Lancs Divisional Signal Company, a training unit based at the third-line depot of the East Lancs Royal Engineers at Carnarvon, North Wales. It was here that men were trained to provide drafts for the first and second-line units. The East Lancs RE history records that 'a great number of returned officers and men came to Carnarvon from hospital in various stages of convalescence, and many of them were used on the administrative and instructional staffs.'

On 26 June 1917, Campbell transferred to the Royal Engineer Signal Depot at Bedford as acting RSM. Promoted to WOII and appointed CSM on 19 November 1917. Transferred to Z Reserve on 3 February 1919.

On his retirement from the army, Campbell moved to London. The 1939 register shows him living with his wife at 9 Olven Road, Woolwich, and working as a clerk in the civil service. He was still living at the same address when he died on 25 January 1947.

Driver 1568 William Dean

No. 4 (Manchester Brigade) Section, 1/1st Signal Company, 42nd (East Lancs) Division, Royal Engineers (TF).
Later Driver 444604, Royal Engineers

Born 1891. Judging by his service number he probably enlisted around 1911. Embodied on 5 August 1914. Signed Army Form E.624, volunteering for foreign service in early September 1914. Embarked with the East Lancashire Division for Egypt on 10 September 1914. Disembarked at Alexandria on 24 September and served with No. 4 Signal Section in Egypt 1914–15. Embarked for Gallipoli on 3 May and arrived off Helles onboard *Derfflinger* on 6 May 1915. In his Gallipoli diary, Riley tells us that 'S. Ridings and Driver Dean were left onboard in charge of some equipment' when No. 4 Section left the ship. Ridings' service records confirm that he returned to Alexandria and disembarked on 19 May. They also state that Dean served continuously in Egypt from 10 September 1914 (his date of embarkation from Southampton) to 31 December 1915. Dean's records give no indication that he re-embarked for Gallipoli and neither S. Ridings nor Driver Dean are referred to again in Riley's Gallipoli diary, so it may be that both men remained in Egypt as part of the base detail.

Admitted to hospital in Egypt (probably Alexandria) on 20 November 1917 suffering from Renal Calculus (kidney stones). His Medal Index Card and entry on the 1914–15 Star Roll confirms he served for the duration of the war. Dean's pension and medical records show that he was granted a pension, for Renal Calculus, on 20 April 1919. At the time, he was unmarried and living at 499 Liverpool Road, Peel Green, Manchester.

Major General Sir William Douglas, KCMG, CB, DSO

GOC, 42nd (East Lancs) Division

Born 13 August 1858 and educated at Bath. Gazetted into 1st Bn, The Royal Scots, on 30 January 1878. Promoted to lieutenant on 25 November 1878, serving as adjutant, 1st Bn, Royal Scots, from 24 March 1880 to 23 March 1887.

Served in the Bechuanaland Expedition, 1884–85. Promoted to captain on 24 June 1885. Appointed adjutant 3rd Royal Scots (Militia), February 1888 to February 1893, and adjutant 1st Royal Scots, 20 February 1893 to 20 August 1894.

Douglas was promoted to major on 24 July 1895 and attended Staff College 1896–97. He served in South Africa, 1900–02, and took part in operations in the Orange Free State, February to May 1900, and in the Transvaal, east of Pretoria, July to 29 November 1900. Took part in the actions at Belfast (26 and 27 August 1900) and Lydenburg (5 to 8 September 1900).

CO to 1st Bn Royal Scots from 24 August 1900, and in command of a column during operations in the Transvaal, November 1900 to November 1901. Promoted to lieutenant colonel on 5 December 1900. Mentioned in Despatches (LG 16 April 1901), received the Queen's medal with three clasps, the King's medal with two clasps, and was created a Companion of the Distinguished Service Order (LG 19 April 1901).

Made brevet colonel 10 February 1904, promoted to colonel on 1 March 1906 and was colonel to the General Staff, 6th Division, and subsequently became (when the title of the appointment was changed) GSO 1st Grade, 8th Division (the 6th Division becoming the 8th Division) Irish Command, from 1st March 1906 to 31 October 1909. Created a CB in 1908.

He commanded the 14th Infantry Brigade from 1 November 1909 to 9 November 1912. Promoted major general on 10 August 1912 and commanded the 42nd Division from May 1913 to 11 March 1917.

Served in Egypt from 10 September 1914 to 5 May 1915 and at Gallipoli from 9 May to 30 December 1915, during which time he was placed in temporary command of VIII Corps on several occasions, the most notable being from 24 July to 8 August (during the last major battle at Helles). Twice Mentioned in Despatches (LG 21 September 1915 and November 1915) and created KCMG in November 1915.

Later served in Sinai, 1916–17, during the battle of Romani and the capture of El Arish. Commanded the Desert Column from 23 October 1916 to 8 December 1916. Twice Mentioned in Despatches (LG December 1916 and July 1917) and awarded the *Croix de Guerre* with Palm (LG 21 May 1917).

Left the division on 11 March 1917 to give evidence in the Dardanelles Inquiry. Douglas later commanded the Western Reserve Centre until retiring on 19 August 1918. He died in 1920.

Known almost universally as 'Little Willie' he was despised by practically all the officers and men in his division. Douglas's ADC, Captain Harold Cawley MP wrote of Douglas in a letter to his father in September:

'My own general is disliked by all his troops, particularly by his officers. He has a third-rate brain, no capacity to grasp the lie of the land and originality or ingenuity. He has been to the trenches three times since he landed, hurried visits on which he saw nothing and he hardly ever goes to an observation point with his field glasses. The result is that he does not understand the lie of the land on his own front. When there is an attack, he works out the details and leaves nothing to the Brigadiers and commanding officers who know the ground. The result last time [August Battle] was that the best Manchester Battalions were sent to an impossible place which every colonel and adjutant regarded as only to be taken after some other commanding trenches had been cleared...'

The other ranks were no less scathing. An unnamed NCO told Chaplain Kenneth Best that 'there are only two ways of General D[ouglas] getting killed—by lyddite on top of [his dugout] direct hit, or by a bullet from one of his own men.'

Notorious for his abrasive nature and for micromanaging his subordinates and local operations (while having little understanding of the ground or firing-line conditions). However, despite Douglas's outward appearance of a brusque, unemotional commander, he was not without feelings and was greatly affected by the losses the division suffered in June and August. Hamilton recalled Douglas as a 'melancholy man before whose eyes stands constantly the tragic melting away without replacement of the most beautiful of the Divisions of Northern England.'

Brigadier General Herbert Cokayne Frith *(CB)*
GOC, 125th (Fusilier) Brigade

Born 12 July 1861 in Gainsborough, Lincolnshire. Commissioned into the Argyle and Bute Artillery (Militia) in 1881. Joined the 2nd Bn, Somersetshire Light Infantry, as a lieutenant on 28 January 1882 and was promoted to captain on 23 September 1887. Employed with the Egyptian Army from 23 September 1885 to 4 October 1895, serving in the Frontier Field Force in Soudan, 1885–86 and was at the Action of Giniss, being awarded the Bronze (Khedive) Star. In 1889 Frith took part in the Action of Toski (Soudan) and was awarded the clasp and 4th Class Medjidie. Posted to the Indian Army as station staff officer class 1 (Punjab district) on 28 July 1897 until 28 July 1902. Promoted to major on 27 January 1900. Listed as a qualified interpreter in Arabic in October 1902, he was also fluent in Turkish, French, Persian, Urdu and Pushtu. Promoted to lieutenant colonel 27 November 1909 and took over command of the 1st Bn, Somerset Light Infantry. Promoted to colonel on 2 June 1913. Relinquished command of his battalion on 27 November 1913 to take command of the Lancashire Fusiliers (125th) Brigade. Listed as temporary brigadier general 5 August 1914.

Frith commanded the brigade in Egypt and arrived with it at Helles on 5 May 1915. He remained in command throughout the campaign. Made temporary major general 30 December 1915 to 20 January 1916. Awarded the CB in 1916 and was twice Mentioned in Despatches for his service on Gallipoli (LG 5 November 1915 and 13 July 1916).

Frith commanded the 125th Brigade in Egypt in 1916–17 and moved with it to France in March 1917. Returned to England on 23 June 1917 to take up command of the Home Service Brigade, an event commemorated in the divisional history:

'General Frith was the last of the General Officers who had served with the Division from the outbreak of war. For three years he had commanded the Lancashire Fusilier Brigade, which had become much attached to him, for he was quick to recognize and give credit for good work, and he possessed a remarkable memory for faces, invariably knowing each officer by name from first meeting.'

Frith was awarded the Order of St. Stanislas, 2nd Class with Swords. He retired on 1 November 1918. He died on 5 March 1942.

Pioneer *(later Corporal)* 3614 Ernest Houghton 'Claude' Hague

No. 4 (Manchester Brigade) Section, 1/1st Signal Company,
42nd (East Lancs) Division, Royal Engineers (TF).
Later Pioneer 267953, Royal Engineers

Estate agent's clerk of Prestwich. Born 19 February 1883 at Ladybarn, Lancashire, the first of three children by John and Jane Hague. Middle name is sometimes given as Horton.

Judging by his service number, Hague probably enlisted in the East Lancs Royal Engineers (TF) on or a little before the outbreak of war. Embodied on 5 August 1914, he signed Army Form E.624 volunteering for foreign service in early September, embarking with the East

Lancashire Division for Egypt on 10 September 1914. Disembarked at Alexandria on 24 September and served with No. 4 Signal Section in Egypt 1914–15. Embarked for Gallipoli on 3 May 1915 and landed at W Beach on 6 May.

'Claude' features prominently in Riley's Gallipoli diary. The last time Claude is mentioned is just a few days before Riley's evacuation on 11 September, so it's probable that Hague served at Helles until that date, if not beyond it.

Hague's main service records appear not to have survived, however, his entry on the 1914–15 Star Roll confirms he served for the duration of the war and was demobilized and transferred to Z Reserve on 4 June 1919. Hague may have married but at the time of the 1939 register he was single and working as an estate agent's cashier. He died in Rochdale, 2 January 1956, age 71.

Driver 1884 Robert Harbour

No. 4 (Manchester Brigade) Section, Signal Company,
42nd (East Lancs) Division, Royal Engineers (TF).
Later Driver 444609 Royal Engineers

Outdoor labourer. Born at 10 Angela Street in the Mill Hill area of Livesey, Blackburn, Lancashire on 29 August 1893, the seventh of eleven children by John, an engine tester, and Mary Ann Harbour.

Judging by his service number, Harbour was probably a pre-war Territorial and may have enlisted in the East Lancashire Divisional Transport and Support Column, based in Rawtenstall, a small town eight miles south-east of Blackburn.

Embodied on 5 August 1914, Harbour signed Army Form E.624, volunteering for foreign service in early September 1914. Embarked with the East Lancashire Division for Egypt on 10 September 1914. Disembarked at Alexandria on 24 September and served with No. 4 Signal Section in Egypt 1914–15.

Riley mentions Harbour only once in his Egypt diary. During Christmas 1914 celebrations, he was 'seen on the floor, searching for a turkey's leg.' He is not mentioned at all in Riley's Gallipoli diary. In addition, Harbour's service records give no indication as to his movements after the division left for the peninsula, so it may be that Harbour was left in Egypt as part of the base detail. If he did serve at Gallipoli, it might have been with another unit.

Robert Harbour married his next-door neighbour, Helen 'Nellie' Sharples, in Burnley on 12 March 1918. His marriage certificate gives his occupation as 'soldier/railway guard' so it may be that some wound or medical condition had rendered him fit for home service only. Demobilized and transferred to Z Reserve on 1 April 1919.

At the time of the 1939 register, Harbour was working in Burnley as a 'colliery digger, surface and below, heavy work.' He died of cardiac failure during a surgical operation in the Victoria Hospital, Burnley, on 13 January 1944.

Sergeant 1126 James (Joseph) Cox Harrop
C Company, 1/9th Bn, Manchester Regt.
Later Lieutenant/temporary Captain

Born in Ashton under Lyne, Lancashire, on 11 January 1891. Christened Joseph Cox Harrop. His father died when he was eight years old and he spent most of his early life living in his paternal grandmother's baker's shop in Old Street, Ashton. There are no records of his enlistment in the 1/9th Manchesters but judging by his rank and number he would have joined at least five or six years before war broke out.

Signed Army Form E.624, volunteering for foreign service in early September 1914 and embarked for Egypt on 10 September. Disembarked at Alexandria on 24 September 1914 and served with his battalion in Egypt 1914–15. Harrop first met Riley at the Abu Zabal Marconi signal station, where Harrop formed part of the guard. The pair would meet a second time at Gallipoli on 22 June 1915.

Embarked with his battalion for Gallipoli on 5 May and landed at V Beach on 9 May 1915. Although the 1/9th Manchesters did not take part in the advance on 4 June, the battalion made two small attacks later that month and Harrop was involved in both actions. The first was on 7 June against Turkish trenches G10 and G11 (between East Krithia Nullah and the Vineyard) and again on 18 June against the Turkish held portions of H11 and H11a (to the left of West Krithia Nullah).

Harrop was promoted to colour sergeant some time before his discharge on 10 December 1915 (either due to sickness or as a 'time expired' man). He re-enlisted in 1916-17 and served as colour sergeant (service number 41447) in the 2nd Bn, Manchester Regt, until being commissioned as second lieutenant into the 12th Bn, Manchester Regt, on 30 May 1917. He was promoted to temporary captain for a month on 28 May 1918 while commanding a trench mortar battery in France, and to temporary lieutenant on 30 November 1918. Harrop continued to command a trench mortar battery until 13 February 1919. He is believed to have died in Colchester in 1953.

Pioneer 1102 James Haworth

**No. 4 (Manchester Brigade) Section, 1/1st Signal Company,
42nd (East Lancs) Division, Royal Engineers (TF).
Later Second Corporal 444595, Royal Engineers**

Judging by his service number he probably enlisted several years before the outbreak of war. Embodied on 5 August 1914. Signed Army Form E.624, volunteering for foreign service, in early September 1914. Embarked with the East Lancashire Division for Egypt on 10 September 1914. Disembarked at Alexandria on 24 September and served with No. 4 Signal Section in Egypt 1914-15.

Embarked for Gallipoli on 3 May and landed at W Beach on 6 May 1915. As one of 'the three Hs' (Haworth, Hossack and Hopkinson) he is mentioned numerous times in Riley's Gallipoli diary, the last time being just a few days before Riley's evacuation on 11 September. It is probable that Haworth served at Helles until that date, if not beyond it.

Haworth's main service records appear not to have survived, however, his entry on the 1914-15 Star Roll confirms he served for the duration of the war and was disembodied on 9 April 1919.

Lieutenant Colonel
Gerald Graham Percival Heywood

1/6th Bn, Manchester Regt—Commanding Officer from 1 September 1911 until the battalion left for Gallipoli on 3 May 1915

Born Denstone, Staffordshire, on 12 January 1867, the fourth son of Sir Percival T. Heywood and Margaret (née Heywood). Grandson of Oliver Heywood (1825–1892), an eminent banker in Manchester, 1st Baronet, High Sheriff of Lancashire, and the first Freeman of Manchester.[98]

Educated at Winchester School, Heywood went on to study architecture and later practised as an architect. In 1898, married Mary 'May' Stanhope, daughter of the Venerable the Hon. Berkley Skudamore Stanhope, Archdeacon of Hereford, brother of the 9th Earl of Chesterfield. Heywood and his wife initially lived at Claremont Cottage on the family estate at Pendleton but later moved to Tickworth Hall, Much Wenlock, Shropshire, and eventually to The Grange, Much Wenlock.

Commissioned second lieutenant into the 2nd Volunteer Bn, Manchester Regt, some time prior to May 1899. Promoted directly to captain on 3 May 1899 and later that year was placed in command of D Company. Promoted to major on 24 May 1907. Heywood retained his rank and seniority when the 2nd Volunteer Bn was redesignated the 1/6th Bn, Manchester Regt, on the formation of the Territorial Force on 1 April 1908. Promoted to lieutenant colonel on 1 September 1911 and succeeded Noel Lee as commanding officer of the battalion on the same day (following Lee's promotion to brigadier).

Volunteered for foreign service in early September 1914 and embarked for Egypt on 10 September. Disembarked at Alexandria on 24 September 1914 and continued to command the battalion during its time in Egypt 1914–15. However, as the battalion prepared to leave for Gallipoli, Heywood's weak eyesight caused him to fail his medical examination and he was forced to hand over command to Major Charles Raymond Pilkington. Heywood returned home and was attached to the

---

[98] Oliver Heywood was an early supporter of the Volunteer Movement. In 1888 he presented the prizes to the 2nd Volunteer Bn, The Manchester Regt (later the 1/6th Bn, Manchester Regt).

Territorial Force Reserve on 2 December 1916 with the rank of lieutenant colonel. He later transferred to the 1st Volunteer Bn, Shropshire Light Infantry, at the rank of captain and was appointed second in command of the battalion. He remained in post until he resigned his commission on 3 October 1919.

Heywood died on 27 July 1954 at The Grange, Much Wenlock, Shropshire, and is buried in Denistone Churchyard, Staffordshire.

Captain *(later Brevet Lieutenant Colonel)* Philip Vaughan Holberton
Adjutant, 1/6th Bn, Manchester Regt

Born Twickenham, Middlesex, on 24 May 1879. Educated at Shrewsbury School and the Royal Military College Sandhurst (January 1900 and passing out on 29 January 1901), where he won the Sword of Honour, which was presented to him by Queen Victoria, as the best cadet in his class. Commissioned second lieutenant on 8 January 1901 into the 2nd Bn, Manchester Regt, which was then serving in South Africa. Joined his battalion at Harrismith, South Africa, in mid-June 1901. In August he was assigned to the battalion's new Mounted Infantry Company and was involved in fighting on 12 November when his company encountered a group of 400 Boers near Schalkie in the Orange Free State. In the action he was hit just over his heart by a bullet, however, his equipment stopped most of the force and he was only slightly wounded. Promoted to lieutenant on 27 November 1901.

Holberton returned to Aldershot with his battalion on 27 September 1902, having qualified for the Queen's Medal with five clasps. Served as adjutant to the battalion from 1 December 1903 until 30 November 1906. Posted to the West African Regt in Sierra Leone on 12 January 1907 and remained with that regiment until 3 July 1910. He re-joined the 2nd Manchesters, then at Mullingar, County Westmeath, Ireland, during July 1910. Appointed adjutant to the 1/6th Manchesters on 4 November 1911 and promoted to captain on 1 December 1911. He was still in post when the battalion was mobilized in August 1914.

Embarked with the 1/6th Manchesters for Egypt on 10 September and disembarked at Alexandria on 24 September 1914. He served with his battalion in Egypt until it embarked for Gallipoli on 3 May 1915. Arrived on V Beach on 6 May 1915 and served there until medically evacuated on 20 October.

On 3 August 1915, Holberton led a small party of men to remove a Turkish traverse in a communication trench running up the north-west side of the Vineyard, to improve the field of fire from the 6th Manchester's barricade. A bombing party successfully kept the Turks back while the digging party completed its work. He took part in the August fighting and moved with the battalion to the left-subsection on 19 August, when the 42nd (East Lancs) Division relieved the 29th Division. On 12 October he took command of the battalion when the CO, Lieutenant Colonel Charles Raymond Pilkington, was admitted to hospital, but was himself evacuated from the peninsula suffering from jaundice on 20 October. Twice Mentioned in Despatches for his service at Gallipoli (LG 5 November 1915 and 28 January 1916).

Promoted to brevet major on 8 November 1915 (substantive 8 January 1916). He re-joined the division in Egypt in 1916 and served as brigade major to the 126th Brigade from 5 April to 19 October 1916. Placed in command of the 1/5th Lancs Fusiliers on 19 October 1916. He moved with the 1/5th Bn, Lancs Fusiliers, to France in March 1917 and was promoted to brevet lieutenant colonel on 3 June 1917. On 21 March 1918, the German Army launched its Spring Offensive (*Kaiserschlacht*) and the 1/5th Lancs Fusiliers were sent to defend the village of Gomiecourt. Around 2 a.m. on 26 March, as Holberton was inspecting defences and encouraging his men, he was shot through the head and killed instantly. He was buried close to where he fell and his grave was identified when the area was recaptured the following September. Almost 40 officers and many men from both the 1/5th Lancs Fusiliers and the 1/6th Manchesters attended his reinternment service, held on 18 September 1918, in what is now the Achiet-Le-Grand Communal Cemetery Extension. Holberton is buried in grave IV.F.8.

Mentioned in Despatches a further three times and awarded the Serbian Order of the White Eagle (with Swords) 4th Class.

Pioneer 1883 Harry Hopkinson

**No. 4 (Manchester Brigade) Section, 1/1st Signal Company,
42nd (East Lancs) Division, Royal Engineers (TF).
Later Sergeant 444595, Royal Engineers**

Judging by his service number Hopkinson enlisted a year or two before the outbreak of war. Embodied on 5 August 1914, he signed Army Form E.624 volunteering for foreign service in early September 1914. Embarked with the Signal Company for Egypt on 10 September 1914 and disembarked at Alexandria on 24 September. Served with No. 4 Signal Section in Egypt in 1914–15. Embarked for Gallipoli on 3 May and landed at V Beach on 6 May 1915. As one of 'the three Hs' (Haworth, Hossack and Hopkinson) he is mentioned numerous times in Riley's Gallipoli diary, who describes Hopkinson as 'always cheerful, being very young.' The last time he is mentioned was just a few days before Riley's evacuation on 11 September, so it is probable that Hopkinson served at Helles until that date, if not beyond it. His main service records appear not to have survived, however, his entry on the 1914–15 Star Roll confirms he served for the duration of the war and was disembodied on 15 March 1919.

Chaplain 4th Class *(later 3rd Class)* Rev. Edwin Thomas Kerby, MC

Chaplain to the 1/7th Bn, Manchester Regt, and the 127th (Manchester) Brigade

Born Aston, Warwickshire, 13 August 1877, the son of William Kerby, a school master, and Ann Mary (née Mosley). Educated at King Edward's School, Birmingham. Matriculated 1896 into Clare College, Cambridge. Graduated with BA in 1899 and gained MA in 1903.

Ordained deacon (Coventry for Worcester) in 1901. Priest (Worcester) 1902. Curate of St. Basil's, Deritend, Walsall, Birmingham 1901–03. Curate of Langley, Worcestershire, 1903–04. Curate of St. James's, Oldham, Lancashire, 1904–10. Organisational Secretary for the Society for the Propagation of the Gospel in Foreign Parts (SPG) for the diocese of Manchester, 1910–19.

Married Marion Boyd in Oldham in December 1909. Their first daughter, Eleanor Nancy Kerby, was born on 26 November 1910. A second daughter, Marion B. Kerby, was born on 13 January 1913.

Appointed Chaplain 4th Class (with the rank of captain), Chaplains' Department of the Territorial Force, and was attached to the 1/7th Bn, Manchester Regt, on 10 March 1914.

Kerby volunteered for foreign service in early September 1914. Embarked with his battalion for Egypt on 10 September 1914 and disembarked at Alexandria on 24 September 1914. When the 1/7th Manchesters were despatched to Cyprus and the Sudan a few days later, Kerby remained in Egypt to act as chaplain to the Manchester Brigade. A third child, Alexander John R. Kerby, was born on 13 February 1915 while he was serving in Egypt.

Kerby embarked from Alexandria with the Manchester Brigade for Gallipoli on 3 May 1915 and landed at W Beach on 6 May. IWGC records show that Kerby (invariably misspelled Kirby) officiated at hundreds of burials right up until the 42nd Division left Gallipoli, including that of five 1/9th Manchesters killed by a single shell while in a reserve trench on Gully Spur on 27 December 1915.

Despite Riley's misgivings towards Kerby, the chaplain showed his true worth at Helles. Major Gerald B. Hurst (1/7th Manchesters) wrote of him in his book, *With The Manchesters In The East*: 'Nor could a Brigade have had a more gallant and untiring padre than Captain E.T. Kerby. He and Captain Farrow [the battalion medical officer] both won the Military Cross. Kerby must have said the burial service over the graves of nearly a thousand Manchesters at Gallipoli.'

Kerby was awarded the Military Cross (LG 3 June 1916) for his service at Gallipoli and was twice Mentioned in Despatches, the first time by Hamilton (LG 5 November 1915) and again by Munro (LG 13 July 1916).

He served again in Egypt from mid-January 1916 until the 42nd (East Lancs) Division embarked for the Western Front on 2 March 1917. He served for the duration of the war. On 25 June 1919, Kerby was made temporary chaplain 3rd class whilst acting as Senior Chaplain to the Forces at Boulogne (substantive on 1 January 1923).

In the years after the war, Kerby resumed pastoral duties in the Manchester area. From 1922 to 1928 he was the vicar at St Mark's, Heyside, Shaw. While in post at St Mark's, on the event of his 50th birthday, 13 August 1927, he was placed on the Territorial Army Reserve of Officers General List.

Kerby was the serving vicar at St Augustine's, Pendlebury, Swinton, when his wife, Marion, died on 15 December 1931. He remarried in September 1935 to Frances Edward (29 years his junior). He retired from the Reserve of Officers List on his 60th birthday having attained the age limit for service. The 1939 register shows Kerby still serving as the vicar at St Augustine's and living in the vicarage at 23 Hospital Road, Pendlebury, with his wife, his eldest daughter, Eleanor, and his son, Alexander. He was still living at St Augustine's vicarage when he died on 12 December 1960.

Major *(later honorary Brigadier General)* Henry Lewkenor Knight, CMG, DSO

Brigade Major, 127th (Manchester) Brigade

Born at Foyhill near Litchfield, Staffordshire, on 24 March 1874. Attended the Royal Military College Sandhurst in 1894. Commissioned as second lieutenant into the Royal Irish Fusiliers on 10 October 1894 and promoted to lieutenant on 3 May 1898. Appointed acting adjutant to the 2nd Bn, Royal Irish Fusiliers, in August 1895 and remained in post until August 1899. Served in South Africa 1899–1900 with his regiment as a captain (substantive captain 1 May 1902) and on staff duties with the Mounted Infantry until invalided on 15 December 1900. Mentioned in Despatches (LG 10 September 1901) and received the Queen's Medal with five clasps.

Appointed adjutant to the 1st Volunteer (City of Dundee) Bn, Royal Highlanders, on 17 May 1901 and remained in post until 15 August 1904. Appointed adjutant to the 4th Bn, Royal Irish Fusiliers, on 19 May 1905. Seconded to the General Staff on 16 April 1912. Promoted to major on 21 January 1914 and appointed as brigade major to the Manchester (later 127th) Brigade on 5 August 1914.

Embarked for Egypt with the brigade on 10 September 1914 and disembarked at Alexandria on 24 September. Served with the brigade in Egypt until it embarked for Gallipoli on 3 May 1915. Landed on V Beach on 6 May 1915 and continued as to serve as brigade major until being temporarily attached to the 125th (Fusilier) Brigade from 20–25 December 1915 (made temporary lieutenant colonel on 20 December 1915). He was described by Gerald B. Hurst in his book *With Manchesters in the East* as 'a tower of strength on Gallipoli.'

After the Manchester Brigade left Gallipoli, Knight was sent to Salonika where he was appointed GSO1 for the 10th Division, holding the post from 30 December 1915 to 15 June 1917. Made brevet lieutenant colonel on 3 June 1916 (substantive 14 March 1917). Served as brigade commander, 80th Infantry Brigade, from 16 June until 24 August 1917. Made temporary brigadier general 16 June 1917, and served on the Staff of XVI Army Corps from 25 August 1917 until 24 February 1919.

Knight was awarded the DSO in the King's Birthday Honours List in 1917, appointed CMG in 1918–19, awarded the Order of the Redeemer 3rd Class, the Greek Military Cross, the Greek Medal for Military Merit, 2nd Class, and was five times Mentioned in Despatches. Promoted to brevet colonel on 3 June 1919 (substantive 4 August 1921) and retired on half pay as an honorary brigadier general on 17 May 1929.

Knight died on 28 March 1945 at Le Court, Liss, Petersfield, Hampshire.

Major *(later Lieutenant Colonel)* Arthur Niven Lawford *(TD, Belgian Croix de Guerre)*

OC, 1/1st Signal Company, 42nd (East Lancs) Division, Royal Engineers (TF). Later Commander Royal Engineers, XV Army Corps

Born 22 November 1884, Oswestry, Shropshire. Son of William Robinson Lawford, an estate agent, and Isabella Harriet Douglas Niven. Educated Colet House, Rhyl, and Cheltenham College.

Served a four years apprenticeship at British Westinghouse Co., Trafford Park. Studied at the Manchester Municipal School of Technology (1903) and from 1907 at Victoria University, Manchester, where he graduated in mechanical and electrical engineering in 1910.

Joined the Institute of Mechanical Engineers in February 1907 (elected Associate Member on 25 October 1912). Became a member of the Old Cheltonian Masonic Lodge (no. 3223) in 1911. Married Vera Margaret Hawson in 1913.

Commissioned second lieutenant into the 3rd Lancashire Royal

Engineers (Volunteers) on 21 February 1903 and promoted to lieutenant on 21 May 1904. He retained his rank and seniority on the formation of the Territorial Force on 1 April 1908 when his unit was redesignated the East Lancashire Divisional Engineers. Promoted to captain on 4 May 1912 and appointed OC, East Lancashire Divisional Telegraph Company (later renamed the East Lancashire Divisional Signal Company). Promoted to major on the East Lancashire Division's mobilization on 5 August 1914.

Volunteered for foreign service in early September 1914. Embarked for Egypt with the Signal Company on 10 September and disembarked at Alexandria on 24 September. Commanded the company in Egypt 1914-15. Embarked for Gallipoli on 5 May 1915 and landed with No. 1 Signal Section (with divisional headquarters) at V Beach on 9 May. Served at Helles until he succumbed to sickness on 22 September 1915 and was evacuated back to England. (Command of the company was taken temporarily by Second Lieutenant A. Roberts, then, from 10 October, by Captain R.W. Dammers, Sherwood Foresters.)

On his recovery (end of 1915, beginning of 1916) Lawford was posted to the 3rd Line Depot of the East Lancs Royal Engineers at Carnarvon, North Wales. It was here that men were trained to provide drafts for the first and second-line units. According to the history of the East Lancs Engineers history, 'a great number of returned officers and men came to Carnarvon from hospital in various stages of convalescence, and many of them were used on the administrative and instructional staffs.'

On 18 May 1916, Lawford was placed in command of the 1/3rd East Lancs Field Company, then at Colchester, Essex. Embarked with his company on 1 June for Egypt, arriving at Alexandria on 13 June, where it joined the 42nd (East Lancs) Division to provide a requisite third field company. On 26 September, Lawford took over temporarily as CRE when Lieutenant Colonel Mozley went on two months leave. Mentioned in Despatches (LG 1 December 1916) presumably for his service at Gallipoli. He again assumed the duties of CRE on 8 January 1917 when Lieutenant Colonel Mozley fell sick. Lawford remained in post until 13 February, when he returned to his company, now redesignated the 429th Field Company.

At the end of February 1917, the 42nd Division (and its divisional engineers) began to move to the Western Front. On 3 March, Lawford

Figure 69. Alexandria, Egypt, 26 December 1915.
Brig. Gen. Noel Lee, GOC Manchester Brigade, and Lt. Col. Gerald Heywood,
CO 6th Manchesters until the battalion left for Gallipoli on 3 May 1915.

was promoted to lieutenant colonel (with precedence from 20 November 1916) and the following day he embarked with 429th Field Company for Marseilles.

At the end of September 1917, the 42nd Division took over the coastal sector of the Nieuport Front and held it for the next six weeks. During this time Lawford's company was engaged in maintaining a number of bridges, with repairs frequently carried out under fire. It was hazardous and difficult work and several of the company's officers and men were decorated. Lawford was awarded the Belgian *Croix de Guerre* (LG 15 April 1918). On 17 November 1917, he again took over temporarily as CRE. On 1 May 1918, he relinquished command of 429th Field Company to take up the appointment of CRE at XV Army Corps.

Lawford remained in the Royal Engineers after the war and was granted the rank of captain in the regular army on 5 October 1921 (with seniority from 5 February 1921). Appointed Assistant Director of Civil and Public Works on 22 December 1919. Attached to the Royal Air Force in Iraq as Works and Buildings Officer from 1 April 1922 to 24 September 1924, qualifying for GSM with Iraq clasp. Awarded the Territorial Decoration (LG 4 July 1922).

Granted the rank of major in the regular army on 18 April 1931 (lieutenant colonel in the TF). Placed on the Retired List (with pay) on 22 November 1934. Granted the rank of lieutenant colonel on 22 November 1934. Died Sussex, 29 March 1950, age 65.

Brigadier General Noel Lee, VD
GOC, 127th (Manchester) Brigade until 4 June 1915

Born Altrincham, 1868, third son of Sir Joseph Lee. Educated at Eton College before going into the family textile business, Tootal Broadhurst Lee and Co.

Having been prevented from joining the regulars by his father, Lee joined the 6th Lancashire Rifle Volunteers (2nd Volunteer Bn, Manchester Regt from 1888) and was commissioned as second lieutenant on 25 December 1886. Promoted to captain on 1 February 1890. Like many of his fellow officers he was a Freemason, having been initiated into the Social Lodge, Manchester, on 17 October 1899. Promoted to major in May 1901 (substantive 2 February 1902), and to honorary lieutenant colonel on 17 May 1906, when appointed CO of the 2nd Volunteer Bn, Manchester Regt. Lee was awarded the Volunteer Officers Decoration (VD) in June 1906 and made honorary colonel in 1907. He retained his rank and seniority on the formation of the Territorial Force when the battalion was renamed as the 1/6th Bn, Manchester Regiment, on 1 April 1908. He was a member of the Territorial Force Advisory Council and the East Lancashire TF Association. In September 1911, Lee was appointed commander of the Manchester Brigade (the first territorial officer to command a brigade) and relinquished command of the 1/6th Manchesters. He was made substantive colonel on 10 March 1914 and temporary brigadier general around the time the 42nd (East Lancs) Division was mobilized in early August 1914.

Lee volunteered for foreign service in early September 1914. Embarked with his brigade for Egypt on 10 September and disembarked at Alexandria on 24 September. Remained in Egypt until embarking with his brigade for Gallipoli on 3 May 1915, landing at W Beach on 6 May. Commanded the 127th (Manchester Brigade) at Helles until seriously wounded around noon on 4 June, during the preliminary bombardment for the Third Battle of Krithia. Lee was evacuated on 4 or 5 June and arrived at Malta about 10 or 11 June. At first his condition seemed to improve but he suffered a haemorrhage and died on 22 June 1915 at the Blue Sisters Hospital in St Julians.

Lee was widely recognised as one of the division's best commanders. When Brigadier General William Marshall was sent by Hunter-Weston to 'tutor' Lee in late May 1915, he found him to be 'a really good Brigadier—and very much liked and trusted by his officers and men.' Lee's divisional commander Major General Douglas (see above) wrote: 'He is a very great loss to the Brigade, he has done splendidly—the most gallant, hardworking, thorough leader that I had, and I don't know how I shall replace him. I am sure that I shall not be able to find his equal.'

Noel Lee is buried in the Pieta Military Cemetery in Malta and received a posthumous Mention in Despatches (LG 5 November 1915) for his service at Gallipoli.

Alec Riley visited Lee's grave in Malta after the war, and took a photograph. A print was among the items he took to a meeting of the 6th Manchesters' Old Members Association in 1932.

Sapper 617 John 'Mall' Mallalieu *(DCM)*

No. 4 (Manchester Brigade) Section, 1/1st Signal Company,
42nd (East Lancs) Division, Royal Engineers (TF).
Private 617, 1/6th Bn, Manchester Regt, later
Sergeant 444594, Royal Engineers

Born around 1884. Some records misspell his surname as Mallalien.

'Mall' had been member of the Volunteers for several years (probably the 2nd Volunteer Bn, Manchester Regt) when, on 29 May 1908, he enlisted in the newly formed 1/6th Bn, Manchester Regt, part of the new Territorial Force. Shown in C Company's year book for 1911 as being in No. 1 Section and living at 22 Oak Road, Lower Broughton, Salford. Awarded the Territorial Force Efficiency Medal on 1 October 1912.

Embodied on 5 August 1914. Signed Army Form E.624 volunteering for foreign service in early September. Embarked with the East Lancashire Division for Egypt on 10 September 1914 and disembarked on 24 September at Alexandria. Served with No. 4 Signal Section in Egypt 1914–15. Embarked for Gallipoli on 3 May 1915 and landed at W Beach on 6 May. He is mentioned numerous times in Riley's Gallipoli diary, the last time being just a few days before Riley's own evacuation on 11 September 1915, so it is probable that Mallalieu served at Helles until that date, if not beyond it.

Awarded the Distinguished Conduct Medal (LG 26 April 1917) while serving on the Western Front. His citation reads 'for conspicuous gallantry and devotion to duty. He has performed consistent good work throughout, and has at all times set a fine example of courage and determination.' He was also Mentioned in Despatches (LG 6 July 1917).

Mallalieu's main service records appear not to have survived, however his entry on the 1914–15 Star Roll confirms he served for the duration of the war. He was discharged on 8 March 1919 under King's Regulations para 392 xvia as 'surplus to military requirements (having suffered impairment since entry into the service).' This indicates that he had been wounded at some time during his service and was entitled to the Silver War Badge (B 341650). His address when discharged was 21 Esmond Road, Cheetham Hill, Manchester.

Second Lieutenant *(later Brevet Colonel)* Robert Saunders Newton *(MC)*

1/6th Bn, Lancashire Fusiliers—Commander, No. 2 (Fusilier Brigade) Signal Section, 1/1st Signal Company, 42nd (East Lancs) Division, Royal Engineers (TF)

Electrical engineer of Manchester. Born Leeds, Yorkshire, 16 October 1879, the son of Alfred Seton, a clergyman and grammar school headmaster, and Ann Saunders. Living in Ramsey, Isle of Man, in 1891, but by 1901 had moved to Stretford, Manchester, where he was training as an electrical engineer. In 1903 Newton became a member of the Society of Telegraph Engineers, later becoming an Associate Member of the Institute of Electrical Engineers. By 1911 he was living in Didsbury, Manchester, and working as an electrical engineer.

Commissioned into the 1/6th Bn, Lancashire Fusiliers, on 19 August 1914 and appointed as battalion signal officer shortly afterwards. Volunteered for foreign service in September 1914 and embarked for Egypt with the 1/1st Signal Company on 10 September 1914. Disembarked at Alexandria on 26 September. Initiated into the Lord Kitchener Masonic Lodge, Cairo, on 14 March 1915. Served in Egypt until the Fusilier Brigade embarked for Gallipoli on 2 May 1915.

Landed with his brigade at V Beach on 5 May 1915 and may have remained at Helles for the duration of the campaign. He served again in Egypt from early-January 1916 and was promoted to lieutenant on 30 January 1916. Embarked with the 42nd (East Lancs) Division when it moved to the Western Front on 2 March 1917. Awarded the Military Cross while serving there (LG 4 June 1917) and also Mentioned in Despatches. Promoted to captain on 10 August 1917. He continued to serve in the (redesignated) Territorial Army after the war, transferring to the Royal Corps of Signals (TA) Reserve on 12 August 1921. Married at the age of 43 in Ealing, London, on 15 January 1923.

Newton retired from the TA on 16 March 1932, at the rank of brevet colonel, but remained a military member of the East Lancashire Territorial Association. On 2 November 1935, while resident in Bramhall, Cheshire, he was made Deputy Lieutenant of the County Palatine of Lancaster. The 1939 register describes him as 'the managing director of an electrical factor and domestic hardware manufacturer, Brevet Colonel (retired) and Committee Chairman of the East Lancashire Territorial Army.'

He died at Ventnor on the Isle of Wight on 27 January 1963.

Sapper 1392 George Richard Noble

No. 4 (Manchester Brigade) Section, 1/1st Signal Company, 42nd (East Lancs) Division, Royal Engineers (TF). Private 1392, Manchester Regt, later Sapper 3618, Royal Engineers (TF) and Lance Corporal 438775, Royal Engineers

Letterpress printer of Salford, Lancashire. Born Pendleton, 19 April 1889, son of George Noble, lorry driver and porter, and Elizabeth Ann.

Enlisted with 1/8th Bn, Lancashire Fusiliers, on 4 August 1908. Attended the School of Signalling and received his Signalling Certificate on 28 June 1908. Transferred to the 1/6th Bn, Manchester Regt, on 10 April 1911, signing a four-year engagement.

Embodied on 5 August 1914, signing Army Form E.624 volunteering for foreign service in early September 1914. Attached 1/1st Signal Company on 10 September 1914 and embarked with the East Lancashire Division for Egypt on the same day. Disembarked at Alexandria on 24 September and served with No. 4 Signal Section in Egypt 1914–15. Landed at W Beach on 6 May 1915. 'Remustered' as a sapper and granted 4th rate engineer pay on 26 June 1915.

Noble is mentioned numerous times in Riley's Gallipoli diary, the last occasion being just a few days before Riley's evacuation on 11 September. Noble's medical records indicate he remained at Helles until the 1/1st Signal Company was evacuated (28 December to 3 January 1916).

Disembarked at Alexandria from Mudros on 16 January 1916. Embarked for England on 25 March 1916 and was discharged 'time expired' on 14 April 1916, having served for five years and five days.

Married Lily Baguley, a cigarette maker of Pendleton, on 8 April 1916 at St John's Wesleyan Methodist, Langworthy Road, Weaste.

Called up under the Military Service Act and ordered to attended a medical board in June 1916 at Pendleton Town Hall. Appointed Lance Corporal, 438775, Royal Engineers, on 18 November 1916. Embarked

Devonport in March 1917 for Basra, Iraq, and joined 14th Divisional Signal Company, 14th (Indian) Division, Mesopotamia Expeditionary Corps, on 10 August 1917. Admitted 23rd British Stationary Hospital, Baghdad, for two weeks in early January 1918. At this time was charged with 'losing by neglect Govt property (i.e.) Jackets Felt Signalling, 1,' for which he had to reimburse the army nine shillings and six pence. Noble contracted malaria in August 1918 and was admitted to the 32nd British General Hospital, Amarah, reported as dangerously ill. He was taken off the dangerously ill list on 15 September, and discharged at Kut in November 1918.

ENoble embarked for England from Basra on 27 February 1919 and was transferred on to Z Reserve on 1 May 1919. He made a claim for disability, due to headaches which he attributed to malaria, and was examined on 19 May 1919. The claim was rejected with the examining physician stating that Noble was of 'normal appearance, seemed quite fit—no physical sign of any diseases.' At this time, Noble and wife Lily were living at 181 Hodge Lane, Seedley, Manchester.

The 1939 register shows Noble working as a rotary machine winder for a newspaper company and living at 72 Chestnut Drive, Woodheys, Sale, Cheshire, with his wife, their two children, Lily and Arthur, and his mother-in-law. He was still living at the same address when he died on 10 April 1941, age 51.

CSM 240 Roland Harry Nuttall

Company Sergeant Major—1/1st Signal Company, 42nd (East Lancs) Division, Royal Engineers (TF), later CSM 426898

Electrician. Born Newent, Gloucestershire, 1884 (perhaps 9 May). By 1901 was living with his family in Gorton, Manchester, and training as an electrician. Enlisted in the 3rd Lancashire Royal Engineer Volunteer Corps on 23 July 1907 and transferred to the East Lancs Division, Royal Engineers (TF), on its formation on 11 April 1908. Promoted to corporal in May 1910 and sergeant in September 1912. Attended each of the seven annual camps held between June 1908 and 1914.

Embodied as sergeant on 5 August 1914 when the division was mobilized. Signed Army Form E.264 on 1 September at Bury camp, volunteering for foreign service. Embarked for Egypt with the Signal Company on 10 September 1914 and was promoted to company sergeant major the same day. Disembarked at Alexandria on 26 September 1914. Initiated into the Lord Kitchener Masonic Lodge, Cairo, on 17 February 1915.

Embarked for Gallipoli on 5 May 1915 and landed (with divisional headquarters) at V Beach on 9 May. Wounded (slightly) by shrapnel on 16 June and evacuated to Alexandria for treatment. Returned to Helles around 26 June and resumed duty. Evacuated again with severe burns to his throat on 27 August 1915 and was admitted to the Citadel Military Hospital, Cairo, on 1 September. Transferred to No. 17 General Hospital, Alexandria on 5 October to be discharged on 20 October. Reported to Divisional Signals at Mustafa Camp in Alexandria on 24 November and was posted to the Base Signal Depot at Cleopatra, Alexandria, on 30 November where he appears to have remained for the remainder of the campaign. Re-admitted to hospital on 22 March 1916 and embarked on a hospital ship for England on 7 April.

Transferred to 71st Division Signal Company at Colchester on 25 November 1916. (Riley was there at the same time.) His period of service was extended on 25 May 1917. There is no evidence of Nuttall serving on the Western Front. He was attached to the 67th Division Signal Company (as was Riley) when demobilized on 12 March 1919. Awarded the Territorial Efficiency Medal on 1 May 1919. Died in Worcester on 10 April 1956.

Sergeant 764 Charles Alfred 'Ormy' Ormesher

No. 4 (Manchester Brigade) Section, 1/1st Signal Company, 42nd (East Lancs) Division, Royal Engineers (TF). Sergeant, 1/6th Bn, Manchester Regt, later CQMS 3721, Royal Engineers (TF) and CQMS 444578, Royal Engineers

Merchant's shipping clerk. Born Manchester, 2 March 1888, son of John Edward Brookes, salesman, and Hannah, of Broughton Road, Salford. May have attended Royal Technical Institute, Salford.

Originally enlisted in the 1/6th Manchesters (his regimental number indicates considerable pre-war service) and later transferred to the Royal Engineers.

Embodied on 5 August 1914, and signed Army Form E.624 volunteering for foreign service in early September 1914. Embarked with the East Lancashire Division for Egypt on 10 September 1914. Disembarked at Alexandria on 26 September 1914 and served with No. 4 Signal Section in Egypt 1914–15. Embarked for Gallipoli on 3 May 1915 and landed at W Beach on 6 May.

Ormesher is mentioned more than any other member of No. 4 Section in Riley's Gallipoli diary and was clearly a close friend of Riley's. The last mention was on the day of Riley's evacuation (11 September) and it is possible that Ormesher remained at Helles until the 1/1st Signal Company was evacuated (28 December to 3 January 1916).

Ormesher's main service records appear not to have survived, however, his entry on the 1914–15 Star Roll confirms he served for the duration of the war. Transferred to the regular RE and served in the Engineers. Disembodied on 9 January 1920.

Married Louisa Bayley in Prestwich in early 1920. A daughter, Jean Brookes Ormesher, was born on 13 September 1920. A city directory of 1929 gives his occupation as bank clerk. The 1939 register confirms this occupation but also records him as a 'mobilized Airforce reservist on leave, no. 760802 A.C. 2,' which suggests that he may have served in the Royal Air Force during the interwar years.

Ormesher was still living at 214 Heywood Road, Prestwich, Lancashire, the same address given on the 1939 register, when he died on 17 April 1971, age 83.

Driver 1121 Edward Pearson

**No. 4 (Manchester Brigade) Section, 1/1st Signal Company,
42nd (East Lancs) Division, Royal Engineers (TF).
Later Driver 440142, Royal Engineers**

Carter and horseman, born Salford, 3 May 1890. Son of Edward Pearson, warehouseman, of Birmingham, and Annie Baldwin of Salford. Eldest of four children.

Pearson's enlistment records appear not to have survived, however, judging by his service number he had served for several years as a territorial before war was declared. Embodied on 5 August 1914, he signed

Army Form E.624 volunteering for foreign service in early September. Embarked for Egypt with the East Lancashire Division on 10 September 1914. Disembarked at Alexandria on 26 September and served with No. 4 Signal Section in Egypt in 1914–15.

Landed at W Beach on 6 May 1915. Admitted to No. 11 Casualty Clearing Station on 3 July 1915 suffering influenza. Transferred to a hospital ship. Re-joined his unit from 'RE details' in August 1915. Pearson is mentioned numerous times in Riley's Gallipoli diary, the last occasion being a few weeks before Riley's evacuation on 11 September 1915. It is probable that Pearson served at Helles until that date, if not beyond it. Following the evacuation of Gallipoli, Pearson served with the 42nd (East Lancs) Division in Egypt 1916–17. Arrived in France with the division from Egypt on 4 March 1917. Later served with a Royal Engineers Cavalry Corps bridging park.

Married Ethel Gate, in the Dock Mission Hall, Salford, on 16 February 1918, while on leave. Taken ill (trench fever and bronchitis) July 1918, evacuated through No. 21 Casualty Clearing Station and No. 2 Canadian General Hospital. Admitted to Toxteth Park Hospital, Liverpool, on 29 August 1918. Discharged from hospital on 31 January 1919 with the medical board considering his condition 'fair'. No pension awarded.

In February 1919, Pearson was living at 531 Eccles New Road, Weaste, Manchester. Sometime later he moved to Lancaster and the 1939 census shows him living with his wife at 59 Cleveleys Avenue, Lancaster, Lancashire. He had two sons with Ethel, Leslie Edward (born 1920) and Stanley William (born 1923). Tragically, both died on active service in WWII: Leslie, an RAF pilot with 77 Squadron and Stanley, a gunner with the Royal Artillery. Pearson died in Lancaster in 1957, age 67.

Figure 70. Edward Fielden Pilkington, known as 'Ned' to family and friends, but 'Pilk' to the signallers under his command.

Captain *(later Major)* Edward Fielden Pilkington

1/6th Bn, Manchester Regt— Commander, No. 4 (Manchester Brigade) Signal Section, 1/1st Signal Company, 42nd (East Lancs) Division (prior to its move to Egypt)

Brother of Capt. Hugh Brocklehurst Pilkington, 1/6th Manchester Regt, KIA 4 June 1915 at Gallipoli, and nephew of Lieut. Colonel Charles Raymond Pilkington, commanding officer of the 1/6th Bn, Manchester Regt, at Gallipoli.

Born Surrey, 23 June 1885, the son of Charles, a colliery proprietor, and Mabel Pilkington. Educated at Winchester School and Trinity College Cambridge. Initiated into the Isaac Newton Masonic Lodge, Cambridge on 6 March 1906. A mining engineer by profession, later colliery director.

Pilkington was commissioned second lieutenant on 1 March 1908 into the 2nd Volunteer Battalion, the Manchester Regt. He retained his rank and seniority when the battalion was redesignated on the formation of the Territorial Force as the 1/6th Battalion, Manchester Regt, on 1 April 1908. Promoted to lieutenant on 12 June 1909. Appointed battalion signals officer in 1912. Promoted to captain on 12 February 1914 and was married around the same time.

Unlike most of his fellow officers, Pilkington did not volunteer for foreign service in September 1914. Riley mentions this in the diary but gives no explanation. 'He told us he was not going himself. As we knew the reasons, we sympathised with him.' It is impossible to know the reason for this, but it's possible he was needed to help run his family's extensive business interests. Instead, he continued to serve at home with the 2/6th Manchesters, a newly formed reserve battalion. In 1915 he was given the acting rank of major and placed in command of the 2/6th Manchesters then training at Crowborough.

Arrived with his battalion in France on 3 March 1917, and was promoted substantive major on 22 September 1917. Returned to England and was demobilized in December 1917, after his father was debilitated by a stroke. His father never recovered and Pilkington was released from Army service in order to carry out the vital work of managing the family coal mining and pottery businesses. He relinquished his commission on 30 September 1921.

Died in Bowdon, Cheshire, on 15 May 1975.

Private 1112 Arthur Poole

No. 4 (Manchester Brigade) Section, 1/1st Signal Company,
42nd (East Lancs) Division, Royal Engineers (TF). Private 1/6th Bn,
Manchester Regt, later Pioneer 1112, Royal Engineers (TF)

Born Patricroft, Manchester, 13 January 1895, son of Frederick and Margaret Norbury Poole, of 30 Trafford Road, Eccles. Attended the Royal Technical Institute, Salford. Poole's main service records appear not to have survived, however, judging by his service number he had served for several years as a territorial before war was declared.

Embodied on 5 August 1914, Poole signed Army Form E.624 volunteering for foreign service in early September 1914. Embarked for Egypt with the East Lancashire Division on 10 September 1914. Disembarked at Alexandria on 24 September and served with No. 4 Signal Section in Egypt in 1914–15. Landed at W Beach on 6 May 1915.

Poole is mentioned numerous times in Riley's Gallipoli diary and was clearly one of Riley's closest comrades. The pair were often in each other's company both on and off duty. They talked, played chess, cooked, and washed together, forming a close bond known to modern-day soldiers as the buddy-buddy system. Riley's last entries regarding Poole are made on the day that he was killed by shellfire and are some of the most poignant in the whole diary. Riley and Poole had been attached to the 1/7th Manchesters. Their signal 'office' was close to where trenches Ardwick Green and Wigan Road ran into Krithia Nullah. Around 8 a.m. on 5 July 1915, Riley was on duty and Poole was cooking breakfast.

> I was at the telephone, so Poole went round the traverse to boil some eggs, and toast some cheese for me, as I didn't like eggs. Stanton, Ralston and Hargreaves were with Poole. A shell blew the mess-kitchen to blazes. I saw it full of smoke and litter. Shells were blowing chunks of parapet away. A whiz-bang burst near our kitchen and I heard Poole say 'If the Turks aren't careful, they'll crack these eggs,' and everybody laughed. When the eggs were boiled, Poole got them out of the mess-tin, saying to Stanton 'Look sharp Serj! They're hot.' Stanton put them on a blanket. Another whiz-bang arrived. There was a cloud of dust, shattered earth, dropping lead and iron. Some

of the balls dropped at my feet. I had huddled up against the wall, as close as I could get. This one had burst over our fire-place. Almost at once I heard 'stretcher-bearers!' from round the traverse. I was a bit dazed, but I knew something had happened. Clifford, the 8th signal sergeant, who happened to be with us at the time, looked round the traverse and said 'Men hit. Round there.'

I said 'Is it Poole?'

'Yes.'

I left the telephone and went round. Poole was lying on his back on the ground, with a ball through one of his eyes. He was dead. Long after, Stanton told me that he caught Poole as he fell, and with his own back to the parapet, supported him for a time. Before he died Poole opened his remaining eye and tried to speak.

Pioneer Arthur Poole is buried at Twelve Tree Copse Cemetery, Special Memorial C.25. He is also commemorated on the honour board of St Andrew's Church, Chadwick Road, Eccles.

Figure 71. Grave marker of Pte 1112 Arthur Poole at Twelve Tree Copse Cemetery, Gallipoli.

Sapper 838 Charles William Ridings

No 4. (Manchester Brigade) Section, 1/1st Signal Company,
42nd (East Lancs) Division, Royal Engineers (TF).
Private 838, 1/6th Bn, Manchester Regt,
later Sapper/Acting Second Corporal 165863, Royal Engineers

Clerk/bookkeeper. Born Salford, 11 November 1887. Son of Sidney James Ridings and Mary Alice Travis.

Attended the Royal Technical Institute, Salford. Enlisted on a four-year engagement in the 1/6th Bn, Manchester Regt, on 12 March 1909, age 21 years. Then a clerk at textile firm S.L. Behrens & Co. Older brother of Sidney Ridings (also No. 4 Section—listed below). Re-engaged for one year with the battalion on 13 February 1913 and again on 20 February 1914.

Embodied as a private in the 1/6th Manchesters in August 1914, attached to the 1/1st Signal Company. Signed Army Form E.624 volunteering for foreign service in early September 1914. Embarked with the East Lancashire Division for Egypt on 10 September 1914. Disembarked at Alexandria on 24 September and served with No. 4 Signal Section in Egypt 1914–15. Embarked for Gallipoli on 3 May 1915 and landed at W Beach on 6 May.

Wounded in the back by a bullet on 10 August 1915. The incident is recalled in Riley's Gallipoli diary.

> We heard, also, that Ridings at brigade headquarters had been wounded the day before. Full details were given me later by a disinterested party. It seemed that nature had called upon him to go a certain distance, just after he finished his duty in the signal office, and he was standing in a low trench when the bullet caught him in the back. Thomas tied him up. Tim came along to see if Ridings would have brandy or whisky. He preferred whisky, and then he was taken away on a stretcher. Noble told me that he had been amused. Riding's parting instructions concerned the disposal of a pair of spurs, of which he was proud, and he asked Ormy to look after them. They found a resting-place in the nullah, however, Ridings got through safely.

Evacuated to Egypt on 11 August 1915 after spending 99 days on the peninsula. Presumably remained in Egypt until 30 January 1916 when he embarked for England to be discharged 'time expired' on 3 March 1916.

On 22 June 1916, Ridings re-enlisted for the 'Period of War' and was posted to the 3/1st East Lancs Signal Company. He married Dorothy Buckley Seddon on 12 December 1916 and embarked for France the following day. Reported to an unidentified 'Signal Depot' on 16 December 1916. Posted to the 6th (Divisional) Signal Company on 15 January 1917, where he appears to have served for the duration of the war. Appointed acting lance corporal in August 1917 and acting 2nd corporal in March 1918. Demobilized and transferred to Z Reserve on 3 March 1919.

The 1939 register shows Ridings working as a sales manager for a chemical dyestuffs company, and living with his wife in Parkside Avenue, Salford. He died in Poole, Dorset, on 17 November 1980, age 92.

Private 3271 Sidney Ridings

No. 4 (Manchester Brigade) Section, 1/1st Signal Company,
42nd (East Lancs) Division, Royal Engineers (TF).
Formerly, Private 1193, 1/6th Bn, Manchester Regt.
Later, Private 23319, 11th Bn, Royal Warwickshire Regt, afterwards,
10th Bn, Royal Warwickshire Regt

Correspondence clerk at an engineering works. Born Broughton, Salford, 2 October 1893. Son of Sidney James Ridings and Mary Alice Travis. Younger brother of Charles William Ridings (also in No. 4 Section — listed above).

Joined the Territorials in 1910 age 18. Embodied into the 1/6th Manchesters, 5 August 1914. Signed Army Form E.624 volunteering for foreign service in early September 1914. Transferred to the 1/1st East Lancs Signal Company on 10 September 1914 and given the rank of pioneer. Embarked for Egypt the same day. Disembarked at Alexandria on 24 September and served with No. 4 Signal Section in Egypt 1914–15. Arrived off Helles on 6 May 1915 aboard the transport *Derfflinger*. In his Gallipoli diary, Riley notes that, when the section left the ship, 'S. Ridings and Driver Dean were left onboard in charge of some equipment.' Ridings' service records show that he returned to Alexandria, disembarking on 19 May. The records also state that he served in Egypt continuously from 10 September 1914 (the date of embarkation) to 31 December 1915. There is no indication that he re-embarked for Gallipoli and there is no further reference to S. Ridings and Driver Dean in Riley's diary, so it may be that both men remain in Egypt as part of the base detail.

Ridings embarked for England from Egypt to be discharged 'time expired' on 31 December 1915. Re-enlisted on 28 November 1916 into the 96th Territorial Reserve Battalion as Private 23319, and transferred to 11th Bn, Royal Warwickshire Regt, on 24 December 1916. He presumably served with the 11th Royal Warwicks during the battalion's time in France, from 30 July 1917 until it disbanded on 7 February 1918, at which time Ridings was transferred to the 10th Bn, Royal Warwicks, then serving in Tidworth, England (later moving to France on 11 November 1918). Disembodied on 8 July 1919, when he gave his address as 2 Douglas Street, Higher Broughton, Salford.

Many of Riding's service records appear to have been lost and those that are available are in places contradictory and contain clerical errors. He has duplicate Medal Index Cards, one of them giving his parent unit incorrectly as the East Lancs Regt and showing his 'entry' date wrongly as 21 May 1915 (errors repeated on his 1914-15 Medal Roll).

The 1939 register shows him living at 22 Rectory Villas, Kirkmanshulme Lane, Longsight, Manchester and employed as a civil servant at the Ministry of Labour. Ridings married Agnes K. Humphreys in Ashton (under Lyne) in October 1941. He died in Ashton (under Lyne) in 1970, age 76.

Lieutenant *(later Brevet Colonel)* Geoffrey Nicolas Robinson *(TD)*

1/4th East Lancashire Regt— Commander, No. 3 (East Lancashire Brigade) Signal Section, 1/1st Signal Company, 42nd (East Lancs) Division, Royal Engineers (TF)

Born in Chatburn near Blackburn on 30 March 1895. Educated at Gresham School, Holt, Norfolk. Went on to study law and was articled to F.D. Robinson of Blackburn. Commissioned as second lieutenant into the 1/4th Bn, East Lancs Regt, on 21 February 1914 and appointed battalion signal officer on 1 May 1914. Volunteered for foreign service in September 1914 and embarked for Egypt on 10 September 1914. Disembarked at Alexandria on 24 September and served with No. 3 Signal Section in Egypt 1914–15. Promoted to lieutenant in November 1914.

Embarked for Gallipoli on 5 May 1915, landing with the East Lancashire Brigade at V Beach on 9 May. Although impossible to be certain, it is likely Robinson remained at Gallipoli until the 1/1st Signal Company was evacuated (28 December to 3 January 1916).

Served in Egypt again from 4 January 1916 until the 42nd Division embarked for the Western Front on 2 March 1917. Promoted to captain on 8 August 1917 (with precedence from 1 June 1916). Gassed at Passchendaele in September 1917 and spent the rest of the war serving at home. Mentioned in Despatches and awarded the Territorial Decoration.

Robinson continued to serve as a Territorial Army officer after the war and was made brevet colonel in June 1938. Employed during the Second World War on 'extra regimental' duties. On 4 June 1955 he reached 'the age of liability to recall' and ceased to belong to the TA Reserve of Officers, while retaining the rank of lieutenant colonel and brevet colonel.

Died on 11 June 1977, age 82, and is buried in Christ Church graveyard, Chatburn, Lancashire.

Sergeant 262 Graham 'Joe' Royle

No. 4 (Manchester Brigade) Section, 1/1st Signal Company,
42nd (East Lancs) Division, Royal Engineers (TF).
Sergeant 262, 1/6th Bn, Manchester Regt, later Sapper/Acting Second
Corporal 238056, Royal Engineers

Sorting clerk and telegraphist at the General Post Office, Manchester. Born Ardwick, 5 March 1885, son of William (some early records give his name as John) and Annie Royle, of 25 Albion Street, Brooks Bar. Royle's father and older sister, Eveline, also worked at the Post Office.

Joined the 2nd Volunteer Battalion, Manchester Regt, sometime around 1903–6. After the formation of the Territorial Force, transferred as lance corporal to the 1/6th Bn, Manchester Regt, on 1 May 1908. Promoted to corporal in 1910 and sergeant in 1912.

Embodied on 5 August 1914, signed Army Form E.624 volunteering for foreign service on 2 September 1914. Attached to the 1/1st East Lancs Signal Company on 10 September 1914 and embarked for Egypt on the same day. Disembarked at Alexandria on 24 September and served with No. 4 Signal Section in Egypt 1914–15.

Embarked for Gallipoli on 3 May 1915 and landed at W Beach on 6 May. 'Joe' is mentioned numerous times in Riley's Gallipoli diary and was clearly one of Riley's closest comrades.

Made sergeant in the Royal Engineers on 30 May 1915 and granted fourth rate of engineer pay. Admitted 1st Field Ambulance suffering from diarrhoea and headaches on 8 August. Transferred to 11th Casualty Clearing Station at W Beach on 11 August 1915, and on to a hospital ship the next day. Royle later stated in a medical examination that he had suffered from dysentery.

Treated in the 21st General Hospital, Alexandria, until 24 November 1915, then transferred to the convalescent depot at Mustafa. Embarked for England 'time expired' in March 1916. Called up under the Military Service Act in March 1917 as Sapper 238056, Royal Engineers, and served with rank of lance corporal for the duration of the war in an unidentified wireless section. Demobilized and transferred to Z Reserve on 4 March 1919.

Initiated into the Richmond Masonic Lodge no. 1011 in the latter part of 1919, at which time he was 34 years of age, living at 39 Norton Street, Brooks Bar, Manchester, and working as a postal clerk. Married Elizabeth Jones (born 11 February 1888) in 1922. The 1939 register shows the couple living at 370 Kings Road, Stretford. 'Joe' died in Manchester in 1961, age 75.

Private 2341 Richard Thomas

No. 4 (Manchester Brigade) Section, 1/1st Signal Company,
42nd (East Lancs) Division, Royal Engineers (TF).
Private 2341, 1/6th Bn, Manchester Regt, later Pioneer 11367,
Royal Engineers (TF), and Pioneer 400528, Royal Engineers

Born 1888. Judging by his service number he enlisted in the 1/6th Bn, Manchester Regt, a year or two before the outbreak of war. Embodied on 5 August 1914, he signed Army Form E.624 volunteering for foreign service in early September 1914. Embarked with the East Lancashire Division for Egypt on 10 September 1914 and disembarked at Alexandria on 24 September.

Thomas' original 'theatre of war' entry date is given on both his medal index card and 1914–15 Star Roll as 22 September 1914. This was later amended to 5 November 1914. Riley's single reference to 'Thomas' in his Egypt diary has them at Abu Zabal 'early in October.' It is likely that Thomas's entry date was amended in error (not unusual in these kinds of records) and that he arrived in Egypt with No. 4 Section on 24 September.

Few of Thomas's service records survive but, whether he arrived in Egypt in September or November, we know he served there with No. 4 Signal Section during 1914–15, and we can be fairly sure he landed at W Beach with No. 4 Section on 6 May 1915. He is mentioned numerous times in Riley's Gallipoli diary, the last occasion being just a few days before Riley's evacuation on 11 September, so it is probable that Thomas served at Helles until that date, if not beyond it.

Thomas was discharged 18 March 1919 and granted a pension for his rheumatism. His Army Form S.B.36 shows that he was married and living at 50 Coupland Street, Hulme, Manchester. However, another note on the same document, added 15 March 1920, states 'man resides in Essex.'

'Tommy'

Pre-war territorial solder who had already signed up for imperial service when Riley reached the headquarters of the 1/6th Manchester Bn on 5 August 1914. Probably a member of the divisional signal company as

Riley describes how 'Tommy' gave his name (a second time) when 'Pilk' (the battalion signals officer) asked his men to volunteer for overseas service. Like the other signallers, 'Tommy' received a bounty for supplying his personal bicycle for active service.

Riley mentions 'Tommy' on eight occasions when in Egypt, typically as his companion when exploring Cairo and Alexandria. He also notes having to help 'Tommy' on the route march to Helouan.

'Tommy' is not mentioned at all in Riley's Gallipoli diary, whereas 'Thomas' is named several times. 'Thomas' features in Riley's nominal roll of the divisional signal company and is referred to on twelve separate occasions in the Gallipoli diary. 'Tommy' and 'Thomas' (Pioneer 11367 Richard Thomas) could be the same man.

Sapper *(later Lance Corporal)* 664 Richard 'Abe' Williams

No. 4 (Manchester Brigade) Section, 1/1st Signal Company, 42nd (East Lancs) Division, Royal Engineers (TF). Sapper (later Lance Corporal) 664 Richard Williams, Royal Engineers (TF)

Iron dresser (foundry worker) of Collyhurst, Manchester. Born 18 October 1889 in the parish of St Michaels, Manchester, the fourth of seven children. Son of Samuel Williams, warehouseman, and Rebecca Biggar.

Attested on 23 March 1911 into the East Lancashire Royal Engineers (TF) on a four-year term of service while employed in the fitting shop at British Westinghouse Electrical and Manufacturing Company, Trafford Park, Manchester. Married Mary Susan Gascoigne, age 27, a core maker (foundry worker), on 4 October 1913, while both were living at 42 King William Street, Salford.

Embodied on 5 August 1914 while attached to the 2nd Field Company, East Lancashire Royal Engineers (TF). Signed Army Form E.624 volunteering for overseas service on 2 September 1914, shortly afterwards transferring to 1/1st Signal Company. Embarked for Egypt on 10 September 1914. Disembarked at Alexandria on 24 September and served with No. 4 Signal Section in Egypt 1914–15.

Embarked for Gallipoli on 3 May 1915 and landed at W Beach on 6 May. Riley mentions 'Abe' (sometimes 'Abie Williams') many times in his diaries. At Gallipoli, Riley gives his rank as lance corporal. The last mention of 'Abe' is 27 August 1915, a couple of weeks before Riley's evacuation from the peninsula on 11 September. Williams' service records show no break in his service at Gallipoli, so he may have remained on the peninsula until the 1/1st Signal Company was evacuated (28 December to 3 January 1916).

Continued to serve with the 42nd (East Lancs) Division in Egypt from 4 January 1916 until embarking for England on 24 March 1916. Discharged 'time expired' on 14 April 1916 having served a total of 5 years and 23 days. It is not known if Williams re-enlisted.

Died 11 February 1958, Headington, Oxfordshire, age 68.

Captain Charles Harry 'Tim' Williamson *(MC)*

Officer Commanding No. 4 (Manchester Brigade) Signal Section, 1/1st Signal Company, 42nd (East Lancs) Division, Royal Engineers (TF). Formerly 1/7th Bn, Manchester Regt, later Royal Flying Corps

Chemist, of Eccles, Manchester. Born Lancashire, September 1887, son of Harry Williamson, chartered accountant, and Mary Elizabeth Blyton.

Commissioned second lieutenant into the 1/7th Bn, Manchester Regt, on 7 February 1911. Promoted to lieutenant on 5 January 1912 and captain on 26 September 1914. Appointed as OC, No. 4 Signal Section, on 31 August 1914. Signed Army Form E.624 volunteering for overseas service in early September 1914. Embarked with No. 4 Signal Section for Egypt on 10 September 1914. Disembarked at Alexandria on 24 September and commanded the section in Egypt 1914–15. Landed at W Beach on 6 May 1915. Continued to command No. 4 Section until evacuated sick in September 1915. Evacuated onwards to England, he married Ada Roberta Ambler, age 25, on 1 November 1915 at St Mary the Virgin, Eccles.

Sometime later he returned to command No. 4 Section. It is not clear if he returned to Gallipoli, but he was definitely in charge of No. 4 Section during the division's second spell in Egypt 1916. In May 1916 he took over command of the Signal Company when Captain Dammers was invalided home. At the beginning of November 1916, Williamson transferred to No. 14 Squadron, Royal Flying Corps, Palestine, as an observer. A few days later he was awarded the Military Cross (LG 26 November 1916) presumably for his actions at Gallipoli. The citation reads: 'for conspicuous gallantry in action. He established and maintained communications under heavy fire with great courage and skill.'

Williamson died in a flying accident at Rafah on the Sinai Peninsula on 27 March 1917. He and his pilot, Second Lieutenant Cecil Charles Gibbs, had just taken off when the engine in their B.E.2e aeroplane stalled and the aircraft fell to the ground killing both men.

Both Williamson and Gibbs are buried in Kantara War Memorial Cemetery, Egypt, grave references B. 159 and B. 177 respectively.

Lieutenant Percy Wolf

Platoon commander, 1/4th Bn, East Lancashire Regt

Born Huddersfield, 1878, to a German father, Dr Alfred Wolf, and a British mother, Emily. Educated at both Blackburn and Manchester Grammar Schools and went on to study law at Victoria University, Manchester.

In 1907, while working as a solicitor for Barrow in Furness corporation, Wolf joined the King's Own Barrow in Furness Volunteers. He returned to Blackburn to work as a solicitor for the town corporation and transferred to the 1/4th Bn, East Lancashire Regt, on the formation of the Territorial Force in 1908. In July 1909, he was appointed as Blackburn's Deputy Town Clerk. On 24 January 1912, he was initiated as a Freemason into the Manor Lodge, Blackburn. Promoted to lieutenant in February 1913.

Volunteered for foreign service at the beginning of September 1914 and embarked with his battalion for Egypt on 10 September. Disembarked at Alexandria on 24 September 1914 and served in Egypt 1914–15. Embarked for Gallipoli on 5 May 1915 and landed at V Beach on 9 May. Killed together with five other men by a single burst of shrapnel on 4 June 1915. Lieutenant Wolf has no known grave and is commemorated on the Helles Memorial, Panel 114–118.

Figure 72. General Sir Ian Hamilton, GCB, GCMG, DSO.

APPENDIX IV

General Sir Ian Standish Monteith Hamilton, GCB, GCMG, DSO

Commander-in-Chief, Mediterranean Expeditionary Force

Much has already been written on Hamilton's involvement in the Gallipoli Campaign. As such, these biographical notes focus instead on Hamilton's early life, earlier military career, and his life after the Great War. Hamilton worked tirelessly for veteran's interests and was 'bombarded with letters by old servicemen begging, pleading for help.' He helped many Gallipoli veterans including Alec Riley, who came to Hamilton for publishing advice.

The failure of the Gallipoli Campaign has done much to obscure the true qualities of Hamilton, the man, and the soldier. He is often perceived as a rather weak and one-dimensional commander, but when Hamilton's earlier career is examined in depth, a far more complex individual is revealed. Here is a man who stood out from his peers as a progressive-thinking military innovator possessed of an original, perceptive and highly analytical mind. Prior to his appointment as C-in-C, Mediterranean Expeditionary Force, Hamilton was widely recognised as one of Britain's most experienced and talented soldiers, highly respected by both the British and German military establishments. After Gallipoli he was 'remembered less and less for his former successes, more and more for his last appointment and only failure.'[99]

These notes draw on Hamilton's own writings, including *Gallipoli Diary*, but mainly his memoirs *When I was a Boy* (1939), *Listening for the Drums* (1944) and *The Commander* (1957). The other important source was John Lee's excellent biography *A Soldier's Life: General Sir Ian Hamilton 1853–1947* (2000).

* * *

Hamilton was born on the island of Corfu on 16 January 1853. His father, Colonel Christian Monteith Hamilton, commanded the 92nd (Gordon) Highlanders. His mother, Maria Corinna Vereker, was the daughter of John, third Viscount Gort, and Maria O'Grady, daughter of Viscount Guillamore. Hamilton's mother Maria died of consumption shortly after the birth of his brother Vereker when Hamilton was three years old.

His father continued to serve with his regiment in India for most Hamilton's childhood and both brothers were brought up by their grandparents and aunts in their home 'Hafton' on the shores of Holy Loch near Dunoon. Here Hamilton was allowed to roam free around the estate in what was an almost idyllic early childhood. This freedom however brought with it the potential for mischief. On one occasion Hamilton attempted to hit an apple balanced on Vereker's head with an arrow (it did not end well) and on another, Vereker succeeded in burning down his grandfather's '£1,000 icehouse.' It was during these pre-school years that Hamilton developed a comparatively egalitarian attitude. He learned to treat the servants with respect and remembered them long after with affection. Their children were his playmates, despite the gulf in social status, and Hamilton treated others respectfully throughout his life.

At the age of ten he was sent to Cheam School, at the time the most expensive private school in England. It was not a happy time for Hamilton who suffered, as did most of his peers, under the school's

---

[99] Anthony Farrar-Hockley, in his preface to *The Commander* (London: Hollis and Carter, 1957).

harsh culture. '*Morally*,' wrote Hamilton, 'the atmosphere of the place was poisonous—deadly—to a certain type of boy, owing to the systematic and cruel bullying, which could hardly have been unknown to the Higher Direction.'

Despite the many troubles and tribulations Hamilton endured at Cheam, the regime ensured he succeeded scholastically.

Towards the end of his time at Cheam, Hamilton suffered the loss of his beloved grandfather and benefactor. 'Suddenly into this fondly planned scheme of life for a Victorian schoolboy (Cheam, Eton, Oxford, heiress, parliament) broke the war pipes and drums ... my grandfather died.' Hamilton had set his heart on Eton but without his grandfather's financial support the famous school was out of the question. Given the choice of attending Rugby, his father's old school, or Wellington College, a piqued Hamilton left the decision to his headmaster, who enrolled him in the latter, a brand-new, red-brick establishment, built in the memory of the 'Iron Duke.'

After the 'over-cramming' doctrine of Cheam, Hamilton found little to challenge him at Wellington and by his own admission wasted most of his four years there. However, he was shaken out of his complacency by some disturbing news near the end of his final year: 'At Easter in 1870, my father, who had now ended his command of the Gordons in India, heard from his friends at the War Office that the purchase of commissions was to be abolished – a revolutionary change which would bring about a reshuffle of all the military cards. To clear the ground one huge exam., would be held that very summer for direct commissions in the Army and then to close down for at least a couple of years.'

Hamilton's military ambitions were rescued by the intervention of Captain Lendy, a French officer who specialised in cramming applicants through Army entrance exams. Hamilton buckled down to his studies and exceeded his own expectations by passing the entrance exam for Sandhurst, placing seventy-sixth out of the four hundred and four examinees who sat that year.

He was still too young to attend Sandhurst proper but, as one of the first one hundred, was entitled to attend 'a year's course of extra special instruction as cadets of the Royal Military College, Sandhurst, to tide them over some of the waiting period.'

Instead, he chose to travel to Dresden and to study under General Dammers. The general was a product of the Military Academy at Hanover. Dammers' father had fought in Halkett's Brigade at Waterloo, and Dammers himself had 'commanded a whole army; a handsome, yellow-haired, square-faced German, still bearing the traces of his Scandinavian ancestry.' This was to be another formative period in the young Hamilton's life with lessons on military history, map reading, surveying, sketching and most importantly German military methods. The knowledge gained under Dammers' instruction would carry him through Sandhurst and open his mind to alternative military doctrines.

After Dresden, Hamilton went onto Sandhurst and soon reverted to his old ways: 'During the year 1872, it was easier to shirk work and to get away with it than at any other period during the history of the Royal Military College. Some of us, like the Cavalry, were already commissioned as 2nd Lieuts. in the Army; others still more or less in the school-boy stage. No system of tuition could cover both lots effectively, and by making clever use of privileges accorded to officers it became easy to run wild at Sandhurst as it had been for quite other reasons, at Wellington.'

However, the solid military grounding Hamilton had received under General Dammers stood him in good stead: 'When H.R.H. the Duke of Cambridge came towards the end of or time to hold his inspection and went through the survey work done during our year, his military secretary drew his attention to a sketch of mine in which the lie of the ground, or *terrain* as we call it, was shown by hachuring or shading in with hundreds of small lines. Thereupon H.R.H. commanded the sketch itself should be sent up to Horse Guards and that the fact should be recorded in R.M.C. orders.'

On leaving Sandhurst, Hamilton was commissioned 'full Lieutenant' and in January 1873, with no place available for him in his father's old regiment, he joined the 12th (Suffolk) Regiment, then serving at Athlone in Ireland. After a few months of garrison life, Hamilton was promised a plum posting. However, fate intervened, as he describes in his memoir *Listening for the Drums*: 'The Quarter-Master General to the Forces, who was going to take me as his A.D.C. when he got his command, was drowned on manoeuvres in Devonshire and my original application for transfer to the 92nd Gordon Highlanders (my father's regiment) which I had made some months earlier, became effective.'

APPENDIX IV

Hamilton sailed for India in November 1873 and after an eventful journey, during which his Indian guide absconded with all his money, he joined his regiment in Mooltan in mid-December. For the next five years he served with the Gordons, alternating from barrack to frontier. Hamilton had little interest in 'routine soldiering' and made no effort to 'master the red books containing the rudiments (drill, law etc.).' Instead he studied for and passed the Lower (and later the Higher) Standard examination in Hindustani, a piece of individualism that 'sent the Adjutant apoplectic'. In those times a junior officer's role was to obey and disseminate orders without question, but from early on Hamilton showed an originality of mind that ran contrary to convention.

An example of Hamilton's ability to think on his feet occurred in 1874. As part of the Gordons' annual inspection, a demonstration attack was to be carried out in front of the inspecting general, Major General Sir Charles Reid, VC.

As Reid and his staff watched, the regiment began to '... advance by Companies, beginning from the left with short sharp rushes of fifty paces. Having made its rush each Company was to fling itself on the ground, fire three rounds rapid 'independent' – make another rush and so *de capo* until we got within 100 yards of the enemy when we would fix bayonets and charge ... By the time we had covered 200 paces we had come within about 70 yards of the stout brick wall some four feet high surrounding the parade ground. Beginning on the left each Company made its rushes; flung itself down and fired its rounds. Seven times this was repeated and now, last of all, it was my turn, but even as I gave the order for the drill-book rush I felt seized with a strong impulse as a sportsman ... to fire over the wall.'

Rather than repeat the 'failure' of the other companies, Hamilton made a snap judgement and on completing the last rush he ordered his men to carry on to the wall where they fired three rounds each and took cover. The Adjutant, Colonel and both Majors rode ominously towards Hamilton who was saved by the Inspecting-General's Bugler sounding the 'Cease Fire' followed by the 'Officer's Call.' The Gordon officers assembled with swords drawn, waiting with trepidation, none more so than Hamilton, for the 'Great Man' to deliver his judgement on the attack.

After criticising the officers on their high mess bills, General Reid went on to praise how the earlier parts of the attack had been carried out, but was critical of the final phase adding: 'A certain amount of make-believe is unavoidable when any field exercise is practised on a parade ground, but to carry this to the extent of treating a brick wall as if it were transparent is to go too far – I hope this criticism will be taken to heart – also in fairness I must praise the officer in command of the right company for his soldierly common sense and I beg his name may be submitted to me for record in the Divisional Office at Lahore.'

Although relieved not to be singled out for criticism, Hamilton was mortified to receive praise in such a public way and later wrote, 'to score in this way over my brother officers – over Inverailort himself [Colonel Cameron, the Gordons' CO] was a most desperate scoop to bring off and one which would demand from me weeks of humility and months of modest behaviour.'

Hamilton broke ranks again when General Roberts sent out a call for volunteers for an expedition against the Looshais hill tribes. Regimental tradition demanded that 'the Gordons either fought collectively as clansmen should – or not at all.' Hamilton was undeterred by protocol and 'was the only creature, officer, N.C.O., or man in the whole regiment who stepped forward.'

Like other officers serving in India, Hamilton received a generous quota of leave. Some of this he spent at Simla, but most was devoted to hunting. In 1875 and again in 1876 he undertook arduous, two-month long expeditions in the high Himalayas, chalking up record bags of antelope and mountain goat.

In 1877, while on six months home leave, he was ordered by the War Office to take a musketry course at Hythe. He achieved an 'extra First' and was 'almost at once gazetted as Musketry Instructor to the Gordons.'

On his return to India, Hamilton set about improving the standards of musketry in his regiment. It was not an easy task. As Hamilton recalled, 'the Gordons were at that time better armoured than anyone nowadays can imagine against enthusiasms or ideas.' At the time the British Army placed little importance on individual marksmanship. 'Professionally speaking, the Colonel, Adjutant, and Sergeant-Major held the bullet to be a fool, and the bayonet to be still the last argument of Kings; the reigning Queen of battles.' As the Gordons' new musketry instructor Hamilton faced 'a mountain of inertia' but later acknowledged the appointment as 'a real turning point in my career.' He applied himself to his new assignment with vigour: 'I sweated; I lectured; I begged; I made bad jokes; I even filled the pouches of the battalion with ball cartridge for private practice out of my own slender purse.'

His efforts began to bear fruit. 'The Adjutant and the Sergeant-Major became first uneasy, next furious, to see so much time lost to the barrack-square for the sake of the rifle range; the field officers, however, were astonished, and not altogether displeased when they saw the musketry returns of the battalion creep up and up to the very top of the tree until we became the best shooting battalion in India.' It was a record that would be noticed in the higher echelons.

Hamilton met his future mentor and benefactor when serving with his regiment in the Second Afghan War (1878–1880). 'In July 1879 during the Afghan War an incident occurred which more than any other single event, was to influence my whole career; for it brought me for the first time into personal contact with Lord Roberts.'

Hamilton was summoned by Roberts to give an account of a small action he had recently taken part in. During the action, Hamilton (recovering from a fever) and a fellow officer riding with him, rallied a party of troops from another regiment who had abandoned their hilltop redoubt to a raiding party of Shinwarris. He led them back to the redoubt only to find it empty. Later, while in pursuit of the raiders Hamilton became isolated and had to fend them off with his revolver. 'I fired six shots altogether but missed as I was very seedy and had just run up a hill, which made my hand shaky.' Taking cover behind a tree while being enfiladed by three raiders, the Shinwarri leader came up and 'fired at point point-blank range with a flintlock *jezail* that missed fire.' Fortunately for Hamilton his party arrived at that moment, killing his attacker, and driving off the other raiders.

His meeting with Roberts resulted in Hamilton being 'gazetted in Field Orders to be A.D.C. to General Redan Massy – commanding the Cavalry Brigade.' But more significantly it led, two and a half years later, to Hamilton being invited by Roberts to 'come onto his staff.'

The Afghan War came to its conclusion after General Roberts decisively defeated Ayub Khan at the Battle of Kandahar on 1 September 1880. Two and a half months later the British Army was again involved in conflict when the First Anglo-Boer War broke out on 16 December 1880. Shortly afterwards the Gordons were ordered back to England.

However, on reaching Cawnpore on 6 January 1881, the Commanding Officer received a 'startling' cable. 'The 92nd Highlanders are to embark for Natal immediately instead of going to England.'

The cause of this bolt from the blue was revealed by Hamilton sixty-eight years after the event: 'As a senior subaltern I had three days previously cabled to Evelyn Wood [Field Marshall Sir Henry Evelyn Wood, VC, GCB, GCMG] in the name of the "subalterns of the 92nd." ... I wrote it myself and paid for it myself. The four senior subalterns agreed on the understanding that I stood the shot if there was a row. The Captains and Majors knew nothing whatever about this plot of mine. Something like this it ran: – "Personal. From Subalterns 92nd Highlanders. Splendid battalion eager service much nearer Natal than England do send." Evelyn Wood was amused and sent us. And so, we went and so I have only one useful arm, but Majuba was worth an arm any day.'

The battle of Majuba Hill was a key event in Hamilton's military career. It began with the bloodless occupation of the hill from which the battle takes its name but ended in a debacle that nearly cost Hamilton his life.

On the night of 26 February 1881, Major General Sir George Pomeroy Colley led a hastily assembled, mixed force of 365 men made up from the 92nd Highlanders, the 58th Regiment and from sailors of the Natal Brigade. The summit was easily captured as the Boers left it unoccupied during the hours of darkness. However, Colley failed to order his men to dig in or build sangars on the sparsely covered hilltop, and they became easy targets when the Boers attacked in force on the following morning. Holding a defensive perimeter of about a mile in circumference, the thin line of defenders was soon forced back. Hamilton reported to Colley, asking for permission to charge the enemy, to which Colley replied, 'we will wait until the Boers advance on us, then give them a volley and charge.' Moments later Hamilton spotted a Boer pointing his rifle at him at close range. He raised his own rifle but was beaten to the shot, and the Boer's bullet went through his left wrist. As he turned round 'in despair' he saw that 'the whole line had given way' and Colley, holding his revolver above his head, shouted orders to the fleeing troops to 'Retire and hold by the ridge.' Hamilton decided to run for it but as he ran, was struck on the head by a spent bullet or stone and knocked unconscious. He awoke to find 'two small Boers, aged about fourteen '... rolling me over and removing my belts, sword, haversack etc.' Colley had been killed in the melee and Hamilton was summoned by Schmidt, one of the Boer commanders, to identify Colley's body. On confirming it was Colley's, Hamilton had his wrist dressed and was told, 'that as I would probably die, they did not want me, and I might go where I liked.'

He spent the next two hours carrying water to the wounded before setting off for the British lines. The following morning, he was discovered by a picquet of the 58th and taken back to camp. Hamilton was admitted to hospital at Newcastle, Natal, and was visited by Sir Evelyn Wood who promised him an honourable mention in dispatches. Wood asked the Commander-in-Chief, HRH the Duke of Cambridge for permission to recommend Hamilton for the Victoria Cross but was refused on the grounds that Hamilton was 'too young, or at least so young that I'd have plenty more chances.'

Hamilton narrowly avoided amputation of his lower arm and his left wrist was permanently debilitated by his wound. He did however take away many valuable lessons: the importance of planning and preparation, unit cohesion, speedy reinforcement, and decisive leadership that he would apply throughout his military career.

The patronage of General Sir Frederick Sleigh Roberts VC was of great benefit to Hamilton's career. In 1881, Hamilton was in England recovering from his wounds and studying for Staff College entrance examinations. Roberts, known affectionately as 'Bobs' by subordinates, then C-in-C Presidency of Madras, had recognised Hamilton's potential in Afghanistan and asked him to serve as his aide-de-camp. At the time the British Army was divided into two factions, the 'Africans' or 'Wolseley Ring' and the 'Indians' or 'Roberts Ring.' The 'Africans' held the greatest influence at the War Office and the keys to higher advancement. Despite reservations, Hamilton accepted Roberts' offer, ended his studies and 'literally burnt his books.' As his biographer John Lee explains, Hamilton was one of the few 'Indians' to serve again in Africa and 'claim a foot in both camps.'

Hamilton's departure was delayed but on 25 February 1882 he received news of his promotion to captain. In June, he joined his new chief in Bangalore, beginning what would be another sixteen years' service in India. He quickly settled into his ADC duties to Roberts who

Hamilton regarded afterwards as the greatest soldier and commander he had served under, and to whom he owed 'militarily everything.'

In 1884, Hamilton became Roberts's Assistant Military Secretary, a role he carried out for six months. However, the Duke of Cambridge, a fervent champion of the Wolseley Ring, refused to confirm the appointment. An indignant Hamilton later recounted: 'Pronounced too young at thirty-one; too inexperienced after two campaigns, wounds and mentions in dispatches...' He resumed his post as Roberts's ADC but was given six months leave in England as compensation.

Hamilton left India in October, 'ostensibly on six months leave but really (if possible) to join the Nile River Column.' He was not alone in his plans: 'Hardly had we cleared Bombay harbour when I found that about half of the Officers who were to be my fellow passengers had hit on the same bright idea as myself; the idea, namely, that we might wangle ourselves into the Gordon Relief Expedition, then about to start for Khartoum.'

However, there were prohibitions. 'There was a ban on "medal hunting"; all and sundry were to be properly appointed from London; if we wanted to relieve Gordon we must do so via Pall Mall: anyone attempting to cut in from any benighted country like India would be summarily dealt with; arrested certainly; probably tried by court martial.'

Undeterred Hamilton jumped ship at Suez and ran 'half a mile with my kit over the soft sand,' to catch the only train that day to Cairo. With the odds stacked against him, Hamilton was lucky to meet a subaltern of the newly formed 1st battalion of his regiment. Through him he secured a place on the expedition with the Gordons who were set to start up the Nile on the following morning.

The ill-fated Nile Expedition comprised two independent forces, the Desert Column and the River Column, and although it ended in failure, the River Column commanded by Major-General William Earle, CB (to which Hamilton was attached) were victorious against a strong Mahdist force at the Battle of Kirbekan.

Hamilton was assigned to D Company, 1st Gordon Highlanders, which during the battle, 'advanced up along the river, parallel to it, opened fire and pinned the Dervishes to their entrenchments...' With the Gordons holding the enemy's attention, Earle led his main force in a wide circular march, round the back of the Kirbekan Ridge and attacked the Mahdists from the rear. 'In open attack formation our men went for them; destroyed their grand counter charge of spearmen by fire then stormed the heights *from the rear!* No one escaped. A few dozen desperate fugitives leaping into the raging Nile, but it is doubtful if any got across.'

British casualties were light. Of the one thousand British and Egyptian troops engaged, only sixty or so were lost, but among them was General Earle who, according to Hamilton, was 'killed by the last shot fired on the field.' However, Hamilton was awarded another mention in despatches, a campaign medal with two clasps and the Khedive's Star.

Hamilton, by now a Brevet Major, returned to India in June 1885. He resumed his duties as ADC to Roberts, who on 28 November 1885, became C-in-C India. In 1886, while at Simla, Hamilton met Miss Jean Muir, then reputed to be 'the loveliest women who ever came east of Suez.' She was already betrothed to an Austrian prince, but Hamilton was undeterred and a few weeks later the couple were engaged to be married.

Writing became an important part of Hamilton's life during his time in India. He entered and won poetry competitions, became the 'Correspondent from Army Headquarters' to the *Madras Mail* and wrote many military pamphlets and speeches for his Chief. He was also generous in promoting the work of others. Hamilton began a lifelong friendship with Rudyard Kipling in 1886 and made efforts to get Kipling's work into print.

In 1885 a dispute over commercial interests broke out between the British and Burmese governments. On 22 October 1885, the British Government issued an ultimatum, the acceptance of which would have effectively ended Burmese independence. Britain declared war a few days later and by 28 November, British forces had captured the capital Mandalay and taken King Thibaw prisoner.

On 1 January 1886, a ten-years-long insurgency was sparked by Britain's annexation of Upper Burma (having already annexed Lower Burma in 1853). Following the death of the C-in-C Burma, Roberts was appointed in his place, embarking with his staff for Mandalay on 3 November. In response to an outbreak of insurgent attacks, Roberts established flying columns of lightly equipped troops and an extensive network of small military posts distributed throughout the country.

In *Listening for the Drums,* Hamilton describes the secrecy surrounding the campaign, perhaps because of its clear imperial purpose. After Burma's annexation, part of the booty looted from the Burmese Government was catalogued by Roberts's staff. Some officers engaged in a little private looting, Hamilton describes one of them 'pulling strips [of gold] off screens or decorations and putting them in his pocket.' When Hamilton was staying at Majionh, the 'ruby mine capital,' he spent his spare time prospecting in temporarily abandoned workings hoping 'to get a good fat ruby out of their mine and give it to Jean.'

Hamilton returned from Burma to marry Jean in India at the beginning of 1887. The ceremony took place on 22 February in Calcutta cathedral and the couple spent their honeymoon in Darjeeling, accompanied to Hamilton's surprise by his mother-in-law.

It would also be a significant year for Hamilton's career. On 1 July he was promoted lieutenant colonel and appointed Assistant Adjutant-General of Musketry at Indian Army headquarters. It was an appointment that would shape Hamilton's career and the innovations he put in place would have a great impact on the training and tactics of the British Army between the late 19th and early 20th centuries.

Hamilton set about remedying the poor state of marksmanship, rewriting completely the musketry regulations for the Indian regiments. Hamilton had laid out his theories on marksmanship and field tactics in a manual, *The Fighting of The Future,* published in early 1885. His ideas on training were radical. They focused on developing an individual soldier's skills on the range, in the classroom and gymnasium, while calling for useless drill to be abandoned. These ideas were later adopted by both British and Indian armies. Hamilton also foresaw an end to the role played on the battlefield by cavalry, which he felt should be used as mounted infantry. He also predicted an end to the forward deployment of field artillery, whose crews were vulnerable to long range rifle fire.

Hamilton was posted to Bengal in 1890, where he remained for the next three years. In 1891 he was awarded the Distinguished Service Order, and in November 1891 was promoted to colonel. In April 1893, Roberts returned to London after forty-one years in India, and Hamilton was appointed military secretary to the new C-in-C India, Sir George White, VC.

Hamilton's new post took him on inspection tours to Nepal and, according to John Lee, 'some spectacular tiger shoots' in December 1893.

In January 1894 he attended ceremonies held in Calcutta for the departure of Lord Lansdown as Viceroy of India, and the arrival of his successor, Lord Elgin. Hamilton took leave in England from May to August and returned to find trouble brewing again on the North-West Frontier. He was unable to secure a place in the expeditionary force that went into Waziristan but was soon in action again.

In early 1895, a small force of five British officers and 400 Indian troops (including men from the 14th Sikhs) were besieged by several thousand Chitralis in the fort at Chitral on the North-West Frontier. A relief force of 15,000 troops under Major-General Sir Robert Low, assembled at Peshawar. Known as the Chitral Expedition, Low's force set off for Chitral at the end of March. Hamilton was appointed by Low as Assistant Adjutant-General and Quartermaster-General on his lines of communications. It was to be a challenging post.

'The Relief Force, as it pushed its way north, had to be supplied over pathless mountains, bridgeless rivers and snow-bound passes swarming with hostile tribesmen. Thousands of animals, donkeys, mules, bullocks, camels had to be kept on the move laden with food, forage, and ammunition for the Force up at Chitral is in constant danger of being cut off. My life was a never-ending struggle to extemporize methods of coping with bandits, fire and flood and it was all I could do to keep my hair on or my head above water.'

Hamilton's next opportunity for action came in 1897, when he given command of the 1st Brigade of the Tirah Expeditionary Force. The force was to punish the Afridi tribe, in the mountain ranges east of the Khyber Pass. First he took a mixed force of infantry and artillery through the Kohat Pass, then then took command of the 1st Brigade. But on the morning the march was to resume, his pony stumbled and fell. Hamilton's leg was broken in the fall, and he was forced to relinquish command until he had recovered.

In February 1898, with the campaign virtually over, Hamilton was placed in command of the 3rd Brigade, by then swollen to seven battalions, a battery and two field companies. It was camped at Gudda Kalai ('the den of thieves') in the Bara Valley and ordered to cover the evacuation of the 20,000-strong main column which stretched 'along a narrow road through a series of deep ravines.'

Hamilton was already friendly with Winston Churchill, and during these operations 'saw young Winston enjoying himself among the bullets: Care and Fear have had no hand in his make-up for which Providence may be praised.' Hamilton would next see Churchill in action while in South Africa and both men's futures were to cross and link from now on. As Hamilton recounted in his last years: 'Setting the fair sex tenderly but firmly on the mantlepiece, nobody, not even Lord Bobs in all his glory, has touched my life at so many points as Winston Churchill.'

As fighting in the Bara Valley ended, Hamilton faced a dilemma. 'The decision I had to make at Gudda Kalai was to be 'the be or not-to-be' of my own career, now at the point at burying itself in a Scottish graveyard.'

One day in March 1898, Hamilton received both 'a cable and a wire.' The wire was from Sir William Lockhart, C-in-C India, offering Hamilton the 'magnificent post' of Quartermaster-General, India, at a salary of £3,000 per annum. The cable was from Sir Evelyn Wood offering the post of Commandant of the School of Musketry at Hythe with the more modest salary of £800. After 'thinking the matter over for twenty-four hours...' he decided on Hythe, a decision pivotal to Hamilton's career. 'Thus, and thus only as it turned out, was I enabled to take part in the South Africa War.'

In April 1898, Hamilton left India for the last time.

Once at Hythe he introduced the British Army to the principles of rifle training he had embedded in the Indian Army.

According to his biographer John Lee, 'realistic battle conditions and individual accuracy summed up the revolution in training instituted by him. He immediately increased the number of full courses at Hythe from four to five a year and drew the militia and yeomanry into the system for the first time.' These innovative methods were arguably the foundations for 'the astonishing efficiency of the British battalions that poured fifteen aimed rounds per minute into the German formations at Mons and Ypres in 1914.'

Hamilton was so successful as Commandant that although appointment was normally for twelve months, he was given a second year. 'Thus, he was in post when the call to arms rang out again in South Africa.'

As tensions rose between the British Government and the two Boer Republics over gold rights and British settlers in Boer territory, Britain prepared for war. Hamilton's old boss, the former C-in-C India, General

Sir George White, was appointed GOC to Natal by the Secretary of State for War, Lord Lansdowne. On 12 September 1899, White appointed Hamilton his Assistant Adjutant-General. Four days later (in circumstances Hamilton would again face on 13 March 1915) he sailed for South Africa 'with no briefing on policy, intelligence or strategy.' British troops began to arrive in Natal during the first week in October and the Boers issued an ultimatum for their removal by 11 October.

White arrived with his staff at Cape Town on 3 October, but en route to Ladysmith the ultimatum expired. The Boers took the offensive, striking to the south and west 'hoping to raise up the Cape Afrikaners in their support.' When Major-General Archibald Hunter arrived at White's headquarters to take over temporarily as chief-of-staff, Hamilton was given the local rank of major-general to command the 7th Infantry Brigade.

Hamilton's brigade included the 1st Devons, the 1st Manchesters and his old battalion, the 2nd Gordons. He immediately ordered three days of intensive training to embed his progressive ideas on musketry, fire control and fire and movement. The lessons learned in these few days were crucial to the outcome of the coming battle and sealed Hamilton's reputation as a modern, forward-thinking commander and leader in the field.

On 20 October 1899, a British column under Lieutenant-General Sir William Penn Symons attacked a 4,000 strong Boer force occupying Talana Hill to the east of the strategically important town of Dundee. Symons was mortally wounded in the battle, which was a tactical victory, but won at a high cost and necessitated a British retirement.

Another Boer force was holding the railway station at Elandslaagte, blocking the route of the retreating column. Sir John French was ordered to attack with his cavalry but found the Boer defenders in greater force than expected. Hamilton's brigade with two batteries of artillery were sent by train to reinforce French and began arriving in the late morning of 21 October. Hamilton assessed the Boer positions and persuaded White and French to accept his plan of attack. John Lee describes how Hamilton roused his troops: 'Hamilton called his soldiers around him and explained to them that they were to put into practice the very wide, very loose formations they had been rehearsing under his direction. He filled the men with enthusiasm, promising them that their fame would be the talk of London the next day.' A war correspondent present reported the men responded eagerly with cries of 'We'll do it, sir. We'll do it.'

The Boers held the eastern half of a horseshoe-shaped ridge that ended in a kopje. The plan was for Hamilton's field guns to bombard the Boer positions whilst the Devons advanced in open order towards the ridge. Hamilton would lead his other two battalions in the main attack—the Manchesters would assault the kopje as the Gordons attacked the Boers' left flank. As the Devons closed on the ridge, the Manchesters, and the Gordons with their pipers playing 'The Cock o' the North,' attacked the kopje.

An intense fight ensued. Lines of farmers' wire slowed the attackers and a storm burst over them. As they neared the top of the hill, some wavered and the attack stalled. Hamilton dashed forward with his aides and ordered buglers to sound the charge. The infantry rose up, surged forward, and won the summit. A white flag was raised and the British sounded 'cease fire.'

Shortly after, some fifty Boers led by General Kock counter-attacked the now relaxed troops. A momentary panic threatened to displace the attackers from the crest. Again, Hamilton rallied his men with a show of personal courage while the Devons stormed up the ridge, putting the Boers to flight. French's cavalry pounced on the retreating Boers, doing 'great execution with their lances.'

The battle would be one of few clear-cut tactical victories by the British in the entire war. Hamilton's role was key in the victory, and this was heralded in the national press. Years later, General von Hindenburg would tell Hamilton that Elandslaagte was 'the only battle fought on orthodox lines in the whole South African campaign.'

However, Hamilton's personal courage was not rewarded. For a second time he was recommended for the Victoria Cross and the recommendation denied. Previously Hamilton had been considered too young, now he was told that as a general officer he was too senior, despite holding the substantive rank of colonel.

The early part of the South African Campaign is a litany of military ineptitude. Within days, the victors of Elandslaagte were ordered to give up their prize and make an exhausting cross-country retreat to join White's main force at Ladysmith. Shortly afterwards the Boers reoccupied Elandslaagte.

On 30 October, White launched an ill-conceived sortie from Ladysmith, resulting in high British casualties and 800 taken prisoner. The Battle of Ladysmith became known as 'Mournful Monday.' In the battle, Hamilton's brigade was to carry out the main frontal attack on Boer positions on Pepworth Hill. However, Colonel Geoffrey Grimwood's force, which had been ordered to support the attack, failed to arrive and the attack was aborted. Four hours later, White ordered his troops to 'retire as opportunity offers' and in the chaos, 'three battalions of British infantry broke and ran for the rear carrying most of the cavalry with them. Only Hamilton's brigade came away with any semblance of order.'

In the siege that followed, Hamilton commanded the largest sector of perimeter, the five-mile-long Section C. Within it was a three-mile-long southern plateau ridge known as the Platrand, with Wagon Hill on its western end and Caesar's Camp to the east. 'With seldom more than a thousand rifles to defend the position at any one time, Hamilton devised the best defence possible according to the latest precepts.' Ever assiduous, Hamilton pressed for more active defence, but his proposals for attacks on enemy lines were all refused.

On 9 November, the Boers launched a heavy attack on Caesar's Camp lasting for most of the day. Hamilton's defences held and the attackers were repulsed. A month later, at 3 a.m. on 6 January 1900, 5,000 Boers under General de Villiers assaulted Wagon Hill and simultaneously Caesar's Camp, as a further force attacked the nek in between them.

Hamilton often slept up on the plateau among his soldiers, and was close to Caesar's Camp when the attacks began. His defences were well placed, and the enemy had little idea of their composition. The 1st Manchesters with some Imperial Light Horse absorbed the initial attack. Hamilton deployed his reserves and pinned back the Boers to the crest of the ridge. The 60th Rifle Brigade came up in support and began a series of costly counterattacks, which Hamilton quickly stopped. After a lull in fighting the Boers resumed their attack. John Lee describes the resulting action: 'Shortly after noon, Hamilton was conferring with local officers at Wagon Hill about an organised counterattack when a determined rush by the Boers, led by De Villiers himself, broke into the position. Hamilton hurled himself into the thick of the fighting, pistol in hand, and in the ensuing melee the Boers were routed, and De Villiers was killed.'

Hamilton had fought off the only major assault made on the garrison and in doing so had increased his stock with White: 'Johnny Hamilton was in command when the principal attack was made and did valuable service, and I have reported on him in the highest terms.'

Shortly after the relief of Ladysmith, Lord Roberts, who had recently been given supreme command in South Africa, asked Hamilton to choose either an infantry brigade or to take charge of Robert's lines of communications. Hamilton opted to command the brigade, and in the event was given a newly created, 10,000 strong division of infantry and mounted infantry. On 30 April 1900, after three weeks training and organising his troops, Hamilton advanced to clear Boer entrenchments at Houtnek and at Thaba mountain. On 1 May, Roberts' main force began its general advance, and Hamilton's command was increased to include a cavalry brigade, a mounted infantry brigade, two infantry brigades and thirty-eight guns.

'Colonel Hamilton was doing the work of a lieutenant-general,' reported the correspondent of the *Morning Post,* Winston Churchill.

Churchill, an astute judge of character and talent, later penned this picture of the soldier in his book *Ian Hamilton's March*: 'His mind is built upon a big scale, being broad and strong and capable of thinking in army corps and if necessary, in continents, and working always with serene smoothness undisturbed alike by responsibility or danger.'

Significantly, Churchill's opinion was supported by Hamilton's subordinates. One, the highly capable Horace Smith-Dorian, wrote of Hamilton: 'From now on I enjoyed every moment of the campaign. He was a delightful leader to follow, always definite and clear in his instructions, always ready to listen and willing to adopt suggestions, and what is more important, always ready to go for the enemy, extremely quick at seizing a tactical advantage, and always in good temper.'

Hamilton's column continued to advance, turning the enemy out of strong lines along the Zand River and taking the important town of Lindley. He forced the Boer resistance leaders Martinus Steyn and Christiaan De Wet to abandon their strong positions at Heilbron, exposing the flanks of the Boer force facing Roberts. This initiated the final stages of the advance to Pretoria.

Hamilton's force was now switched to the left. He defeated a strong Boer force at Doornkop, opening the way to Johannesburg which fell on 30 May. The advance to Pretoria resumed on 3 June, with Hamilton's force at the centre. Two days later Pretoria fell. Shortly after, Hamilton's column was key to defeating 7,000 Boers under General Botha at the Battle of Diamond Hill.

On 23 June, Hamilton fell from his horse and broke his collar bone. Unable to continue, he relinquished command. He returned to duty on 14 July, to command a division of infantry and mounted infantry, and was promoted to local lieutenant-general, and to Hamilton's delight, his pay increased to £7 per day.

From early on, Hamilton believed the war could be concluded by offering the Boers terms to allow them to return to their farms. Letters to his wife Jean confirm 'he was again fulminating against the folly of demanding unconditional surrender of all the Boer leaders.'

After the British took Middleburg on 27 July, Hamilton was ordered to secure the mountain passes in the Magaliesberg range against a Boer force operating to the British rear under General De Wet. A delay in intelligence allowed De Wet's force to elude Hamilton's troops, who managed only to harry De Wet's rear-guard.

Hamilton was ordered to re-join the main force and advance along the railway line to Komati Poort. His column arrived on the 24 September, but the Boers had fired their supply depot and fled. The fall of Komati Poort and dispersal of the main Boer forces changed the nature of the campaign, as the Boers adopted guerrilla warfare tactics.

Roberts heard from London he would succeed Lord Wolseley as Commander-in-Chief. All the main towns in both Boer Republics were now occupied. With the war all but over, Roberts handed command to Lord Kitchener on 12 December 1900. Roberts asked Hamilton to become his Military Secretary, an important post with significant influence over promotions and appointments. He agreed, but on condition that the posting was limited to two years. Any regret he felt on leaving his field command was amply compensated by the order of a KCB and substantive promotion to major-general on 12 October 1900.

In early November 1901, Hamilton's new posting was cut short when he was asked to return to South Africa as Chief of Staff to the Commander-in-Chief, Lord Kitchener. He took up the post in late November, with the local rank of lieutenant general. In addition to his new duties Hamilton remained Roberts' Military Secretary and passed back to London regular reports on officers serving in South Africa. He held nothing back in his assessments and was particularly critical of Douglas Hague. Hamilton reported he had little to say about Hague, 'because he did so little with his troops, who might as well have been in winter encampments, so reluctant was their commander to use them in action!'

Hamilton was soon running the day-to-day business of the war, 'the organising of patrols between blockhouses and the sweeps of columns, which he reduced from large-scale efforts to more concentrated work against particular local commandos.'

In April 1902, Hamilton took overall command of the thirteen columns as they tightened their grip on De La Rey's commandos. He sent four 'super columns,' composed of his best units and most trusted commanders, in a drive towards the Boers' last refuge, the Great Hart's River Valley. With several commandos ranged against him Hamilton, reading the situation perfectly, saw through a feint made by the Boers, and warned his column commanders to prepare for an attack at any moment. On 11 April, Hamilton was with Kekewitch's column near Rooiwal when hundreds of Boer horsemen charged across the veld, 'knee to knee and rank upon rank,' in what appeared a show of contempt for British marksmanship. The Boers had miscalculated. 'The charge was shattered; the leader, Potgieter, was killed; the commandos flew asunder and were pursued, losing what remained of their artillery.' Hamilton, who had been deeply involved in the first great victory of the war, Elandslaagte, had taken part in the last.

On 31 May 1902, the Boer leaders, having been promised representative government, signed a peace treaty ending the war. Hamilton had admired the 'rifles and religion' stance of the Boers and advocated they be given generous terms. Magnanimous in victory, he 'genuinely felt no malice towards his former enemies and sought only to ensure that Britain would never have to fight them again.'

Hamilton returned to England with Kitchener in July 1902, to a triumphant welcome. Kitchener had paid tribute to Hamilton's contribution a few days earlier in his final South Africa despatch: 'At much personal inconvenience, Lord Roberts lent me his Military Secretary, Sir Ian Hamilton, as my Chief of Staff. His high soldierly qualities are already well known, and his reputation does not require to be established now. I am much indebted to him for his able and constant support to me as Chief of Staff, also for the marked skill and self-reliance he showed later, when directing operations in the Western Transvaal.'[100]

His star was reaching its zenith, as John Lee describes: 'Hamilton's return to London saw him at the very height of his fame; he seemed to be going from success to success. His victories in the field were complimented by his brilliant staff work; he was in liaison with powerful figures in the Liberal Party; his ideas on policy show him to be a far-sighted thinker on military and imperial affairs. He was surely destined for high office.'

Hamilton resumed his post as Military Secretary to Roberts, and in April 1903, he was appointed as Quartermaster General of the British Army.

By the end of 1903, war between Japan, an ally of Great Britain since 1902, and Tsarist Russia appeared imminent. Hamilton's post of Quartermaster General was coming to an end. In January 1904, with no other appointments on the horizon, he took leave and sailed for Japan, hoping to secure the position of official British observer with the Japanese army.

En route he learned the post had been filled by Lieutenant-General Sir William Nicolson, with Lieutenant-Colonel Aylmer Haldane as Military Attaché. But whilst steaming to Hong Kong he received a cable offering him an appointment as representative of the Indian Army to the Japanese. He accepted the post, which came with a salary of over £3,000, and the assistance of a staff officer and an ADC.

His subsequent observations of the Japanese Army in its training, organisation and operations in Manchuria would lead him to draw important lessons for the conduct of modern battle. Although Hamilton would later alter his opinion, he was initially impressed by the Japanese

---

100 *The London Gazette*, Lord Kitchener's Despatch, 23 June 1902, published 29 July 1902, p.4835.

generals and the fighting qualities of the ordinary Japanese soldier and expressed these views in a letter to Winston Churchill in April 1904. Throughout his time with the Japanese, Hamilton kept a daily diary which provided the main reference source for his two-volume study of the war, and second military treatise, *A Staff Officer's Scrap Book*.

Hamilton returned to Britain in April 1905 to take up the post of GOC Southern Command. He remained in post for the next four years, during which time both volumes of *A Staff Officer's Scrap Book* (Vol. I in 1905 and Vol. II in 1907) were published, defining new standards for a work of this type, and becoming a worldwide success. Shortly after the second volume's publication he received promotion to full general on 24 October 1907.

While GOC Southern Command, Hamilton served on the Advisory Council for the recently formed Territorial Force, for which he became a powerful advocate. The TF's second annual camp was held on Salisbury Plain with Hamilton in overall command. 'After only a week he had them performing well in manoeuvres with his regular divisions. At a review held on Whit Monday 1909, the East Lancashire Territorial Division [with Riley among its ranks] moved with such precision that a French observer of the exercises mistook their artillery for regular soldiers.'

On 1 June 1909, Hamilton was appointed Adjutant-General to the Army and the Second Military Member of the Army Council. A first duty was to write, at the request of Lord Haldane, a defence of the volunteer principle.[101] Hamilton produced a text of a hundred pages, which Haldane prefaced with his own introduction.

Hamilton embarked that August on an overseas tour as an official observer at manoeuvres being held separately by the Russian and German armies.

In October 1910, Hamilton took over as GOC Mediterranean and was also appointed Inspector-General of Overseas Forces, for all forces of the Empire outside the United Kingdom and India. He would occupy the post for almost four years, during which time he made extensive tours of inspection throughout the Empire.

---

101 The volunteer principle advocated using the TF and Yeomanry organisations to expand Britain's land forces, rather than by the introduction of national conscription.

APPENDIX IV

Hamilton returned to England on 15 July 1914, with his appointment due to end on 1 August. He expected to be reinstated in the combined roles of Inspector-General of Overseas Forces and Inspector-General of Home Forces, but that new position was given to Sir John French. Instead, Hamilton was offered and declined the post of GOC Ireland.

On 30 July 1914, Sir John French was confirmed as C-in-C, British Expeditionary Force. Hamilton was given command of the Home Army, a demanding role which Hamilton tackled with energy and efficiency. In addition to organising home defence, he had to deal with the consequences of Kitchener's sudden appeal for 100,000 volunteers, and with the urgent mobilisation and further training of the Territorial Force.

On 12 March 1915, Hamilton describes in his *Gallipoli Diary* how he was summoned at short notice to a meeting with Kitchener, then Secretary of State for War. In a 'matter-of-fact tone,' Kitchener said, 'we are sending a military force to support the Fleet now at the Dardanelles, and you are to have Command.'

Kitchener's words took Hamilton by surprise. He had seen Kitchener daily over the preceding six months but knew nothing of the Mediterranean Expeditionary Force, let alone its deployment at the Dardanelles. Hamilton learned from Kitchener that his force was to incorporate; 30,000 Australians and New Zealanders under Lieutenant General William Birdwood, the 29th Division under Major General Aylmer Hunter-Weston, the Royal Naval Division under Major General Archibald Paris, and a French contingent of indeterminate strength under General d'Amade. In total, the force would number 80,000 men.

Kitchener told Hamilton he could not take his own staff including his Chief of Staff Ellison who was to be replaced by General Walter Braithwaite. In laying out criteria for the operation, Kitchener emphasised that the army would be subordinate to the navy, adding, 'The sailors are sure they can force the Dardanelles on their own and the whole enterprise has been framed on that basis.' He cautioned Hamilton that 'all things ear-marked for the East are looked on by powerful interests both at home and in France as having been stolen from the West.'

Hamilton accepted his assignment knowing little of the Gallipoli Peninsula, the nature of its ground or the Turkish defenders he faced. It was soon clear that little planning or preparation had been made for the campaign, and there was scant intelligence to inform the task. As Hamilton recalled, 'Braithwaite set to work in the Intelligence Branch at once. But beyond the ordinary textbooks those pigeonholes were drawn blank. The Dardanelles and Bosphorus might be in the moon for all the military information I have got to go upon.'

He was dispatched in haste on 13 March 1915 (Churchill had wanted Hamilton to leave a day earlier) via France to Marseille and onward by light cruiser to Tenedos. He reached Tenedos Bay on the 17th, to learn General d'Amade had also arrived. Both generals transferred to the *Queen Elizabeth* for an immediate conference with Admiral de Robeck, Admiral Wemyss and Commodore Keyes. After de Robeck had briefed Hamilton and d'Amade on the naval and military situation, he asked to see Hamilton's instructions. Braithwaite read out his chief's nebulous orders. 'When he stopped, Roger Keyes, the Commodore, inquired, "Is that all?" And when Braithwaite confessed that it was, everyone looked a little blank.' It was an inauspicious start to a campaign that would ultimately end Hamilton's distinguished military career.

His initial remit, to support naval operations, was short lived. Within a few weeks Hamilton was commanding one of the largest amphibious operations ever undertaken. What followed has been recorded in official histories and many personal accounts, including Hamilton's *Gallipoli Diary* and Alec Riley's own account of the same name.

Hamilton remained as C-in-C of the MEF until his recall on 17 October 1915. Initially scapegoated for the failed campaign, Hamilton's reputation was chiefly restored after the findings of the Dardanelles Commission were made public.

After the war, Hamilton's part in founding the British Legion, and his committed efforts to ensure that Gallipoli veterans received the recognition they deserved, further enhanced his reputation. He also ensured each campaign veteran received the 1914–15 Star.

He remained popular with those who had served under him and in the country as a whole and was asked to unveil hundreds of war memorials.

Hamilton's attitude towards his former enemies was pragmatic and prescient. He cautioned against the 'hate propaganda of war' and argued for a generous peace towards the Germans and their acceptance into the League of Nations. Even before the war had ended, Hamilton was developing these arguments in a small book entitled *The Millennium* which he published in 1919. John Lee describes how Hamilton warned that 'great wars invariably led to bad peace settlements,' and 'poured scorn on capitalist combines, likening them to vampires battening on the people for their own selfish ends.'

The years immediately after the war were intensely busy for Hamilton. As well as his work with the British Legion, he championed other ex-servicemen's causes, inaugurated war memorials, and spoke at Old Comrades Association meetings. Hamilton often used these opportunities to voice progressive opinions. On one occasion, while unveiling a memorial in 1922, he vented his frustration at France's attitude towards Germany: 'It is from the contempt and harshness of the Victor that the spirit of revenge is bred in the defeated as surely as dirt breeds disease.'

He was busy with his writing. In 1920, he published *Gallipoli Diary*, his two-part memoir of the campaign. Other works at that time included *The Soul and Body of an Army* in 1921, *The Friends of England: Lectures to Members of the British Legion* in 1923, and a collection of his poetry *Now and Then* in 1926. Such was Hamilton's literary reputation that in 1929 he received an advance copy of the English translation of Erich Maria Remarque's *All Quiet on the Western Front* from the book's publisher G.P. Putnam. This opened an exchange of letters between the two authors.

In 1928, Hamilton became a founding member and vice-president of the Anglo-German Association, an organisation created to promote closer ties between the former enemies. He made several visits to Germany during the early 1930s, driven by his commitment to reconciliation. This mission distracted him from the brutality of the Nazi regime. Hamilton met Rudolf Hess and other party officials in 1934. Later, in an address to the Yorkshire West Riding British Legion, he referred to Hess as 'a very fine young fellow ... far more than the mere mouthpiece of Herr Hitler.'

Despite his unremitting schedule, Hamilton still responded to pleas for help and advice from veterans.

Alec Riley first wrote to Hamilton in December 1923. Hamilton responded with a thoughtful letter, and a signed photograph of himself. An exchange of friendly, informal correspondence continued for almost a decade. Rank and social status separated the two men and made this a profoundly significant exchange, revealing much about Hamilton's fairness and generosity.

In a letter dated 15 December 1923, Riley described his own service at Gallipoli, and how he was in the honour guard when Hamilton unveiled the South African War Memorial in Manchester in 1908. With the letter were seven photographs Riley had taken at Gallipoli during the campaign. In his reply, written two days later, Hamilton thanked him for the 'interesting photographs,' and chided him, tongue in cheek. 'I suspect you were defying my regulations when you snapped them!'

Years later, in 1931 or early 1932, Riley sent Hamilton a copy of what is now a lost manuscript 'Return to Cape Helles', and fifteen photographs he had taken in May and June of 1930, during one of his independent visits to Gallipoli. Riley's purpose was to ask Hamilton to write an introduction to his book. Hamilton agreed and sent Riley his proposed introduction. An exchange of letters followed in April 1932, with Riley reporting on publishers' rejections and Hamilton replying with words of consolation and encouragement: 'Anyway don't lose hope about it and keep on trying. Let me hear from you once in a blue moon.'

Riley wrote again on 27 October 1932, with news of further rejections, and asking (perhaps at the request of his literary agents) for certain words in Hamilton's introduction to be altered. Hamilton made the changes, only to have Riley write back on 29 October, suggesting further alterations. It is a measure of Hamilton that he complied, but his patience was wearing thin. His letter of 31 October begins: 'You must do as you wish in these matters.' Riley returned the final revised draft for Hamilton's approval and apologised for his 'impertinence.' It is uncertain if Hamilton replied and it is possible that the chain of correspondence ended there.

In 1938, as part of the British Legion's efforts to promote peace between the former enemies, the 85 years old Hamilton led a party of forty of its members on a wreath laying visit to Germany. At each memorial he delivered reconciliatory speeches in fluent German, saying that 'if the world was run by old soldiers instead of autocrats and bureaucrats there would be no more wars.' A few days later, when Hamilton was in Berlin, John Lee describes a surprise invitation: 'He was suddenly whisked off by air to Munich to lunch with that "fine young fellow," Rudolf Hess. Within a few hours he was taking tea with

Adolf Hitler at Berchtesgaden ... Hitler was said to be awe-struck at being in the presence of a man who had learned his German amongst the heroes of 1871.'

The two men spoke privately for ninety minutes, with Hitler launching a 'charm offensive' towards the old general. Hamilton recognized this for what it was, but later took Germany's side over 'Czech provocations.'

Through the lens of history, Hamilton's engagement with Nazis is problematic. Considered against his sincerely held pacifist beliefs (born of personal experience of brutal conflicts) Hamilton's actions demonstrate his desperate compulsion to prevent another world war. As his biographer John Lee explains: 'Let us just remember that, as Hitler came to power in 1933, Hamilton was eighty years old and had spent nearly fifteen years unveiling monuments to the dead, giving speeches to their memory and being bombarded with letters by old servicemen begging, pleading for help as they sank into poverty in "the land fit for heroes." These letters are painful to read even today and there really were a great many of them. Even a certain naivety might be forgiven him.'

Hamilton continued to write. In 1939, his first autobiographical work, *When I was a Boy*, was published. When his wife Jean died in early 1941, he dedicated a memoir to her that was printed privately. The second part of his autobiography, *Listening for the Drums*, was published in 1944. His final work, *The Commander*, was edited by Anthony Farrar-Hockley and published posthumously in 1957.

Although Hamilton and his wife had no children by birth, they fostered then adopted two children in 1919, Harry and Rosalind. Their adopted son Harry (Knight) was killed in action in 1941 while an officer in the Scots Guards in North Africa.

Hamilton died in London on 12 October 1947. His friend Churchill described him as a 'brilliant and chivalrous man' who had served his country well. Ten years after his death the nation recognised his service with a memorial in St Paul's Cathedral.

APPENDIX V

East Lancashire (42nd) Division Field State at embarkation Southampton, 10 September 1914

Unit strengths, recruiting centres and names of officers have been compiled using the divisional history, the history of the divisional engineers, Harts Army Lists, and medal index lists and cards. The numerical designations for the division and infantry brigades, shown in brackets, are given for reference only and did not apply until 25 May 1915. The main recruiting centres for each unit are shown in square brackets.

Divisional Headquarters

25 officers and 128 other ranks.
National Buildings, St. Mary's Parsonage, Manchester.

GOC, Major General William Douglas, CB, DSO

Captain H.T. Cawley, MP, ADC

Captain A.W. Tufnell, GSO (2nd Grade)

Captain R.S. Allen, DAA & QMG

Colonel J. Bentley-Mann, ADMS

Lieutenant Colonel G.T. Rawnsley, DADMS

Major E. Sergeant, Sanitary Officer

Cavalry

6 officers and 132 other ranks.

'A' Squadron [Oldham and Rochdale], Duke of Lancaster's Own Yeomanry

Divisional Artillery

55 officers and 1,289 other ranks.

1/1st East Lancs Brigade RFA (Headquarters: 50 King St, Blackburn)

4th Lancs Battery [Blackburn]

5th Lancs Battery [Church] – Major J.C. Browning

6th Lancs Battery [Burnley]

Ammunition column [Blackburn]

1/3rd East Lancs (Bolton) Brigade RFA (Headquarters: Bolton)

18th Lancs Battery [Bolton]

19th Lancs Battery [Bolton]

20th Lancs Battery [Bolton]

3rd Ammunition Column [Bolton]

Divisional Engineers

19 officers and 568 other ranks. Headquarters: Old Trafford.

Lieutenant Colonel C.E. Newton, CRE

1/1st East Lancs Field Company – Major J.H. Mousley

1/2nd East Lancs Field Company – Major L.F. Wells

Divisional Signal Company – Major A.W. Lawford

Lancashire Fusiliers (125th) Infantry Brigade

120 officers and 3,962 other ranks.

> Brigade Commander – Colonel H.C. Frith, CB
> Brigade Major – Brevet Major A.J. Allardyce
>
> > 1/5th Bn, Lancashire Fusiliers [Bury]
> > – Lieutenant Colonel J. Isherwood, VD
> >
> > 1/6th Bn, Lancashire Fusiliers [Rochdale]
> > – Lieutenant Colonel Lord Rochdale
> >
> > 1/7th Bn, Lancashire Fusiliers [Salford]
> > – Lieutenant Colonel A.F. Maclure, TD
> >
> > 1/8th Bn, Lancashire Fusiliers [Salford]
> > – Lieutenant Colonel J.A. Fallows, TD

East Lancashire (126th) Infantry Brigade

120 officers and 3,978 other ranks (correct to within one or two officers and a few tens of other ranks).

> Brigade Commander – Colonel D.G. Prendergast, CMG
> Brigade Major – Major C.J. Hickie
>
> > 1/4th Bn, East Lancs Regiment [Blackburn]
> > – Lieutenant Colonel F.D. Robinson, VD
> >
> > 1/5th Bn, East Lancs Regiment [Burnley]
> > – Lieutenant Colonel J. C. Hoyle
> >
> > 1/9th Bn, Manchester Regiment [Ashton under Lyne]
> > – Lieutenant Colonel D.H. Wade
> >
> > 1/10th Bn, Manchester Regiment [Oldham]
> > – Lieutenant Colonel J.B. Rye, VD

Manchester (127th) Infantry Brigade

120 officers and 3,978 other ranks (correct to within one or two officers and a few tens of other ranks).

> Brigade Commander – Colonel Noel Lee, VD
> Brigade Major – Major H.L. Knight
>
>> 1/5th Bn, Manchester Regiment [Wigan]
>> – Lieutenant Colonel H.C. Darlington
>>
>> 1/6th Bn, Manchester Regiment [Stretford]
>> – Lieutenant Colonel G.G.P. Heywood
>>
>> 1/7th Bn, Manchester Regiment [Manchester city centre]
>> – Lieutenant Colonel H.F. Gresham, TD
>>
>> 1/8th Bn, Manchester Regiment [Ardwick]
>> – Lieutenant Colonel W.G. Heys, TD

East Lancashire Divisional Train ASC

16 officers and 276 other ranks.
Headquarters: Hulme Barracks, Manchester.

> Lieutenant Colonel J.G. Needham
>
>> No. 1 (Headquarters) Company – Major A. England
>>
>> No. 2 (Lancs Fusiliers) Company – Captain A. Gillibrand
>>
>> No. 3 (East Lancs) Company – Captain H.M. Kenyon
>>
>> No. 4 (Manchester) Company – Captain F. Howard

East Lancashire Royal Army Medical Corps

30 officers and 655 other ranks.

Headquarters: Upper Chorlton Road, Manchester.

1/1st Field Ambulance
– Lieutenant Colonel H.G. Parker

A and B Section [Manchester]

C Section [Bolton]

1/2nd Field Ambulance
– Lieutenant Colonel W.B. Pritchard / Major H.W. Pritchard

A and B Section [Manchester]

C Section [Burnley]

1/3rd Field Ambulance
– Lieutenant Colonel W.M. Steinthal

A and B Section [Manchester]

C Section [Bury]

Total strength

511 officers and 14,966 other ranks.

ABBREVIATIONS AND ACRONYMS

A/	Acting
ADC	Aide-de-camp
AF	Army Form
AIF	Australian Imperial Force
ASC	Army Service Corps
AZ	Signal station at Abu Zabal
BMR	Battalion Manchester Regiment
Bn	Battalion
C-in-C	Commander-in-Chief
CB	Companion of the Order of the Bath
CMG	Companion of the Order of St Michael and St George
CO	Commanding Officer
Coy	Company
CQMS	Company Quartermaster Sergeant
CRE	Commander Royal Engineers
CSM	Company Sergeant Major
CVO	Commander of the Royal Victorian Order
DCM	Distinguished Conduct Medal
DR	Despatch Rider
DSO	Distinguished Service Order
Dvr	Driver
GA	Signal station on Gebel Ahmar
GCB	Knight Grand Cross of the Order of the Bath

GCMG	Knight Grand Cross of the Order of St Michael and St George
GHQ	General Headquarters
GN	Signal station at Polygon Barracks
GOC	General Officer Commanding
GSM	General Service Medal
GSO1	General Staff Officer (Grade 1)
HQ	Headquarters
HM	His Majesty's
HMT	His Majesty's Transport
HRH	His Royal Highness
IWM	Imperial War Museum
KCB	Knight Commander of the Bath
KCMG	Knight Commander of the Order of St Michael and St George
KIA	Killed in action
LF	Lancashire Fusiliers
LG	*London Gazette*
MEF	Mediterranean Expeditionary Force
MC	Military Cross
MO	Medical Officer
NCO	Non-Commissioned Officer
OBE	Order of the British Empire
OC	Officer Commanding
OHMS	On His Majesty's Service
Pnr	Pioneer
Pte	Private
QM	Quartermaster
RAMC	Royal Army Medical Corps
RE	Royal Engineers
Regt	Regiment
RFA	Royal Field Artillery

RMC	Royal Military College Sandhurst
Spr	Sapper
TA	Territorial Army
TD	Territorial Decoration
TF	Territorial Force
VC	Victoria Cross
VD	Volunteer Officers' Decoration
WOII	Warrant Officer Second Class

BIBLIOGRAPHY

Archival sources

Imperial War Museum, 'Private Papers of A Riley', Documents.14130

—, battlefield relics, EPH 6758-84, EPH 6786-99, EPH 6808-18, EPH 6820-25, EPH 6828-41, EPH 6849, EPH 6856, EPH 6858, EPH 6860-62, EPH 6864-77, EPH 6891, EPH 6913

—, photographs, Q 81419-62

Liddell Hart Military Archives, King's College London, HAMILTON, Gen Sir Ian Standish Monteith (1853-1947), GB0099 KCLMA Hamilton, 14/7/6, 15/5/17, 18/22

Published sources

'The Silent Nullahs of Gallipoli', *Twenty Years After: The Battlefields of 1914-18, Then and Now*, 1936-38, pp. 1224-1235

A History of the East Lancashire Royal Engineers / Compiled by Members of the Corps (London: Country Life, 1921)

Aspinall-Oglander, C.F., and Archibald F. Becke, eds., *Military Operations, Gallipoli, History of the Great War Based on Official Documents / by Direction of the Historical Section, Committee on Imperial Defence* (London: William Heinemann, 1929-1932)

Behrend, Arthur, *Make Me a Soldier: A Platoon Commander in Gallipoli* (London: Eyre & Spottiswoode, 1961)

Best, Kenneth, and Gavin Roynon, *A Chaplain at Gallipoli: The Great War Diaries of Kenneth Best* (London: Simon & Schuster, 2011)

Bigwood, George, *The Lancashire Fighting Territorials (in Gallipoli)* (London: 'Country Life' & George Newnes, 1916)

Bonner, Robert, *Volunteer Infantry of Ashton-under-Lyne: Including the Biography of William Thomas Forshaw VC* (Knutsford, Cheshire: Fleur de Lys Publishers, 2005)

Bonner, Robert (ed.), *Great Gable to Gallipoli – The Diary of Lieutenant Colonel Claude S Worthington DSO, 5 October 1914 – 25 September 1916. 6th Battalion The Manchester Regiment* (Knutsford, Cheshire: Fleur de Lys Publishers, 2004)

Campbell, Captain G.L., *The Manchesters* (London: Picture Advertising Co. Ltd, 1916)

Cherry, Niall, *I Shall Not Find His Equal: The Life of Brigadier-General Noel Lee, The Manchester Regiment* (Knutsford, Cheshire: Fleur de Lys Publishing, 2001)

Darlington, Henry, *Letters from Helles* (London: Longmans, Green and Co., 1936)

Gibbon, Frederick P., *The 42nd (East Lancashire) Division: 1914–1918* (London: Country Life, 1920)

Hamilton, General Sir Ian, *Gallipoli Diary* (London: E. Arnold, 1920)

—, *When I was a Boy* (London: Faber and Faber, 1939)

—, *Listening for the Drums* (London: Faber and Faber, 1944)

—, ed. Anthony Farrar-Hockley, *The Commander* (London: Hollis and Carter, 1957)

Hartley, John, *6th Battalion, the Manchester Regiment in the Great War: Not a Rotter in the Lot* (Barnsley: Pen & Sword Military, 2010)

Hurst, Gerald B., *With Manchesters in the East* (Manchester: The University Press, 1918)

Lee, John, *A Soldier's Life: General Sir Ian Hamilton 1853–1947* (London: Macmillan, 2000)

Purdy, Martin, and Ian Dawson, *The Gallipoli Oak* (Ramsbottom, Lancashire: Moonraker Publishing, 2013)

Sheffy, Yigal, *British Military Intelligence in the Palestine Campaign 1914–1918* (Oxfordshire: Routledge, 2014)

Watkins, Charles, *Lost Endeavour* (Eldenbridge, Kent: Promotion House, 1970)

Westlake, Ray, *The Territorials 1908–1914, A Guide for Military and Family Historians* (Barnsley, Yorkshire: Pen & Sword Books, 2011)

Image sources

Front cover: Battalion signallers, August 1914, from John Hartley, *6th Battalion, the Manchester Regiment in the Great War*; Sunset on the river Nile from Kasr El-Nil Barracks by CQMS 2755 Frank Leonard Edmonds, Camel Transport Corps, AIF, attached to Capt. Frank Hurley, official war photographer. Photo probably taken 1917–1918. Mitchell Library, State Library of New South Wales, PXB 232.

Back cover: Photograph from an album compiled by an unnamed soldier in the 6th Manchesters, 42nd (East Lancashire) Division. Tameside Local Studies and Archives Centre, Manchester Regiment Archive, MR4/23/102.

Figures 1, 2, 3, 6 and 72: Images from the editors' personal collections.

Figures 7, 9, 18, 38, 57 and 60: Photographs from an album compiled by L/Cpl 953 (later Sergt 444050) E.W. Robert Harrison, Divisional Signal Company, 42nd (East Lancashire) Division. Stephen Chambers collection.

Figures 8 and 26: Photographs from an album compiled by Pte George Oliver Harrison, 6th Manchesters, 42nd (East Lancashire) Division. Tameside Local Studies and Archives Centre, Manchester Regiment Archive, MR2/17/52.

Figures 10, 12, 25, 37, 42, 43, 47, 48, 50, 54 and 64: Photographs from an album compiled by an unnamed soldier in the 6th Manchesters, 42nd (East Lancashire) Division. Tameside Local Studies and Archives Centre, Manchester Regiment Archive, MR4/23/102.

Figures 11, 29, 30, 40 and 49: Photographs from an album compiled by Capt. (later Major) John Murray Rose, 1st New Zealand Expeditionary Force, who served at Gallipoli with the Wellington Infantry Battalion as commander of the machine gun section. Museum of New Zealand, Te Papa Tongarewa, AL.000563.

Figures 13, 14, 17, 27, 28, 31 and 68: Photographs taken 1914–1915 by Second Lieut. John Bolton or Capt. H. Hargreaves Bolton, both 1/5th Bn, East Lancashire Regt, and a studio portrait of John Bolton (fig. 68) taken in Egypt 1914–1915. The Bolton Archive. View online at The Gallipoli Association website.

Figures 15, 16, 19, 23, 24, 33, 35, 36, 39 and 41: Photographs taken 1915–1916 by Capt. William Saunderson Cooper who served with the Wellington Infantry Battalion and New Zealand (Maori) Pioneer Battalion. Museum of New Zealand, Te Papa Tongarewa.

Figure 20. 'Imperial wireless communications', *Modern Wireless*, vol. 1, no. 2, March 1923.

Figures 21, 22 and 58. Photographs by L/Cpl 4458 Albert William Savage, No. 3 Australian General Hospital, AIF, compiled in an album titled 'Photographs of the Third Australian General Hospital at Lemnos, Egypt & Brighton (Eng.)' Egypt photos probably taken 1916. Mitchell Library, State Library of New South Wales, PXE 698.

Figure 32. Photograph by CQMS 2755 Frank Leonard Edmonds, Camel Transport Corps, AIF, attached to Capt. Frank Hurley, official war photographer. Photos probably taken 1917–1918. Mitchell Library, State Library of New South Wales, PXB 232.

Figure 34. Photograph taken circa 1917 by Lieut. John Frederick Clifford Hunt, East Yorkshire Regt. The British Museum, Af,A52.81.

Figures 44 and 45. Photographs from an album compiled by Spr 1393 (later Lieut.) Thomas Gerald George Fahey, 12th Light Horse (later 2nd Light Horse Signals Troop), AIF. Photos taken between 1916 and 1918. The University of Newcastle (Australia), Living Histories, Robinson Family Collection.

Figure 46. Photograph from an album titled 'Souvenir of Sinai & Palestine, 1916–1917' and named to 'Trp. J. Ellis 7th L.H.'. National Library of Australia.

Figures 51, 52 and 53. Photographs from the E.W. Searle collection of photographs. National Library of Australia.

Figures 55 and 56. Photographs taken 1917–1918 by Capt. Frank Hurley, official photographer, AIF, which were exhibited in Sydney in early 1919. Mitchell Library, State Library of New South Wales, PXD 31/120–128.

Figure 59. Photograph taken by Pte 577 Henry Charles Marshall, 1st Bn, AIF, compiled in an album titled 'Kensington to Cairo and from Cairo to Gallipoli : album of photographs, 1914–1915'. Pte Marshall died 10 June 1915 of wounds received in action at Gallipoli, and the album and photos were among the effects returned to his family. Mitchell Library, State Library of New South Wales, PXA 1861.

Figure 61. Photograph attributed to Bugler J.F. Smith, 7th Light Horse, AIF. Mitchell Library, State Library of New South Wales, PXB 242.

Figures 62 and 63. Photographs from an album compiled by John Lindsay Ross, 27th Bn, AIF, and titled 'With the Twenty-Seventh Battalion Australian Imperial Force 1915–1919'. State Library of Victoria, 2647811.

Figure 65. Photograph attributed to 'Kerboul', possibly a Frenchman aboard the hospital ship *Duguay-Trouin*. Ministère de la Culture, Médiathèque du patrimoine et de la photographie, APOR020568.

Figure 66: Photograph sent by Alec Riley to Sir Ian Hamilton. Liddell Hart Military Archives, King's College London, 18/22.

Figures 67 and 69. Photographs from the collection of Capt. William Wynne, 6th and 2nd battalions, Manchester Regt. Tameside Local Studies and Archives Centre, Manchester Regiment Archive, MR4/17/263/4.

Figure 70. Portrait of Major E.F. Pilkington. Family collection.

Figure 71. Photograph by Bill Sellars, November 2021.

ACKNOWLEDGEMENTS

Mike and Bern thank Peter Hart, Stephen Chambers, Jim Grundy, Michael Robson, Warren Smith and The Gallipoli Association for their help publicising *Gallipoli Diary 1915*. In preparing Riley's diaries for print, the editors have benefited greatly from the contributions and advice of Bill Sellars, Norma Wallworth and R.W. Filla. Many of the soldiers' photographs that illustrate this account have been preserved and made available to modern-day researchers through the diligence of archivists and librarians whose work cannot be valued highly enough. The help and advice given by the staff at Tameside Local Studies Library, holders of the Manchester Regiment Archive, is especially appreciated. Stephen Chambers, John Hartley and the Bolton family were generous in permitting us to reproduce photographs from their private collections. Last but definitely not least, Mike and Bern would like to thank their respective spouses: Viv Lacey for her assistance with the introduction and biographies and Cheryl Ward for creating the logo and artwork for the book's cover, and both for their continued toleration of two Gallipoli Campaign obsessives.

INDEX

42nd (East Lancashire) Division ix, 18, 118, 130–131, 208, 215–219
Divisional Headquarters 215
Cavalry 216
Divisional Artillery 216
Divisional Engineers 216
Divisional Signal Company 17, 18, 39, 86, 105, 117, *118*, 125
   No. 4 Section ix, 15, 36, 39, 46–47, 64, 95
Lancashire Fusiliers (125th) Infantry Brigade 125, 217
   1/6th Lancs Fus 18, 23, 28
   1/7th Lancs Fus 18, 23, 28
East Lancashire (126th) Infantry Brigade 217
   1/5th East Lancs Regt *41*, 62, 70
   1/9th Manchesters 32, 57
Manchester (127th) Infantry Brigade 123, 218
   1/6th Manchesters vii, 14, *93*, 95, 96, *99*, 101, 113, 123, 140
   1/7th Manchesters 95
   1/8th Manchesters 15
East Lancashire Divisional Train ASC 218
East Lancashire Royal Army Medical Corps 219

A

Abbassia xi, 1, 35, *40*, 45, 70, 79, 105, 111, 112, 113, 124
Abe/Abie. *See* Williams, Spr R.
Abercrombie, Gen., monument 101
Ablitt, 2/Lt W.J. *46*
Aboukir *100*, 101–102, *102*
Abu Zabal 1, 52–53, 55–68, *56*
Aldous, Lieut. F.C. *140*
Alexandria 1, 32–33, 93–102, 125
Allen, Pte C. 23, 26
American sailors 101
Andrews 8
Arabic words 33, 35, 42, 43, 48, 56, 58, 62, 65, 67, 68, 75, 77, 82, 88, 107
Aragon, HMT 24, 26, 32
Ardwick Drill Hall 10
Ardwick Green 15
Army Form E.624 15, *20–21*
Ataba el-Khadra 45, 48, 107
Atlantian, HMT 24, 26
Australian soldiers 50, 52, 101, 119, 125
Avon, HMT 24, 26

B

Baron, 2/Lt J. *41*
Barrage du Nil *114*, 114–115
Bazley, Capt. W.N. *140*

Bedouin 65, 91
bicycles viii, 6, 8, 9, 13, 14, 17, 33, 43, 47, 52, 79, 87, 95, 111
Blatherwick, Lieut. F.M. *140*
Blatherwick, Lieut. T. *140*
Bolton, 2/Lt J. 46, 62, *76*, 141–143, *142*
Bolton, Capt. D.C. *140*
Bolton, Capt. H.H. *76*
Bombardier Wells 9
Bridge, Pte J. 32
Bristol Hotel *80*, 81
Broad, Lieut. G.L. 17, 39, 87, 144–145
Brown, Gurkha Rifles *46*
Bury 1, 17

C

Cairo Museum 73, 75
Cairo railway station *120*, 122
cakes 10, 45, 81
Caledonian, HMT 24, 26
Californian, HMT 24, 26
Campbell, Sgt J.E. 39, 86, 87, 119, 145–146
canteens 27, 28, 36, 39, 40, 42, 48, 56, 57, 65, 67, 81, 86, 119
Catacombs of Kom-el-Shukafa 97
Challinor, Spr J.W. 65
Chesham Camp 1, 17
Chevington, ammunition boat 24, 26, 30
church parades 14, *70*, 71, 87, 96
cinemas 75–76, 117
Citadel 35, 61, *77*, 79, 85
City of Westminster Yeomanry 24
Claude. *See* Hague, Pnr E.H.
Coates, Col. 111
Collins, Capt. C.H.G. 15–16
Coptic quarter 82–83
Corsican, HMT 24, 26

D

Davies, Capt. O. St L. *140*
Dead City 79

Dean, Dvr W. 72, 146–147
Delta 33, 35
Derfflinger, SS 126
Deseado, HMT 24, 26
Donald, 2/Lt A.J.I. *140*
Douglas, Maj. Gen. Sir W. 57, 113, 123, 147–149

E

Edgar, Capt. R.A. *140*
Egyptian cavalry 42
El-Azhar 107
El-Bedreshein 88, 91
El Marg 53, 55
English Winter Hotel 123
Ezbekiyeh Gardens 81, 119

F

Fallowfield 6
ferries. *See* rivercraft
Ferry Post, Ismailia 120, *121*
field telephones 105, 111
Fish market. *See* Waz'a
Flatters 32
Frith, Brig. Gen. H.C. 18, 31, 149–150
funerals 31, 32, 71, 117

G

Gallipoli ix–xi, 1, 209–210
gamoose 59, *60*, 62, 68, 88
Garden of Antoniadis 95
Gebel Ahmar 52, 72, 117
gharry *41*, 43, 81
Gibraltar 29–30
Grantully Castle, HMT 24, 26

H

Hague, Pnr E.H. 'Claude' 16, 27, 58, 64, 150–151
Hales, Cpl 67
Halliwell, 2/Lt W.A. 125

236

Hamilton, Gen. Sir I. vii, x, 118, 130, 133, *186*, 187–213
Harbour, Dvr R. 88, 151–152
Harrison, RAMC 111
Harrop, Sgt J.C. 68, 152–153
hawkers. *See* vendors
Haworth, Pnr J. 16, 58, 153
headquarters, 3 Stretford Road 5–10
Heliopolis 43, 77, 79, 83, *84*, 111
helios 53, 61, 72, 101, 111
Hell-faced Bill 25
Helouan 122–124
Herts Yeomanry 24
Heywood, 2/Lt H.C.L. *140*
Heywood, Lt. Col. G.G.P. 10, 123, *140*, 154–155, *162*
Hocking, Gurkha Rifles 46
Holberton, Capt. P.V. 10, 123, *140*, 155–156
Holden, Lieut. N.V. 46
Hollingworth Camp 1, *12*, 13–17
Holt, Capt. J. *140*
Hopkinson, Pte H. 7, 112, 123, 157
Hossack, Pnr E.F. *49*, 153
Hoyle, 2/Lt H.K. 46
Humphries 27

I

Imperial Service Badge 6, *7*, 28
Indian soldiers 24, 26, 32, 120–121
Ionian, HMT 24, 26, 126
Isherwood, Margaret 9, 16, 139
Ismailia 72, 120
Ismailia Canal 52, 55

J

Jackson, Capt. S.F. *140*
James, Lieut. G.S. or F.A. 46
Joe. *See* Royle, Sgt G.

K

Kait Bey *94*, 96

Kasr el-Nil 57, *74*, 75, 79
Kelly, Lieut. W. 46
Kerby, Rev. E.T. 96, 157–159
Kessler, Capt. E. *140*
khaki drill 6, 15, 18, 33, 40, 55, 101
khamâsîn 115, 120
Khan el-Khaleli 107–108
Khedivial 58, 64
Killick, Lieut. R. *140*
Knight, Maj. H.L. 15–16, 159–160

L

Lake Timsah 120, 122
Lawford, Maj. A.N. 31, 39, 64, 65, 71–72, 87, 117, 119, 160–161, 163
Lee, Brig. Gen. N. 10, 15, 123, *140*, *162*, 163–164
Lillie, 2/Lt W.H. 46, 57
limelight 52, 64–65
locusts 108, 111
Lomas, Pte 113

M

M. *See* Isherwood, Margaret
Maadi 122
Mahmoudiyah Canal 95
Mallalieu, Spr J. 15, 165
Marconi company 55, 56, 61, 62, 64, 65, 68
Mataria 83, *84*
Maxwell, Gen. Sir J. 44, 64, 118
M Block 124
Memphis 88–91
Mesaba, HMT 24, 26
Midan el-Khazindar 81
Middleton, 2/Lt A.C. 46
military police barracks 82, 110
  See also Red Caps
Minerva, HMS 24, 26, 32
mobilization 1, 6, 8, 10
Mokattam Hills 35, *77*, 85, 112
Molesworth, 2/Lt W.N. 46, *140*

Moslem festivals 72, 120
mosques 35, 82, *106*, 107
  Giyushi Mosque 85
  Mosque of Amru 82
  Mosque of Mahmud Pasha 109
  Mosque of Mohamet Ali 35, 61, 77
  Mosque of Rifaiyeh 107, *109*
  Sultan Hassan Mosque 107, *109*
Museum of Arab Art 85
Music and musicians 62-63, *78*, 79. *See also* songs
Mustafa Barracks 93, 95, 99, 101

N

native police 45
Netley, Royal Victoria Hospital 11, 132
Neuralia, HMT 24, 26
newspapers 6, 39, 42, 58, 75, 108, 116, 117
  Reuters' news 39
Newton, Lieut. R.S. 5, 39, 53, 55, 63, 71-72, 87, 166-167
New Zealand soldiers 52, *74*, *90*, 101, 119
Nick. *See* Robinson, Lieut. N.
Nileometer 83
Noble, Pnr G.R. 6, 28, 72, 86-87, 167-168
Norris, Capt. A.H. *140*
Norseman, HMT 24, 26
North Carolina, USS 33, 101
Nuttall, CSM R.H. 39, 168-169
Nuzha Garden *94*, 95

O

Ocean, HMS 24, 26, 30
Old Cairo *110*
Ormesher, Sgt C. 7, 31, 57, 64, 112, 113, 123, 169-170
ostrich farm 83

P

pay 6, 10, 63, 99, 105-106, 125
Pearson, Dvr E. 64, 170-171
piastres 40, 42, 65, 71, 72, 81, 86, 108, 124, 125
Pilk. *See* Pilkington, Capt. E.F.
Pilkington, Capt. E.F. 5, 6, 7, 9-10, 13, 15, 16, *172*, 173
Pilkington, Capt. H.B. *140*
Pilkington. Maj. C.R. *140*
Pindar 64
Plymouth 4, 24
Polygon Barracks 39-40, 42-43, *43*, 71-72, 222
Pompey's Column 97
Pompey's Pillar *97*
Pont Limoun Station 53, 65
Poole, Pte A. 16, 17, 64, 174-175
Pyramids of Gizeh 35, 48-50, *51*, 52

Q

Quibell, J.E. 73

R

Ramleh *98*, 99
Red Blind Street. *See* Wagh el-Birket
Red Caps 82, 119 *See also* military police barracks
Ridings, Pte S. 7, 27, 177-178
Ridings, Spr C.W. 23, 27, 83, 85, 176-177
Riley, 2/Cpl A. vii-xii, *128*, 129-136, 187, 208, 211-212
rivercraft 34, 55, 68, *74*, 75, 120
Robinson, Capt. C. *41*
Robinson, Lieut. G.N. 39, 58, 87, 178-179
Rochdale 1, 13, 14, 18, 216-217
Rosthwaite 6, 7, 129, 132, 139
route march 72, 118, 122-124
Royle, Sgt G. 'Joe' 6, 7, 9, 13, 63, 86, 179-180

S

sakiehs 35, 58, *59, 60*, 62, 63, 67, 83
Saturnia, HMT 18, 22, 23–33, *24, 30*
schools 67, 114
Severn Tunnel 3
shadoofs 35, *60*, 63, 66, 67, 89
Sharia Kamel 81, 119
Shepheard's Hotel *80*, 81
signalling viii, 8, 10, 14, 47, 64–65, 79, 105, 111–112. *See also* field telephones, helios, limelight, telescopes
signal stations 79
  Abdin Barracks 79
  AZ 52, *56*, 57, 58, 64
  British Agency 79
  Citadel 79
  Egyptian State Telegraphs 79
  Flagstaff Hill 79
  GA 52, 58, 62, 64, 65, 67, 72
  GN 52, 72
  Kasr el-Nil Barracks 79
  Military Police Station 79
  Police and Fire station 79
  Telephone Exchange 79
Simpson, 2/Lt I.L. 46
Soldiers' Home 39
songs 5, 17, 26, 47, 62–63, 67, 86–88, 113. *See also* music and musicians
Southampton 1, 17, 18, 23, 132, 135
Sphinx 50, *51*, 52
Sphinx of Memphis 88, *89*
Step Pyramid *90*, 91
Suez Canal ix, xi, 55, 64, 72, 120, 135
Suez Road 46, 79, 105, 111, 124
  Second Water Tower 79
  Third Tower 111

T

tarbouche 82
Taylor, Lieut. A.C.B. *140*

telescopes 53, 61
Tennessee, USS 101
tennis court *56*, 62–63
Territorial Force vii–viii, 1, *20, 21*, 208
Thomas, Pte R. 57, 181
Thomson, Lieut. A.D. *140*
Thornber, 2/Lt J. *41*
Tim. *See* Williamson, Capt. C.H.
tombs 35, 49–50, 61, 62, 67, 73, 75, 77, 79, 82, 88–89, 91, 107
Tommy 15, 50, *98*, 114, 119, 122, 181–182
trams 43, 45, 48–49, *98*, 99, 101
Turkish prisoners of war 122
Turner, Shoeing-smith A. 31

V

vaccination 27, 28, 105, 111
vendors 44, 45–46, 55, 81, 112, 116
Virgin's Breasts *104*, 105, 112

W

Wagh el-Birket 81
water buffalo. *See* gamoose
Waz'a 81, 119
Welldon, Bishop 11
Weymouth, HMS 32
Wilde, Lieut. R.W. 46
Williamson, Capt. C.H. 'Tim' 15, 16, 39, 86, 87, 183–184
Williams, Spr R. 'Abe' 65, 123, 182–183
Wolf, Lieut. P. 58, 61, 184
Worthington, Maj. C.S. *140*
Wynne, Lieut. W. *140*, 230

Y

Yates 23

Z

Zoo 48, 76

www.ingramcontent.com/pod-product-compliance
Lightning Source LLC
Chambersburg PA
CBHW022049290426
44109CB00014B/1038